INFORMAL CRIMINAL JUSTICE

Advances in Criminology
Series Editor: David Nelken

Titles in the Series

Informal Criminal Justice

Edited by
DERMOT FEENAN
University of Ulster, Northern Ireland

Ashgate

DARTMOUTH

Published by
Dartmouth Publishing Company
Ashgate Publishing Limited
Gower House
Croft Road
Aldershot
Hants GU11 3HR
England

Ashgate Publishing Company
131 Main Street
Burlington VT 05401-5600 USA

Ashgate website: http://www.ashgate.com

British Library Cataloguing in Publication Data
Informal criminal justice. - (Advances in criminology)
    1.Crime prevention - Citizen participation 2.Criminal
    justice, Administration of - Citizen participation
    3.Vigilantes
    I.Feenan, Dermot
    364.4'0457

Library of Congress Cataloging-in-Publication Data
Informal criminal justice / edited by Dermot Feenan.
    p.cm. -- (Advances in criminology)
    Includes bibliographical references.
    ISBN 0-7546-2220-7
    1.Criminal justice, Administration of. I. Feenan, Dermot. II. Series.

HV9443 .I53 2002
364--dc21

2002020617

ISBN 0 7546 2220 7

Printed and bound by Antony Rowe Ltd., Chippenham, Wiltshire

Contents

Contributors

Ray Abrahams is a Fellow of Churchill College, University of Cambridge, and author of *Vigilant Citizens: Vigilantism and the State* (Polity Press, 1998).

Arthur D. Brenner is Associate Professor of History at Siena College in Loudonville, New York. He is co-editor (with Bruce B. Campbell) of *Death Squads in Global Perspective: Murder with Deniability* (St. Martin's, 2000).

W. Fitzhugh Brundage is a Professor at the University of Florida, where he is also Chair of the History Department. Most recently, he edited *Where These Memories Grow: History, Memory, and Southern Identity* (University of North Carolina Press, 2000).

Dermot Feenan is a Lecturer in Law at the University of Ulster, and a Visiting Scholar at Cornell Law School, Cornell University, 2002.

Colin Harvey is Professor of Constitutional and Human Rights Law at the University of Leeds. His most recent book is an edited volume, *Human Rights, Equality and Democratic Renewal in Northern Ireland* (Hart, 2001).

Susan Jean, a recipient of a Mellon Fellowship, is a doctoral student at Columbia University.

Rebekah Lee is a doctoral student in South African history at Queen's College, Oxford.

Kieran McEvoy is a Reader in the School of Law, and Assistant Director of the Institute of Criminology and Criminal Justice, at The Queen's University of Belfast. He is co-author of *Crime, Community and Locale: The Northern Ireland Communities Crime Survey* (with David O'Mahony, Ray Geary and Jon Morison)(Ashgate, 2000).

Harry Mika is a Professor at Central Michigan University and has conducted research on restorative justice in Northern Ireland.

Anthony Minnaar is Director of the Institute for Human Rights and Criminal Justice Studies, Technikon, South Africa.

Jeremy Seekings is an Associate Professor in the Departments of Political Studies and Sociology at the University of Cape Town. His publications include *The UDF: A History of the United Democratic Front in South Africa, 1983-1991* (2000) and (with Nicoli Nattrass) *From Race to Class: Unemployment, Social Change and Inequality in South Africa* (2002).

Sandra Walklate is currently Professor of Sociology at Manchester Metropolitan University and Honorary Research Fellow in the Centre for Comparative Criminology and Criminal Justice, Bangor, University of Wales. Her most recent publication is (with Karen Evans) *Zero Tolerance or Community Tolerance? Managing Crime in High Crime Areas* (Ashgate, 1999).

Acknowledgements

I am grateful to the contributors to this book for their trust, labour and co-operation, to Pat McKee and David Pettigrew for help in formatting the manuscript, to Karen McCann for work on the index, and to Dr. Venkat Iyer for advice on the book proposal. Thanks are due also to John Irwin and Pauline Beavers of Ashgate for their co-operation.

Dermot Feenan
Jordanstown

1 Re-introducing Informal Criminal Justice

Dermot Feenan

The field of informal criminal justice is a key area of concern to those interested in law, criminology, policing, public policy and the sociology of crime. Its contemporary relevance can be seen in the emergence of restorative justice programmes, characterized by informal mediation between victim and offender (Morris and Young, 2000), and throughout continuing debates in legal pluralism regarding the relationship between state law and non-state law. The significance of informal criminal justice lies also in its potential to act as a theme by which to analyse developments in the governance of crime. The hollowing out of the state in many advanced capitalist countries in late modernity re-focuses attention on the peripheral exercise of governance (Braithwaite, 2000). There is evidence of a risk that formal, open and accountable systems of justice will be replaced and concealed by a range of bureaucratic sites (Hillyard and Gordon, 1999). The reactionary culture of the late twentieth and nascent twenty-first centuries is characterized in the sphere of criminal justice by control and confinement (Garland, 2001), much of which is evident in the rise of relatively informal private policing and formal incarceration. The persistence of incarceration as a function of criminal justice, despite its penological failures (Garland, 1990), underlines the need for non-legal forms of punishment. The interest in informalism as part of the access to justice movement in the 1970s, is renewed by the recent reiteration, as in Britain, of a need for alternatives to lawyers and courts to resolve disputes (Lord Chancellor's Department, 1998). Yet, the shift towards responsive criminal justice is contained within an administrative *mentalité* that requires centrally defined needs and priorities, efficiency, and evaluation (James and Raine, 1998; Hughes, 1998; Crawford, 1998). A reminder of informal justice may serve to counter-balance the proliferation of regulation and the ascendancy of managerial values in the criminal justice system.

The relevance of informal justice lies, too, in the appreciation that law as a form of power has been subsumed within a Foucauldian understanding of governmentality (Foucault, 1991; Matthews, 1988). Informal aspects of ostensibly formal legal processes vie with formal law to deliver power, coercion and justice (van Krieken, 2001). Purported informal crime management may be revealed as state action. Thus, the description by Guang-cai and Ming-kai (1993) of an informal mass movement of people against crime in People's Republic of China appears instead to be part of a government policy of 'comprehensive administration'. The centrality of law to government is displaced by complex systems of power. Similarly, the conventional view of a criminal justice *system* is problematized by recognition of variation in ways of controlling crime. An account of criminal justice in terms of differences between complex informal approaches to justice destabilizes totalizing assumptions about crime. It ruptures the idea that criminal justice is a single system (Elechi, 1996), a view more thoroughly explained by anthropologists in relation to law generally (Pospisil, 1971). This acknowledgement of plurality, including indigenous systems of law, allows a critical de-centring of the state as the primary focus of concern in conventional criminology. Yet, an understanding of the operation of official legal regulation is enhanced through knowing more about indigenous law and its interaction with official law (Galanter, 1981). This critical approach also resists the tendency of law to grab more ground and to impose unity, where there is 'dis-unity' (Shamir, 2000).

The continuous flux within states undergoing constitutional and political transition such as Northern Ireland and Yugoslavia underlines the need to sort alternative, popular and informal systems of justice. The history of political conflict demonstrates that states undergoing political or ethnic conflict often experience a conflict over the legitimacy of justice. Informal justice often flourishes where the transitional state has its eyes on bigger constitutional and political issues, as in South Africa, Northern Ireland and the Weimar republic, 1919-1933. Popular revolutionary justice may in time become part of the formalized system (Isaacman and Isaacman, 1982), reflecting Teitel's (2000) view that justice in transition will often import prior senses of justice.

In recognizing previous conceptions of informal justice it is necessary to acknowledge two principal landmarks within the broader literature on informal justice; Abel's two-volume *Politics of Informal Justice* (Abel, 1982a, 1982b) and Matthews' *Informal Justice* (1988). This present edited collection seeks to build on that literature by providing critical examination of concepts, contemporary research and historical studies.

Informal Criminal Justice

Any attempt at defining 'informal criminal justice' presents a challenge. Even to split the term and attempt a simple definition at criminal justice is problematic. It may be assumed that one is referring to a set of formal institutions such as the prosecutors, courts, prisons and probation services (Williams, 2001; Davies *et al*, 1998), but criminal justice (and criminal law) reflects and shapes historically variable and constantly changing fields of conflicting political forces (Sumner, 1990). Moreover, concepts of criminal justice are so heavily weighted in favour of the 'official' that 'informal' categories are measured with reference to the state. This is a variant on legal centralism. A more open rendering of criminal justice, in terms of broad concepts of enforcement, punishment, adjudication, dispute-processing, prevention, deterrence, rehabilitation and restoration will facilitate a richer understanding of informal processes.

The concept of informal justice developed particularly in the 1970s and 1980s to describe the shift towards community-justice, delegalization and informal dispute processing, though the call for less bureaucratic law had early support in the writings of Roscoe Pound. A wider appreciation of informal methods of resolving what would be regarded in the West as crimes was already established in the work of ethnographers (Merry, 1988). Abel (1982c) viewed informal justice as non-bureaucratic, de-professionalized, commonsensical, flexible, ad hoc and particularistic. It was characterized by substantive and procedural rules that were vague and unwritten. He described it as a reaction against all formal legal institutions, not just the courts. In Britain, a similar shift was expressed in the proliferation of law centres, arbitration and conciliation (Matthews, 1988). Informalism was linked to the wider 'access to justice' movement. However, the promise of informal justice was tempered by an increasing realization that most of the schemes sought to expand judicial power (Harrington, 1982), consolidated the justice system at the expense of community empowerment (Wahrhaftig, 1982) or formalized the informal (Matthews, 1988). In terms of political economy, informalism was seen as a mechanism whereby advanced capitalist states expanded their power, while appearing to be in retraction and, thus, diffused resistance (Abel, 1982a; Santos, 1982a). Cain (1985) argued that actual attempts at informalism and definitions of informalism had failed to advance a working class 'collective justice'.

The term 'popular justice' has sometimes been used synonymously with informal justice to describe processes and rules which are informal in ritual, non-professional and local (Merry, 1993). However, popular justice is more often used to describe justice that is community-based (Longmire, 1981) or justice that is based on widespread public support (Hillyard, 1985). Santos (1982b) offers the most thorough typology, identifying five types. These encompass justice in pre-capitalist societies; popular participation in the administration of justice in democratic capitalist societies, such as neighbourhood tribunals; exceptional justice in fascist regimes which is designed to eliminate enemies; all or part of the administration of justice in state socialist regimes; and, revolutionary justice. It is clear then that these types of justice are not necessarily informal. If one were to add to Santos's typology examples of smaller scale popular justice, such as the Knights of Labor courts in the US in the latter half of the nineteenth century which followed relatively formal procedures (Garlock, 1982), it is clear that 'popular' does not necessarily connote 'informal' processes.

Popular justice also may be distinguished from 'populist' justice. Cain (1985) equates the latter with fascist and repressive tendencies. It is characterized by its lack of accountability, restricted institutionalization, and concern to see the 'other side' as outsider. It is more prone to targeting the scapegoat, whose stigmatization and elimination allows society survive its tensions and conflicts. Nonetheless, with its lack of rules or theory, populist justice can constitute a form of informal justice and thus is closely related to vigilantism. Indeed, it could be said that vigilantism, represents a sub-set of informal criminal justice. The 'term' vigilantism, however, carries heavy political connotations and resists easy definition (Abrahams, 1998, 2002). Johnston (1992), has offered the most thorough definition, arguing that it comprises: planning and premeditation by participants; voluntary engagement by private citizens; autonomous citizenship; use or threat of the use of force; reaction when an established order is under threat from a transgression of institutionalized norms; and, an aim to control crime or other social infractions by offering guarantees of security to participants and others. Participants may specifically invoke notions of justice to justify their actions, as in the case of the *justiceiros* ('justice makers') and 'street' lynchings of Brazil (Fernandes, 1991; Martins, 1991). Some purported vigilantism may be less about justice than organized political resistance. Kowalewski (1996) argues that it is best conceived as an unconventional countermovement against a dissident movement, a view that is well-illustrated with reference to the counter-insurgency groups in the Philippines in the late 1980s and early 1990s (Kowalewski, 1990; Hedman, 2000). It may also represent self-defence initiatives, involving policing by residents of communities under threat – as in Israeli communities in late 1973 (Yanay, 1994) and West Belfast in late 1969. The overlapping of motivations and functions of self-styled 'vigilantes' is complex, reflecting the local anxieties about place (Girling *et al*, 1998) and broader understandings of the constitutional legitimacy of such action (Fritz, 1993).

While an attempt has been made here to preserve the validity of the concept of informal justice, there are a number of reasons to question whether the concept is sound. Arguably, it preserves the privileged position of law 'because it reinforces belief in the law' (Dezalay, 1994, p. 165). Benton (1994) dismisses the distinction between informal and formal in relation to the informal sector, arguing that 'it would be sensible simply to abandon the "informal sector" as an *a priori* construct linked to a separate legal level or sphere' (p. 239). Other commentators critique the dyad while preserving its usefulness as a working framework (Abel, 1982a; Matthews, 1988). The distinction suggests fixed categories where there is a need to examine variation (Galanter, 1981). It can conceal the exercise of state power in the guise of informalism. The idea that informal justice stands apart from state power is therefore problematic. Indeed, Abel (1982c) argues that resort to informal criminal dispositions not only increases state control but also has been accompanied by a substantial expansion of the formal apparatus, such as prisons, police, prosecutors and judges. In this sense, informal justice is a 'mythology accommodating a conflict' (Fitzpatrick, 1993). Moreover, the apparent boundaries between formal and informal are permeable, with confluent formal and informal practices. For instance, in the contested terrain of criminal justice in Northern Ireland, the state's need to maintain watertight boundaries between formal criminal justice and informal justice in order to maintain its legitimacy in the face of violent ethno-national resistance is undermined by numerous examples of such permeability. On occasions, the state has allowed paramilitary organizations to police their communities (Munck, 1984; Hillyard, 1985). According to one crime prevention officer in Belfast, '[o]n the record, no we don't do that, but I don't doubt that a policeman on the street, being human, would say, well, if that's the way you want to deal with it, then go ahead' (Brewer *et al*, 1997, p. 186).

Nonetheless, the distinction between on the one hand formal criminal justice as state or official justice and on the other informal criminal justice as popular or alternative justice remains a valuable, if only rough, way of examining criminal justice. The distinction underlines the real opposition of state and non-state law, and foregrounds the reality that the state generally exercises dominant coercive power. It recognizes that formal justice can more easily monopolize the symbolic power associated with state authority (Merry, 1988). While there can be inter-penetration and reliance between the two spheres (Henry, 1983), the distinction is useful, subject to an acknowledgment that the exercise of power is fluid and crosses conceptual boundaries.

Blurred Boundaries

The blurring of the boundary between formal and informal occurs in a number of ways, through: symbiosis; formal exploitation of the informal; informal exploitation of the formal; informal operation in the interstices of the state; and, informal operation independent of the state. The relationship between the state and non-state actors may be symbiotic where this involves those working informally to do the work that the state may believe it cannot carry out publicly. This occurs in the links between the *justiceiros* and the police in Brazil (Martins, 1991) or where the police turn a blind eye to the actions of vigilantes, as in South Africa (Minnaar, 2002; Lee and Seekings, 2002). In some circumstances, where the formal system has little leverage over informal, local methods of crime control and the informal mechanisms require access to state resources, both must rely on co-operation between state and indigenous systems. An example is the programme established by the Alaskan state government to deliver criminal justice, law enforcement and public safety in Alaska's Native villages. It provides resources to communities placed under strain by economic and cultural erosion but must rely on the informal norms and law-ways of the Eskimo, Aleut and Indian peoples alongside formal Western law for its operation (Marenin, 1993).

The official system has used parallel informal systems directly to consolidate its overall rule. This was a feature of colonial rule but aspects can be seen elsewhere, as in the South African apartheid state's delegation of authority to chiefs as part of a policy of establishing different political systems for different political groups. A similar development is the absorption of informal systems into the formal through the introduction of codes, standards, and management by lawyers (Auerbach, 1983; Spitzer, 1982). The formal system may also call in aid the informal methods or symbols of justice to achieve its own ends. Thus, in their study of Gypsy law, Caffrey and Mundy (1985) recount that the police would bring 'errant' boys to the Romani owner of a halting site for punishment. As long as parents of the boys would agree to 'punishment', the site owner would run the boys around a trotting track twice a day and the police would not prosecute. In the Philippines, the state appropriated the symbols of traditional informal modes of dispute resolution in order to develop its judicial institutions (Silliman, 1985). The borrowing of informal methods may follow transitions in government, where the subaltern class achieves power. In South Africa following apartheid the South Africa Police Service partially incorporated the local civilian street patrols which had developed in the townships in the absence of legitimate state policy as a second tier of policing to deal with the low level problems of crime and disorder (Brogden, 1995).

Occasionally, indigenous informal systems will use the official system to reinforce the operation of the indigenous, as illustrated in the study, now somewhat dated, of residents of favelas in Brazil creating their own law but adopting the forms and symbols of the state (Santos, 1977). More often the informal system will simply reflect the formal. This can be seen in the hierarchy of local mechanisms mirroring the conventional criminal justice system (Walklate, 2002), through to indigenous systems incorporating cultural elements from official law (Galanter, 1981). Even in ostensibly revolutionary forms of justice the informal alternatives to the state can mimic the former state. Thus, while Castro's popular tribunals in 1962 allowed popularly elected judges a great deal of discretion, in time the tribunals were replaced by more formalized courts (Salas, 1983).

Where the state leaves a vacuum in controlling crime this gap can be filled by informal, local methods of crime control. The ingress of informal methods may develop where there is a lack of political will to deal with perceived violations. For instance, Brenner (2002) argues that the failure of the Reichstag and Land parliaments to address political violence in the Weimar period encouraged the rise of often brutal informal reprisals against perceived enemies of the state. Informal systems also operate independently of the state (Caffrey and Mundy, 1997), and include many examples of informal methods of crime control (Brewer *et al*, 1997; Foster, 1993; Findlay and Zvekic, 1988). Braithwaite's recounting of 'reintegrative shaming' within small scale village society underlines the social processes that maintain criminal justice (Braithwaite, 1989). Informal criminal justice is also shaped by the informal processes of law-making, for instance in decisions about prosecution arising within police gossip. This sense of 'informal' facilitates a move away from a study of law which is centred on disputes to one where legal change is shaped dynamically. Ditton's ethnography of informal management of employee theft, for instance, reveals a complex matrix of informal factors mediating fiddling, based on, variously, a calculative basis, profit orientation, an eclectic ad hocness, and a rough sense of justice (Ditton, 1977).

Structure of the Book

This book seeks to acknowledge the diversity of perspectives on informal criminal justice by offering a range of studies that explore contextual and historically-situated, even if highly contested, notions of justice. They range from contemporary accounts of paramilitary punishment in Northern Ireland to political murders in Weimar Germany. In the early part of the book dealing with conceptual issues, Harvey (2002) views as problematic 'justice systems' operating in tension with state law within a constitutional democracy, and, more provocatively, questions whether justice can ever be informal. 'Justice systems must find a place within this bigger picture of state law if they are to be regarded as legitimate or acceptable within a constitutional democracy', he argues. His reasoning for privileging constitutional democracy is based on what he sees as the 'ideal of democracy' whereby 'the participation of every person in the formulation of the values which regulate community life is at least possible'. He contrasts this understanding of constitutional democracy with authoritarianism or autocratic rule, which he sees as based on a belief in the rule of 'the superior few' without systems of regulation. The place of justice systems within the state raises fundamental questions for those concerned about law, social control and government, and is leading to new analyses of statism and pluralism within criminology (Hirst, 2000). A further challenge for those supporting constitutional democracies is how nominally representative governments can address the diffuse sites of legal ordering within a hollowed out state which is increasingly subject to globalization.

Abrahams (2002) seeks to develop in his chapter the definition of vigilantism as a form of informal criminal justice. He posits an 'ideal' type involving 'an organized attempt by a group of "ordinary citizens" to enforce norms and maintain law and order on behalf of their communities, often by resort to violence, in the perceived absence of effective official state action through the police and courts'. He bases his definition upon the features of language used historically and recently by participants and commentators to characterize both vigilantes and their targets. His aim is to illuminate how language is employed to legitimate and defend or oppose and control vigilante behaviour. The concern with legitimation arises in Feenan's chapter on community justice and paramilitary punishment in Northern Ireland (Feenan, 2002). Here the contest over legitimacy is not about vigilantism but rather the broader contests over state legitimacy in relation to policing and crime control within ethno-nationally divided communities in parts of the North of Ireland. Feenan argues that the policing of communities by Republican and Loyalist paramilitaries represents a form of community justice that is based on more complex relations between communities and paramilitaries than is acknowledged in much of the existing literature. This theme is developed in McEvoy and Mika's chapter on restorative justice initiatives in Northern Ireland, with reference to Nationalist and Republican areas (McEvoy and Mika, 2002). They argue that traditional analyses of and responses to paramilitary punishment have failed to acknowledge four related facts. First, that the IRA has undertaken responsibility for the defence of their community against Loyalist and security force attacks. Secondly, that a parallel culture of dependence on the IRA developed within Republican communities. Thirdly, that in respect of state policing, the former Royal Ulster Constabulary lacked legitimacy in working class Republican and Nationalist communities. They conclude that the cessation of military operations by the IRA in 1994 placed greater political pressure on the Republican movement in relation to such activities. Recent restorative justice projects that work with paramilitary acquiescence serve to divert targets from paramilitary punishment. McEvoy and Mika see the restorative justice projects as an opportunity, within the context of a reformed policing service in Northern Ireland, to develop organic links between state policing and those communities, but at the pace of the latter.

The importance of crime as a local problem to be managed at a national level with greater understanding of local ways is stressed by Walklate (2002) in her chapter on informal crime management in a northern British city. She studies two urban communities and cautions against either universalistic or simplistic solutions to crime. Her close study of responses to crime reveal different processes of trust within the communities about informal crime management and the role of the state. This suggests the need for more nuanced mechanisms which 'enable not only the informal processes to work but which may also be necessary for more formal processes to work' (*ibid*), such as those under the Crime and Disorder Act 1998. This more nuanced appreciation of local crime management allows Walklate to test assumptions made about communities within the official system and to challenge objectives in the legislation, such as the notion of getting young people to 'make amends' and the concept of 'partnership'.

Lee and Seekings (2002) open two chapters on informal criminal justice in South Africa, drawing particular attention to the under-researched role of women in their study of popular justice after apartheid in the street committees of Guguletu and Khayelitsha. They note that even after the transition to democratic government there remain high levels of support throughout South Africa for popular vigilantism, which they treat as a form of popular justice. They note that the persistence in vigilantism corresponds with high levels of no confidence among the population in the government's control of crime. Minnaar (2002) continues the attempt to explain the persistence of vigilantism in South Africa following apartheid with a detailed study of the vigilante groupings *Mapogo a Mathamaga* and PAGAD (People Against Gangsterism and Drugs). Minnaar maintains that the vigilantism occurring throughout South Africa does little for law and order or of upholding any vision of justice in the community. Nonetheless, he acknowledges that the aims of groupings such as *Mapogo* reflect particular notions of justice that are instant and retributive.

An attempt to emphasize notions of justice in particular historical circumstances informed the choice of the final two chapters. The first, by Brenner (2002), examines the legitimation of political murders during the Weimar government in Germany, 1919-1933. While some of the early murders were justified on the grounds of national emergency or national self-defence, Brenner's historical study posits devastating longitudinal effects of such legitimation. He argues that the ineffectual intervention of the state and criminal justice system to the murders paved the way for the legal justifications of the Röhm purge in 1934. The jurist Carl Schmitt was reported as stating that the murder of Röhm was a 'true execution of justice. It was not carried out under the administration of justice, but was itself the highest justice' (*ibid*). In turn, such justification established precedents on which the persecution and murder of Jews and others could take place. The rhetoric surrounding the extra-judicial executions and subsequent criminal trials, Brenner concludes, are a major part of what connected the violence of the early period with Nazi concepts of justice. The issue of legitimation is studied further in an historical context by Jean and Brundage (2002) in their chapter on lynchings in the southern US in the late nineteenth and early twentieth centuries. In particular, they find that the reporting of lynchings by newspapers in Florida granted legitimacy to lynchings and yet held mobs accountable to notions of 'honourable' lynchings. This legitimation of lynching as a form of popular justice finds echoes in the attempt of the state in the late 1970s in Argentina to equate summary execution with 'popular justice' (Ietswaart, 1982). From an historical point of view, Jean and Brundage's excavation of the role of newspapers is extremely valuable because there were so few public documents about lynchings given the dearth of prosecutions and corresponding paucity of court records. Jean and Brundage locate their study within an explanation of racism and the economic protection of slavery that reveals much about white southeners' exercise of power and understanding of justice.

Issues for Further Research

This edited collection adds to the existing literature on informal justice, but there are many further lines of inquiry worthy of pursuit. Abel's (1982c) identification of the promising aspects of informal justice remain relevant in the twentieth-first century. He named mechanisms that offer equal access to the law to the many rather than the few, that operate quickly and effectively, that limit professionalization, that are familiar rather than esoteric and that strive for substantive justice rather than formal procedure. Much remains to be done to implement such aims. Further research is required on the nature of constraints on informal power and the strategies of the state to subvert informal justice, such as recourse to the 'rule of law', and co-opting concepts such as 'partnership'. The concept of governmentality provides a further productive, if not essential, seam for richer inquiry. The link between informal justice and private security in late modernity remains largely unexplored, even when the rise of the latter has been explained in terms of an informal amelioration of state fiscal crises (Olgiati, 1993) and the implications for public interest and peace have been flagged (Shearing, 1993).

The experience of certain groups is under-researched in the work on informal justice, though they receive increasing attention in studies of the formal system. Thus, young people receive little attention, despite being the predominant group targeted, for instance in paramilitary punishment in Northern Ireland (Feenan, 1998) and vigilantism in South Africa (Lee and Seekings, 2002). The place of women is largely neglected, as Lee and Seekings acknowledge in their study of the street committees of Guguletu and Khayelitsha townships in South Africa.

More penetrating analysis is required in determining who sets the rules in informal justice. While the community may call for general types of punishment, the enforcers may set the type and severity of punishment. In Northern Ireland, while there is demand within communities for paramilitary policing, the paramilitaries largely determine the nature of punishment. The norms of punishment will also mirror the interests of the enforcers. In Walklate's chapter the local enforcers refer to a 'moral code' by which it is acceptable to grass to the police regarding child abuse or a rape but not a ram-raid or post office robbery. Ethnographic study, characterized by in-depth participant observation, may assist in researching these issues. Some of the more penetrating recent field studies, such as Starn's (1999) account of the rondas in Peru, reveal complex influences in informal justice that go beyond traditional explanations. Similarly, ethnography may better reveal the symbolic and cultural importance of informal punishments.

Whichever methodology is employed, the changing governance of crime in late modernity and the tendency of formal power to infiltrate informal mechanisms re-introduces the field of informal criminal justice as a valid and significant subject of study.

References

Abel, R. L. (ed.) (1982a), *The Politics of Informal Justice, Volume 1, The American Experience*, Academic Press, New York.

Abel, R. L. (ed.) (1982b), *The Politics of Informal Justice, Volume 2, Comparative Studies*, Academic Press, New York.

Abel, R. L. (1982c), 'The Contradictions of Informal Justice', in Abel, R. L. (ed.), *The Politics of Informal Justice, Volume 1, The American Experience*, Academic Press, New York, pp. 267-320.

Abrahams, R. (1998), *Vigilant Citizens: Vigilantism and the State*, Polity Press, Cambridge.

Abrahams, R. (2002), 'What's in a Name? Some Thoughts on the Vocabulary of Vigilantism and Related Forms of "Informal Criminal Justice"', in Feenan, D. (ed.), *Informal Criminal Justice*, Ashgate, Aldershot, chapter 3.

Auerbach, J. S. (1983), *Justice without Law? Resolving Disputes without Lawyers*, Oxford University Press, New York.

Benton, L. (1994), 'Beyond Legal Pluralism: Towards a New Approach to Law in the Informal Sector', *Social and Legal Studies*, Vol. 3(2), pp. 223-42.

Braithwaite, J. (1989), *Crime, Shame and Reintegration*, Cambridge University Press, Cambridge.

Braithwaite, J. (2000), 'The New Regulatory State and the Transformation of Criminology', *British Journal of Criminology*, Vol. 40, pp. 222-38.

Brenner, A. (2002), 'From Informal Justice to Formal Injustice: The Decriminalization of Political Murder in Weimar and Nazi Germany', in Feenan, D. (ed.), *Informal Criminal Justice*, Ashgate, Aldershot, chapter 9.

Brewer, J. D., Lockhart, B. and Rodgers, P. (1997), *Crime in Ireland 1945-95: 'Here be Dragons'*, Clarendon Press, Oxford.

Brogden, M. (1995), 'An Agenda for Post-Troubles Policing in Northern Ireland — The South African Precedent', *Liverpool Law Review*, Vol. XVII(1), pp. 3-27.

Caffrey, S. and Mundy, G. (1997), 'Informal Systems of Justice: The Formation of Law within Gypsy Communities', *American Journal of Comparative Law*, Vol. 45(2), pp. 251-67.

Cain, M. (1985), 'Beyond Informal Justice', *Contemporary Crisis*, Vol. 9, pp. 335-73.

Crawford, A. (1998), *Crime Prevention and Community Safety: Politics, Policies and Practices*, Longman, London.

Davies, M., Croall, H. and Tyrer, J. (1998), *Criminal Justice: An Introduction to the Criminal Justice System in England and Wales*, 2nd edn., Longman, London.

Dezalay, Y. (1994), 'The Forum should fit the Fuss: The Economics and Politics of Negotiated Justice', in Cain, M. and Harrington, C. B. (eds), *Lawyers in a Postmodern World: Transition and Transgression*, Open University Press, Buckingham, pp. 155-82.

Ditton, J. (1977), *Part-time Crime: An Ethnography of Fiddling and Pilferage*, Macmillan, London.

Elechi, O. O. (1996), 'Doing Justice Without the State: The Afikpo (Ehugbo) Nigeria Model of Conflict Resolution', *International Journal of Comparative and Applied Criminal Justice*, Vol. 20(2), pp. 337-55.

Feenan, D. (1998), 'Punish or Restore', *Fortnight*, May, 13-14.

Feenan, D. (ed.) (2002), 'Community Justice in Conflict: Paramilitary Punishment in Northern Ireland', *Informal Criminal Justice*, Ashgate, Aldershot, chapter 4.

Fernandes, H. R. (1991), 'Authoritarian Society: Breeding Ground for *Justiceiros*', in Huggins, M. K. (ed.), *Vigilantism and the State in Modern Latin America: Essays on Extra-Legal Violence*, Praeger, New York, pp. 61-70.

Findlay, M. and Zvekic, U. (eds) (1988), *Analysing (In)formal Mechanisms of Crime Control: A Cross-Cultural Perspective*, United Nations Social Defence Research Institute, Rome.

Fitzpatrick, P. (1993), '*The Impossibility of Popular Justice*', in Merry, S. E. and Milner, N. (eds), *The Possibility of Popular Justice: A Case Study of Community Mediation in the United States*, University of Michigan Press, Ann Arbor, pp. 453-74.

Foster, J. (1995), 'Informal Social Control and Community Crime Prevention', *British Journal of Criminology*, Vol. 35(4), pp. 563-83.

Foucault, M. (1991), 'Governmentality', in Burchell, G., Gordon, C. and Miller, P. (eds), *The Foucault Effect: Studies in Governmentality*, University of Chicago Press, Chicago.

Fritz, C. G. (1993), 'Popular Sovereignty, Vigilantism, and the Constitutional Right of Revolution', *Pacific Historical Review*, Vol. 63(1), pp. 39-66.

Galanter, M. (1981), 'Justice in Many Rooms: Courts, Private Ordering, and Indigenous Law', *Journal of Legal Pluralism*, Vol. 19, pp. 1-47.

Garland, D. (1990), *Punishment and Modern Society: A Study in Social Theory*, Clarendon Press, Oxford.

Garland, D. (2001), *The Culture of Control: Crime and Social Order in Contemporary Society*, Oxford University Press, Oxford.

Garlock, J. (1982), 'The Knights of Labor Courts: A Case Study of Popular Justice', in Abel, R. L. (ed.), *The Politics of Informal Justice, Volume 1, The American Experience*, Academic Press, New York, pp. 17-33.

Girling, E., Loader, I. and Sparks, R. (1998), 'A Telling Tale: A Case of Vigilantism and its Aftermath in an English Town', *British Journal of Sociology*, Vol. 49(3), pp. 474-90.

Guang-cai, S. and Ming-kai, C. (1993), 'Alternative Policing and Crime Control in China', in Findlay, M. and Zvekic, U. (eds), *Alternative Policing Styles: Cross Cultural Perspectives*, Kluwer, Deventer, pp. 71-90.

Harrington, C. B. (1982), 'Delegalization Reform Movements: A Historical Analysis', in Abel, R. L. (ed.), *The Politics of Informal Justice, Volume 1, The American Experience*, Academic Press, New York, pp. 35-71.

Harvey, C. (2002), 'Legality, Legitimacy and the Politics of Informalism', in Feenan, D. (ed.), *Informal Criminal Justice*, Ashgate, Aldershot, chapter 2.

Hedman, E-L. (2000), 'State of Siege: Political Violence and Vigilante Mobilization in the Philippines', in Campbell, B. B. and Brenner, A. D. (eds), *Death Squads in Global Perspective: Murder with Deniability*, Macmillan, New York, pp. 125-51.

Henry, S. (1983), *Private Justice: Towards Integrated Theorising in the Sociology of Law*, Routledge and Kegan Paul, London.

Hillyard, P. (1985), 'Popular Justice in Northern Ireland', *Research in Law, Deviance and Social Control*, Vol. 7, pp. 247-67.

Hillyard, P. and Gordon, D. (1999), 'Arresting Statistics: The Drift to Informal Justice in England and Wales', *Journal of Law and Society*, Vol. 26(4), pp. 502-22.

Hirst, P. (2000), 'Statism, Pluralism and Social Control', *British Journal of Criminology*, Vol. 40, pp. 279-95.

Hughes, G. (1998), *Understanding Crime Prevention: Social Control, Risk and Late Modernity*, Open University Press, Buckingham.

Ietswaart, H. F. P. (1982), 'The Discourse of Summary Justice and the Discourse of Popular Justice: An Analysis of Legal Rhetoric in Argentina', in Abel, R. L. (ed.), *The Politics of Informal Justice, Volume 2, Comparative Studies*, Academic Press, New York, pp. 149-79.

Isaacman, B. and Isaacman, A. (1982), 'A Socialist Legal System in the Making: Mozambique Before and After Independence,' in Abel, R. L. (ed.), *The Politics of Informal Justice, Volume 2, Comparative Studies*, Academic Press, New York, pp. 281-322.

James, A. and Raine, J. (1998), *The New Politics of Criminal Justice*, Longman, London.

Jean, S. and Brundage, W. F. (2002), 'Legitimizing "Justice": Lynching and the Boundaries of Informal Justice in the American South', in Feenan, D. (ed.), *Informal Criminal Justice*, Ashgate, Aldershot, chapter 10.

Johnston, L. (1996), 'What is Vigilantism?', *British Journal of Criminology*, Vol. 36(2), pp. 220-36.

Kowalewski, D. (1990), 'Vigilante Counterinsurgency and Human Rights in the Philippines: A Statistical Analysis', *Human Rights Quarterly*, Vol. 12, pp. 246-64.

Kowalewski, D. (1996), 'Countermovement Vigilantism and Human Rights: A Propositional Inventory', *Crime, Law and Social Change*, Vol. 25, pp. 63-81.

Lee, R. and Seekings, J. (2002), 'Vigilantism and Popular Justice After Apartheid', in Feenan, D. (ed.), *Informal Criminal Justice*, Ashgate, Aldershot, chapter 7.

Longmire, D. (1981), 'A Popular Justice System: A Radical Alternative to the Traditional Criminal Justice System', *Contemporary Crisis*, Vol. 5, pp. 15-30.

Lord Chancellor's Department (1998), *Modernising Justice: The Government's Plans for Reforming Legal Services and the Courts*, Cm 4155, Lord Chancellor's Department, London.

Marenin, O. (1993), 'Policing Rural Alaska', in Findlay, M. and Zvekic, U. (eds), *Alternative Policing Styles: Cross Cultural Perspectives*, Kluwer, Deventer, pp. 45-70.

Martins, J. de S. (1991), 'Lynchings — Life by a Thread: Street Justice in Brazil, 1979-1988', in Huggins, M. K. (ed.), *Vigilantism and the State in Modern Latin America: Essays on Extra-Legal Violence*, Praegar, New York, pp. 21-45.

Matthews, R. (ed.) (1988), *Informal Justice*, Sage Publications, London.

McEvoy, K. and Mika, H. (2002), 'Republican Hegemony or Community Ownership?: Community Restorative Justice in Northern Ireland', in Feenan, D. (ed.), *Informal Criminal Justice*, Ashgate, Aldershot, chapter 5.

Merry, S. E. (1988), 'Legal Pluralism', *Law and Society Review*, Vol. 22(5), pp. 869-96.

Merry, S. E. (1993), 'Sorting Out Popular Justice', in Merry, S. E. and Milner, N. (eds), *The Possibility of Popular Justice: A Case Study of Community Mediation in the United States*, University of Michigan Press, Ann Arbor, pp. 31-66.

Morris, A. and Young, W. (2000), 'Reforming Criminal Justice: The Potential of Restorative Justice', in Strang, H. and Braithwaite, J. (eds), *Restorative Justice: Philosophy to Practice*, Ashgate, Dartmouth, pp. 11-31.

Minnaar, A. (2002), 'The "New" Vigilantism in Post-April 1994 South Africa: Searching for Explanations', in Feenan, D. (ed.), *Informal Criminal Justice*, Ashgate, Aldershot, chapter 8.

Munck, R. (1984), 'Repression, Insurgency, and Popular Justice: The Irish Case', *Crime and Social Justice*, Vol. 21-22, pp. 81-94.

Olgiati, V. (1993), 'Control for Hire: Private Security Agencies in Italy', in Findlay, M. and Zvekic, U. (eds), *Alternative Policing Styles: Cross Cultural Perspectives*, Kluwer, Deventer, pp. 181-202.

Pospisil, L. (1971), *The Anthropology of Law: A Comparative Theory of Law*, Harper Row, New York.

Salas, L. (1983), 'The Emergence and Decline of the Cuban Popular Tribunals', *Law and Society Review*, Vol. 17, pp. 587-613.

Santos, B. de S. (1977), 'The Law of the Oppressed: The Construction and Reproduction of Legality in Pasagarda', *Law and Society Review*, Vol. 12, pp. 5-125.

Santos, B. de S. (1982a), 'Law and Community: The Changing Nature of State Power in Late Capitalism', in Abel, R. L. (ed.), *The Politics of Informal Justice, Volume 1, The American Experience*, Academic Press, New York, pp. 249-66.

Santos, B. de S. (1982b), 'Law and Revolution in Portugal: The Experiences of Popular Justice after the 25th of April 1974', in Abel, R. L. (ed.), *The Politics of Informal Justice, Volume 2; Comparative Studies*, Academic Press, New York, pp. 251-80.

Shamir, R. (2000), *The Colonies of Law: Colonialism, Zionism and Law in Early Mandate Palestine*, Cambridge University Press, Cambridge.

Shearing, C. D. (1993), 'Policing: Relationships Between Public and Private Forms', in Findlay, M. and Zvekic, U. (eds), *Alternative Policing Styles: Cross Cultural Perspectives*, Kluwer, Deventer, pp. 203-28.

Silliman, G. S. (1985), 'A Political Analysis of the Philippines' Katarungang Pambarangay System of Informal Justice Through Mediation', *Law and Society Review*, Vol. 19, pp. 279-301.

Spitzer, S. (1982), 'The Dialectics of Formal and Informal Control', in Abel, R. L. (ed.), *The Politics of Informal Justice, Volume 1, The American Experience*, Academic Press, New York, pp. 167-205.

Starn, O. (1999), *Nightwatch: The Politics of Protest in the Andes*, Duke University Press, Durham, NC, and London.

Sumner, C. (ed.) (1990), *Censure, Politics and Criminal Justice*, Open University Press, Milton Keynes.

Teitel, R. (2000), *Transitional Justice*, Oxford University Press, Oxford.

Van Krieken, R. (2001), 'Legal Informalism, Power and Liberal Governance', *Social and Legal Studies*, Vol. 10(1), pp. 5-22.

Wahrhaftig, P. (1982), 'An Overview of Community-Oriented Citizen Dispute Resolution Programs in the United States', in Abel, R. L. (ed.), *The Politics of Informal Justice, Volume 1, The American Experience*, Academic Press, New York, pp. 75-97.

Walklate, S. (2002), 'Informal Crime Management in a Northern British City', in Feenan, D. (ed.), *Informal Criminal Justice*, Ashgate, Aldershot, chapter 6.

Williams, K. S. (2001), *Textbook on Criminology*, 4th edn., Oxford University Press, Oxford.

Yanay, U. (1994), 'Co-opting Vigilantism: Government Response to Community Action for Personal Safety', *Journal of Public Policy*, Vol. 13(4), pp. 381-96.

2 Legality, Legitimacy and the Politics of Informalism

Colin Harvey

Introduction

The formalism-informalism debate is never far from the concerns of legal scholars. Formalism, in particular, has come in for severe criticism from waves of recent legal scholarship. Critical scholars have joined the long line of opponents. It is not always clear what is meant by formalism when it is used. There are generally two broad strands to critical argument. The first stresses the impact which formalism (usually termed 'legalism' for these purposes) has on societal relations. Here formalism is used pejoratively as the cause of major problems in modern society. The problems identified are familiar ones: selfishness; atomism; and individualism. The second strand is sceptical of the argument that there could ever be an escape from 'the political'. The argument here is that there is no 'other worldly' and detached position for formalism to place a foothold in. Formalism is thus cast as an attempt to mask the political nature of the legal enterprise. This is often directed against liberalism, with the argument that it is a political theory which tries to disguise its own politics and which attempts to de-politicize social life. Formalists are thus involved, it is claimed, in an exercise in denial. These critical arguments have provoked a mixed response, examined in more detail below.

The aim here is to explore these issues in three basic stages. First, I examine familiar debates in legal theory about the rule of law. Secondly, I place these in the context of modern debates on legality, as this has been reflected in consideration of the work of Carl Schmitt. Finally, I address the relevance of this for critical thought on the law and politics of informalism. While this chapter does not directly address specific examples of informal justice, the issues examined have relevance for current debates on criminal justice policy. The tentative, if banal, conclusion is that everything depends on context. Talk of the negative or positive consequences of formalism-informalism is misplaced without reference to the practical use of the concepts in particular contexts. Viewed contextually the informalism-formalism debate seems less like an argument and more like a basic misunderstanding of the issues. One question raised here is whether justice can ever truly be 'informal'. In addition, caution is urged on collapsing legality into pure power struggles. While the meaning of legality is shaped by local contexts, the stress on standards and values has an important place. In democratic societies connections exist between legality, as a particular form of constraint, and notions of legitimacy. So, while law is arguable in nature, this is an inherent aspect of the rule of law rather than being opposed to it. Disagreement about the meaning of law does not merit the radical conclusion that the rule of law is a sham.

Legality in Question

When informal justice is debated the rule of law is regularly raised as an argument against it. Arguments about the rule of law, and how it fits with informalism, continue unabated. In popular discourse the rule of law is widely regarded as a 'good thing'. Politicians and lawyers consistently call for the rule of law in societies the world over. This popular call scarcely reveals any deep-seated concern about the alleged oppressive impact of a culture of legalism. The assumption tends to be that the rule of law is something that everyone must have. There is however another side to this. Combined with the spirited defence of the rule of law one also hears a different, more critical, argument. In this line of thought legalism is to be avoided, where possible. To say that an individual or a society is legalistic is to be critical. In practice, however, we find calls for the global export of the rule of law at the same time as many are decrying the legalism of modern societies. The rule of law is something that everyone should celebrate, but, it would seem, in moderation only. In order to clarify this one needs to probe what precisely we mean by the rule of law.

Liberal conceptions of the rule of law tend to stress its value as a frame of reference for a democratic society. In other words, citizens should know the rules which govern them and be able to order their lives within the context of these rules (Hayek, 1976). What is important in this conception is legal certainty as well as predictability. Citizens must be able to conduct themselves in accordance with known rules, and be able to predict, with reasonable precision, the implications of the rules for their lives. The rule of law has 'thin' and 'thick' versions. The 'thin' version is purely procedural. The stress is on the rule of law as a procedure only (Raz, 1983). According to this 'thin' version, a belief in the rule of law does not commit you to a particular view of the good life. To say that a political community is governed by the rule of law is to say nothing about the particular political theory which that community ascribes to. This procedural understanding of the rule of law remains neutral as to substantive views of the good life.

The process-based conception of the rule of law can be contrasted with the 'thick' version. According to the 'thick' version, the rule of law is not a purely procedural device. The 'thick' understanding is committed to a substantive theory of justice. This substantive theory of justice is liberal in nature and the argument is that no theory of the rule of law can defend a position which does not address the good life. The rule of law therefore reflects a particular ideological commitment to a version of democratic life. If a political community attaches significant weight to the rule of law, then it is committed to a particular political position. It is not a technical device for achieving objectives, it is an end in itself. The values of this democratic tradition are immanent in law and emerge through processes of ongoing interpretation. This version of the rule of law is rooted in an understanding of legality as reflecting a democratic tradition with constraints attached. In contrast to the 'thin' version, this approach defends a version of the good life of which the rule of law is a central part. Both these understandings of the rule of law presume two things: that legalism is a 'good thing'; and that rules have a measure of certainty which renders the idea of the rule of law meaningful in practice. These positions are not accepted by all. Some would question both the idea that legalism is desirable and the argument that rules guarantee certainty. As noted, legalism is often used pejoratively to refer to a basic problem in modern society. A society which is legalistic is viewed by many as one that is dysfunctional. A person who is critical of legalism is not necessarily someone who rejects the idea of a society governed by law. But the critique does highlight problems when rule-governed behaviour is taken to extremes. It is difficult to imagine how complex modern societies would manage without sophisticated mechanisms of legal regulation.

The second criticism perhaps has more force. Modern critical scholarship in law has highlighted the extent to which contestation goes all the way down. The argument is that legal reasoning is not distinct and does not differ in its basics from political reasoning. The argument is that approaches to legal interpretation are anchored in substantive political positions. This does not mean that a particular approach to legal interpretation results in a definitive political result. Critical scholars have noted that the same approach to legal interpretation can have a different result, depending on context. The critical argument is that law is indeterminate (Hutchinson, 2000). The focus then turns to the strategic uses of law in particular political contexts. On this view law is little more than a game. The key to success is judged by how well the game is negotiated. The focus turns to concepts such as 'playfulness'. In this game there are said to be no real constraints and thus everything rests on the creativity of judges, for example (Hutchinson, 2000). The direct implication must be the belief that people have been fooled into believing there is more to constitutional democracy than arbitrary decision and pure power relations.

The radical indeterminacy critique springs from a recognition of the arguable nature of law. But is this the only conclusion to reach? Neil MacCormick comes to a rather different conclusion and one that is more persuasive (MacCormick, 1999). He sets out to provide a reconciliation between the arguable nature of law and legal certainty. He argues that setting these against each other is a misstatement in emphasis (MacCormick, 1999, p. 176). Law has a 'defeasible certainty' only (*ibid*). The ideology of the rule of law has built into it the arguable nature of modern law. Individuals expect to be able to challenge legal decisions. In the criminal process the rights of the defence are constructed around this very idea. It is the arguable nature of the rule of law which in fact protects people against arbitrary government (MacCormick, 1999, p. 177). The rule of law can hold on to the idea of constraint without compromising its dynamism. Disagreement about the meaning of legality thus becomes one key part of its intrinsic nature. Far from undermining the rule of law this is what gives the concept its dynamism. In this sense, it makes democracy possible. Dyzenhaus put it best when he says that the rule of law 'is the institutional mechanism of democracy' (Dyzenhaus, 1999, p. 89).

Is there an ethics of legalism? In terms of the morality of the rule of law, the mechanism encourages what Christine Sypnowich has termed an 'ethic of civility' (Sypnowich, 1999, p. 194). The rule of law helps to ensure that we are accorded worth and dignity in the public sphere (*ibid*). The argument is that there is an ethic of legalism which is essential to modern democratic life. As she notes, this has an important function in 'safeguarding boundaries' (*ibid*). She argues that some utopian appeals to transparency and openness pay scant regard to the value of privacy. What is noteworthy about the arguments presented above is that they are advanced as progressive defences of the rule of law. There is a tendency in critical scholarship to attack formalism and everything that is said to come with it. Traditionally, the rule of law has been written-off as an ideological mask by many critical scholars. This presents a challenge to those who believe that legality matters for marginalized groups. The argument is not that the rule of law is to be uncritically welcomed. It is a commitment to legality without illusions. The idea that there are constraints on power, contained in the legal form, is difficult to deny. That this is a desirable state of affairs is also hard to reject. People disagree about the meaning of law, and for good reason. But this does not mean that people therefore reject the idea that there are limits within the context of a constitutional democracy (Waldron, 1999).

The debate about the rule of law is endless. Perhaps this is precisely the point. Arguments within law are also continuing conversations based on persuasion, negotiation and re-negotiation. There are, however, some versions of the rule of law which are more persuasive than others. The radical indeterminacy thesis is not simply a political dead-end, but it also underestimates the strength of feeling that citizens have about the concept of legality. The call for the law to be applied does not solely come from the powerful. Those who are disadvantaged and marginalized also make strong claims about the applicability of the rule of law. Are legal scholars really telling individuals to view all this as a game in which they must make strategic moves? The difficulty is that many citizens of modern democracies believe the 'noble lie' and make strong claims on the legal system to live up to the ideals of justice in practice. While much of this argumentation can be considered strategic, there is the real attempt to reach a mutual understanding about what it means to live in a constitutional democracy. In terms of scholarly development, the key lies in contextual analysis of legality as it functions within specific democratic contexts. To do this is not, however, to support the radical indeterminacy thesis or accept that law is a game without limits. All games have rules, and these rules make the ongoing development of the game possible.

No Escape from 'the Political'

The idea that we should be governed by law and not by persons is directed, in much of the literature, against politics. One way of depicting this is to say that rules provide objective standards for stable government, and that politics is the sphere of the messy and chaotic. It is vital that this position is not the subject of caricature. There are progressive as well as conservative sentiments in play here. The progressive defence of the rule of law is based on the role of impersonal rules in protecting the weak against the strong. This view, which surfaces frequently, is a plea against the conception of a world in which 'might equals right'. The fear which underpins this is based on a particular reading of the argument that all law is politics. This argument has recently resurfaced in an interesting guise with increasing interest in societies where law is under stress. For example, the Weimar Republic has attracted considerable attention from legal and political scholars in recent years. One leading participant in the events of that period figures prominently in the current debate: Carl Schmitt.

There has been a remarkable resurgence of interest in the work of Schmitt. In legal scholarship this was evident in 2000, for example, when the *Cardozo Law Review* published the papers from a Symposium oddly entitled 'Carl Schmitt: Legacy and Prospects'. Numerous books and articles on this subject have been produced. These range from the extremely critical to pure apology for Schmitt's actions in Germany in the 1930s. Some argue that Schmitt's involvement with German fascism resulted directly from his legal and political beliefs, while others express surprise by his turn to the Nazis. One might justly ask why the work of a prominent legal scholar in post-World War I Germany is of any relevance to this chapter. The main reason for engagement is Schmitt's sustained critique of liberal democracy and his agonistic view of democracy. There are important lessons to be drawn from his work for building a defensible conception of democracy. This has important implications for how we think about informal justice. This is particularly so in the modern context where internal conflict has replaced inter-state conflict as the main form of contestation. Schmitt remains of interest because his work prefigures many arguments which are currently in vogue in modern legal scholarship.

Dyzenhaus persuasively labels Schmitt's approach as 'communitarian existentialism' (Dyzenhaus, 1997, p. 2). This captures perfectly Schmitt's belief in the decision as the basis of political and legal order, as well as his support for ethnic homogeneity against any notion of pluralism. Schmitt's authoritarianism should be of particular concern to those interested in legal pluralism. Schmitt was explicitly against pluralism as an approach to political life.[1] His response was to view pluralism as a threat to stability and his demand was for the 'sovereign decision' (Hirst, 1999). He wanted to be known as the modern day Hobbes, and given his friend-enemy conception of politics his search for decision is perhaps unsurprising. What Schmitt's work does is to disturb complacency in democratic thought and arrest the idea that we are moving consensually to a new cosmopolitan world order. Schmitt expressed impatience and irritation with parliamentary democracy, which he viewed as a form of endless discussion (Schmitt, 1985a; Schmitt, 1985b). His critique of democracy is mirrored in modern neo-conservative distaste for deliberation and dialogue.

The idea of an 'end to politics' confronts Schmitt's agonistic view of the world. His argument has direct implications for the rule of law. What he effectively tried to do was reveal the original moment of force which underpins constitutional legal order (Zizek, 1999). His focus was on the constituent power upon which liberal constitutionalism was based. This power could not be captured by the rule of law because it was the pure decision which preceded the formation of the legal order.

His work was presented as a critique of Hans Kelsen's normativist legal theory. Schmitt rejected, as many modern legal scholars now do, the idea that law can be regarded as a gapless normative system. The sovereign decision stands behind all legal order and emerges in times of crisis and emergency. Schmitt tried to reveal the historical contingency of the Weimar constitution in particular (one can debate his motivations for this line of argument), but his position must be assumed to have wider applicability (Cristi, 1998). This approach runs directly counter to those who suggest that it is the constitution that becomes sovereign. Schmitt rejected the idea that the constitution, once agreed, stood over the sovereign. His argument was rather that the role was in practice reversed.

What Schmitt's 'them' and 'us' conception of politics does is rock any wishful thinking about the consensual origins of constitutional democracies. His theory of democracy brings us back to the constituent power of the people in the wilful establishment of a constitutional order. Schmitt's work has at least two implications for consideration of informal justice. The first is his stress on the politics of law. For Schmitt liberal constitutionalism tries to bring politics to an end, and the rule of law ideology is part of this process. The second is his antipathy to pluralism within the state. One suspects that legal pluralism would also run counter to his search for stability and order. The attraction of Schmitt for theorists of the Left lies in the commitment to the strong state. At a time when international and internal processes are challenging traditional notions of sovereignty Schmitt's theory of the state can seem attractive. For those who view the state as the prime site for a potentially progressive politics, then modern trends can seem excessively constraining. Schmitt's work therefore offers the idea of a return to the strong state acting on behalf of a unified order to secure stability.

The increased interest in the 'decisionism' of Schmitt has been met by a revival of interest in the democratic tradition in modern law. This work does not deny the power of Schmitt's insights, but it favours other legal theorists from the same period. One might say that Schmitt has provoked some legal scholars into more robust defences of the democratic tradition in modern law. A number of scholars, most notably David Dyzenhaus and William Scheuerman, have sought to resurrect a critical understanding of legality which can deal with Schmitt's arguments. In undertaking this task they have drawn extensively upon other intellectual figures from Weimar Germany (such as Franz Neumann and Hermann Heller). This work is critical in the sense that Dyzenhaus in particular has sought to argue in support of a connection between legality and legitimacy and to draw a direct link to progressive political values. He has developed a thesis which stands in opposition to the dominant position of Anglo-American legal positivism (Dyzenhaus 1991, 1997). Drawing upon the work of Hermann Heller, among others, Dyzenhaus advances the argument for law as a genuine constraint on political power (Dyzenhaus, 1997, p. 2). This does not mean that law can prevent authoritarianism or always stem abusive political power. Law is enmeshed in a political and democratic culture. Where these are weak, or non-existent, then appeals to legality will do little to assist. His argument is that if lessons are to be learned from Weimar then they must come from those on the Left like Heller and not Schmitt (Dyzenhaus, 1999).

Scheuerman is explicit in linking Schmitt's work to modern trends in legal scholarship (Scheuerman, 1999, 1994). He draws direct parallels with those who claim that law is inherently arbitrary, an empty vessel filled with power relations. As with modern theorists, Schmitt too was interested in deconstructing the liberal rule of law (Scheuerman, 1999, p. 137) While some modern theorists are content to leave it at that, Schmitt took the trouble to reconstruct a concept of law for the postliberal order. Schmitt's way to overcome indeterminacy was through increased ethnic homogeneity (*ibid*). The way to eliminate indeterminacy, for Schmitt, was through the eradication of moral and political pluralism. Scheuerman believes that the experience of Schmitt should be a lesson to all those who believe that the indeterminacy thesis has a liberating impact on practical politics.

The fear which underpins criticism of Schmitt has a modern resonance. Scheuerman's position reflects a popular reaction to informal processes. Rather than view these as opportunities for flexibility and justice in the individual case, they are seen as potential sites of injustice where the powerful will always defeat the marginalized. There is merit in this argument. It is unclear who would find the deformalized landscape of some 'utopias' the most liberating. Marginalized groups are often the vocal advocates of legality. For example, those who call for the legal protection of human rights are expressing a desire for, and belief in, the notion of law as a constraint. Disagreement continues to exist on the meaning of the constraint that law imposes, but few reject the idea of a political community without legal limitations. The acceptance of this ideal is political, as is the commitment to the use of the legal form. Interpretations of law also reflect political positions crafted within legal language. However, this does not mean that law can be reduced to pure power relations. This cynical conclusion is far removed from the dynamic reality of struggles over legality in modern democracies.

Can Justice Really be Informal?

In the final part of this chapter I want to raise some concerns about the use of the term 'informal justice'. We all appear to know what we mean when we refer to systems of informal justice. However, there is a real issue whether justice can ever be informal. The focus thus far has been on legality and central issues in legal theory. My argument is that legality retains its importance as a constraint, albeit contested, on the actions of the powerful. The arguable nature of law can be accepted without abandoning the notion that law can make a real difference in practice. However, there are other issues which arise in the context of informal justice. From the perspective of legal pluralism can justice ever be truly informal? It is difficult to imagine any structured form of social interaction as being entirely informal. To simplify, one could argue that norms structure social relations in every sphere. These need not be norms which meet the exacting tests of legal validity, however, they do infuse social processes. A local system of restorative justice, for example, may function with its own rules which are routinely followed and enforced. This normative order is outside of state law, but it would be difficult to argue that everything about it was informal and arbitrary. This may well be the case, but we cannot assume in advance that the absence of state law necessarily renders the process arbitrary. The system might not be legitimate, or it might even be illegal (on human rights law grounds, for example) but neither would render the process entirely informal.

Introducing this element of legal pluralism brings other issues with it. For example, it presents a challenge to the traditional way of conceiving the relation between law and discretion. It is usual for lawyers to see discretion as a problem. Discretion is to be eradicated or limited as much as possible. But if social processes function with their own rules (albeit non-legal ones) then the view of discretion must alter to reflect this fact. The focus shifts to understanding how these social processes work and what role law can play in relation to them. This is a rather different and more subtle argument which seeks to cast doubt on the rigid distinction drawn between formalism and informalism. The rule of law model sketched above is hierarchical in nature. It is statist in that the sovereign state makes the law which is imposed on the political community. This view of law confronts the multiplicity of normative orders which exist in modern societies. The norms which structure modern life are not simply legal. Customs and traditions within communities also shape the actions of individuals. No individual is completely removed from this societal context. It is the sanctions which follow violation that distinguish legal order. In democratic societies the coercive power of the state acts as the main, and legitimate, sanction on the individual for norm violation. Within this context the individual, at least in theory, has the opportunity to challenge the imposition of a sanction on the basis of rules which would be applied equally to others. This system of accountability is important in making a clear distinction between the legal form and other normative orders.

It is open to doubt whether justice can ever be accurately described as informal. Most justice systems, no matter how arbitrary, normally function within a rule-governed context. This does not mean that all normative orders are equally legitimate. Such relativism mistakes the particular legitimacy which attaches to state law in a constitutional democracy. There are sound reasons for the formal processes of criminal justice which have emerged in constitutional democracies. These processes offer legal guarantees to the individual which are essential to the concept of, for example, a fair trial. Justice systems must find a place within this bigger picture of state law if they are to be regarded as legitimate or acceptable within a constitutional democracy. Regulatory systems can accommodate pluralism in modern societies.

The argument that law is arguable does not, as I suggest, lead to radical indeterminacy or a deformalized world. Individuals expect law to be arguable and for institutions to be open to persuasion about the meaning of law. This fact, which is fundamental within criminal justice systems, is also central to the concept of legality. Law is, however, not the only normative order in a political community. It exists within the context of other normative orders. Law engages with these orders and both shapes and is itself shaped by them. However, this pluralism does not sanction practices within the state which violate basic constitutional principles relating to, for example, the legal protection of human rights. The legitimacy of law within the state rests in part upon its universal applicability within the territory. It also rests on the reasons which are provided to support the norm. What may seem like an order to the government, must appear as a norm to the individual. The individual should, in the ideal context, see this norm as a sound basis for action. The individual is not the passive recipient of a command, but an active participant in the process of democratic governance. Legitimacy is thus also connected to the process which produces the norm. Individuals are correct to insist that it is the democratic process which produces legitimate legal norms. The ideal of democracy is that the participation of every person in the formulation of the values which regulate community life is at least possible. At the core of the ideal is a profound faith in the individual and the belief that people develop best within the context of a healthy democracy. The ideal may seem a long way from reality in the modern context, but it remains the ideal nonetheless. This is to be contrasted with authoritarian or autocratic rule, where there is a belief in the rule of the 'superior few' within systems of regulation. This has implications for justice systems which function within constitutional democracies. This does not mean that the state cannot recognize and accept pluralism.

Conclusion

The debate about the rule of law is endless. The aim of this chapter is to raise some questions rather than provide comprehensive answers. The debate over informalism tends to rest on assumptions about how political communities work and rests on a monolithic conception of legal order. There are few, if any, areas of modern life which are not governed by rules, of one kind or other. Normative orders are not confined to state law. This is not to defend a relativist understanding of legal order, but to acknowledge that the relationship between law and society is more complicated than is often presented. Law does not come out of nowhere and it does not enter a world without customs, traditions, and habits. In modern complex societies the continuing conflict over the meaning of law can appear as the ultimate argument for the demise of the rule of law. This is a mistake. Citizens, particularly those who confront the criminal process, wish to be able to challenge both legal and factual interpretations. This arguable nature of law is central to the rule of law and not, as is sometimes argued, counter to it. The idea of legal certainty is frequently overstated in arguments about the nature of the rule of law.

The result of my argument is that informal justice systems must find a place with the legal and political orders of constitutional democracies. They cannot function entirely outside of the legal order and they must be consistent with, and responsive to, the constitutional and other values of the particular political community.

Note

1 He did acknowledge pluralism in the sense of a world of states. He described the international community as a 'pluriverse' as opposed to a 'universe' (Schmitt, 1996, p. 53).

References

Cristi, R. (1998), 'Carl Schmitt on Sovereignty and Constituent Power' in Dyzenhaus, D. (ed.), *Law as Politics: Carl Schmitt's Critique of Liberalism*, Duke University Press, Durham, NC, and London, pp. 179-95.
Dallmayr, F.R. (2000), 'Borders of Horizons? Gadamer and Habermas Revisited', *Chicago Kent Law Review*, Vol. 76(2), pp. 825-51.
Dyzenhaus, D. (1991), *Hard Cases in Wicked Legal Systems: South African Law in the Perspective of Legal Philosophy*, Clarendon Press, Oxford.
Dyzenhaus, D. (1984), 'The Legitimacy of Law: A Response to Critics', *Ratio Juris*, Vol. 7, pp. 80-94.
Dyzenhaus, D. (1994), '"Now the Machine Runs Itself": Carl Schmitt on Hobbes and Kelsen', *Cardozo Law Review*, Vol. 16(1), pp. 1-19.
Dyzenhaus, D. (1996), 'The Legitimacy of Legality', *University of Toronto Law Journal*, Vol. 46, pp. 129-80.
Dyzenhaus, D. (1997), *Legality and Legitimacy: Carl Schmitt, Hans Kelsen and Hermann Heller in Weimar*, Oxford University Press, Oxford.
Dyzenhaus, D. (1999), 'Putting the State Back in Credit', in Mouffe, C. (ed.), *The Challenge of Carl Schmitt*, Verso, London, pp. 75-91.
Hayek, F. (1976), *The Constitution of Liberty*, Routledge and Kegan Paul, London (originally published in 1960).
Hayek, F. (1976), *The Road to Serfdom*, Routledge and Kegan Paul, London (originally published in 1944).
Hutchinson, A. (2000), *It's All in the Game*, Duke University Press, Durham, NC, and London.
Hirst, P. (1999), 'Carl Schmitt Decisionism', in Mouffe, C. (ed.), *The Challenge of Carl Schmitt*, Verso, London, pp. 7-17.
Kalyvas, A. (1999), 'Who's Afraid of Carl Schmitt?', *Philosophy and Social Criticism*, Vol. 25, pp. 87-125.
Rasch, W. (2000), 'Conflict as Vocation: Carl Schmitt and the Possibility of Politics', *Theory, Culture and Society*, Vol. 17, pp. 1-32.
Raz, J. (1983), 'The Rule of Law and its Virtue', in Raz, J. (ed.), *The Authority of Law: Essays on Law and Authority*, Oxford University Press, Oxford, pp. 211-29.
Schmitt, C. (1985a), *Political Theology*, The MIT Press, Cambridge and London.
Schmitt, C. (1985b), *The Crisis of Parliamentary Democracy*, The MIT Press, Cambridge, MA, and London.
Schmitt, C. (1996), *The Concept of the Political*, The University of Chicago Press, Chicago and London.
Waldron, J. (1999), *Law and Disagreement*, Oxford University Press, Oxford.
Wright, R. G., (2000), 'Traces of Violence: Gadamer, Habermas, and the Hate Speech Problem', *Chicago Kent Law Review*, Vol. 76, pp. 991-1014.
Wheeler, B. R. (2001), 'Law and Legitimacy in the Work of Jurgen Habermas and Carl Schmitt', *Ethics and International Affairs*, Vol. 15, pp. 173-83.
Zizek, S. (1999), 'Carl Schmitt in the Age of Post-Politics', in Mouffe, C., *The Challenge of Carl Schmitt*, Verso, London, pp. 18-37.

3 What's in a Name? Some Thoughts on the Vocabulary of Vigilantism and Related Forms of 'Informal Criminal Justice'[1]

Ray Abrahams

Introduction

Social action is rarely if ever unambiguous and uncontentious, and the vocabulary used by actors to designate themselves and others and their actions often occupies a fuzzy zone somewhere between the truth and hocus-pocus.[2] This is arguably especially so in the realms of politics and order maintenance, where public service provision and sectional power seeking are notoriously difficult to disentangle from each other. It is certainly quite commonly the case with vigilantism. In the present essay, I explore some features of the language used historically and recently by actors and by commentators to characterize both vigilantes and their targets.[3]

Such a focus is not in any way intended as a scholastic diversion of attention from the often harsh practicalities of vigilante behaviour and the conditions in which it arises. Rather, it aims to illuminate how language is employed to legitimate and defend or oppose and control such behaviour in important ways. In its many guises and configurations, vigilantism commonly has very serious real world implications – often of life and death – for both its practitioners and their targets. It also poses difficulties for the governance of the state, raising awkward questions about the state's claims to provide efficient, just and honest law enforcement, and it illustrates some puzzling qualities of local-level social life. It does this both through its pursuit of law and order and defence of moral values by typically violent and illegal means, and also through its often complex and confusing combinations of opposing elements – sectional and common interests, conservatism and radicalism, elitist and populist values, and intolerance and caring decency. It is not surprising that, with such a heady and at times manipulable mixture, vigilantism typically provokes conflicting responses within and between individuals and groups, and that rhetoric and labelling play a significant role in the arguments it generates.

What 'are' Vigilantes?

Defining 'vigilantism' poses problems for disinterested discussion and analysis. 'Vigilante', 'vigilantism', and a range of other comparable terms, are variously used by those immediately concerned – the 'vigilantes' and their targets – and by politicians, academics, and the general public, sometimes carefully but often loosely, sometimes neutrally and sometimes not, and sometimes but not always in good faith. The fact that such variable, and at times contested, usage is accompanied by, but by no means simply reflects, considerable behavioural variation both within and between different historical and cultural settings, makes it particularly difficult to arrive at a descriptive definition or taxonomy that will satisfactorily encompass the wide range of phenomena involved.

For this reason, as an academic self-consciously trying to work with such terms analytically and comparatively, while at the same time recognizing their ambivalent emotive power and the shifting spectrum of their referents 'on the ground', I have found it useful to resort to the Weberian strategy of 'ideal' or 'pure' types which provide a measure rather than a simple picture of reality. From this perspective, 'vigilante' and 'vigilantism' can then be said 'ideally' to involve an organised attempt by a group of 'ordinary citizens' to enforce norms and maintain law and order on behalf of their communities, often by resort to violence, in the perceived absence of effective official state action through the police and courts.[4] This last point is a key one, which sharply differentiates the 'vigilante' from the 'anarchist'.[5] For whereas anarchism is fundamentally opposed to the state as such, vigilantism is much less radical, since it is typically more critical of the state's actual performance than of the state itself. As such it tends to fall politically between two stools. For the truly conservative, and typically for the state itself, taking the law into one's own hands is quite unacceptable, while for the truly radical, it may appear too conservative and reactionary. At the same time, its wide distribution warns us not to underestimate the force of popular concern for law and order, to which vigilantes typically are or claim to be responding.

As the chapters in this book reveal, and as my own comparative studies show, real life provides numerous examples of groups and their activities which approximate to and deviate from the above 'ideal' in interestingly differing ways while still appearing, and often claiming, to merit inclusion within a single frame of discourse.[6] One key variable in the present context is the degree to which such groups really represent the interests of a whole community or only part of it – perhaps defined in faction, party, generation, gender, ethnic, class or sectarian terms. Thus even in a case like that of Tanzanian Sungusungu vigilantes, which I have studied in some depth and which approximate relatively closely to the ideal type, it is arguable that their activities have often reflected the interests of senior males in the society rather than those of their wives and of younger men (Abrahams, 1998, p. 36). In many other cases, such as the 'informal justice' meted out by paramilitary 'punishment groups' in Northern Ireland, this question of representation has been debated and contested by both actors and observers.[7] Of course, in an extreme case like that of covert governmental 'death squads', and comparable groups, which sometimes masquerade as vigilantes, claimed membership of a community ultimately becomes no more than a cloak of mystifying political propaganda. Another variable, which I discuss below and which has sometimes proved contentious, is the extent to which vigilante activity is disciplined and organized as opposed to that of an unruly mob.

The Vocabulary of Vigilantes and their Critics

In the world of actors and more partisan observers, the word 'vigilante' is one of a set of 'emic' terms within the political vocabulary of those concerned.[8] For particular groups of actors in different historical settings, other members of this word-set have included, 'vigilance committee', 'regulators', 'moderators', 'neighbourhood watch', 'rondas' (patrols) in Italian and Spanish speaking areas, 'punishment groups' or 'squads', 'mobs', 'death squads', and 'stranglers', as well as more specific proper names such as 'Ku Klux Klan' in the American South and Mid-West, 'White Caps' also in the Mid-West, 'Alsa Masa' (*Masses Arise*) in the Philippines, and 'Sungusungu' or 'Basalama' (the people of peace and security) in West-central Tanzania. Similarly, a range of terms has been used to describe the activities of such groups, including 'vigilance' and 'vigilantism', 'lynching', 'informal justice', 'justice sommaire' (in France), and 'charivari' or 'rough music' (with a long history in continental Europe and Britain, and later the American South).[9]

The connotations of such terms are by no means always uniform and stable, as the history of the word 'vigilante' – probably the most widespread of them – illustrates. The word is originally a Spanish adjective meaning 'watchful', and as a noun it mainly seems to mean a 'watchman' in that language. It was taken into English in the nineteenth century, and entered popular vocabulary through the writings of Thomas Dimsdale (1866) about the 1860s Vigilantes of Montana – a group of concerned citizens, many of them freemasons, who organized themselves initially against the allegedly corrupt local Sheriff and his band of 'road agents', and later against other criminals and 'undesirables' who crossed their path. At that time, the word, like its grander sounding contemporary 'vigilance committee', seems to have had a mainly positive significance, and those who were opposed to such groups tended to refer to them by more pejorative words such as 'stranglers'. More recently in North America, there appears to be a growing tendency to view the term 'vigilante', and the violence associated with it, more critically, and it has negative connotations for many Britons, notwithstanding quite widespread feelings that individuals should be relatively free to defend themselves against muggers and burglars. An interesting distinction in this context was drawn by Tony Blair, as shadow Home Secretary in 1993, when he commented, in a broadcast interview on rising popular anxiety about crime, that 'We do not need vigilantes, but we do need vigilance'.[10] Again, in South Africa during the Apartheid period, the term was commonly used negatively for regime-supporting gangs employed by local political leaders to keep their opponents in order, while the term 'comrades' was widely used in contrast as a positive term for often comparably violent groups of African National Congress supporters.[11] As I understand it, the term is now used there more generally. It is also sometimes used in English to refer to lone seekers after vengeance, and this seems partly to hark back to the influence of films and comic-books, such as the 'Death Wish' series and to Batman and other such 'heroes'. Beyond this, the term also has a wide range of use well outside the strict realm of vigilantism itself, for instance in such phrases as 'the impatient monetary vigilantes' of the bond market and the name 'Vigilantes of Love' adopted by an American folk-rock and soul group. It is also perhaps worth noting that in English, the set of words including 'vigil', 'vigilance' and 'vigilante', which derive originally from Latin, co-exists with a second set, with partly overlapping meanings, including 'wake', 'watch' and 'watchful'. These words are of Germanic origin, but they appear to share ancient Indo-European roots with their Latin counterparts. At the same time, the idea of 'neighbourhood watch', with its connotations of non-violence and collaboration with the police, has come to be contrasted strongly with vigilantism in contemporary English.

Those who have sought to defend vigilantism, have naturally tended to stress concepts like 'community', and 'justice', and to highlight the local inaccessibility or the 'incompetence' and 'corruption' of state institutions and officials, the 'threat' to decent society posed by vigilante targets, and their own concern for the 'victims' of offences as opposed to their perpetrators. Claims to efficiency are also sometimes made, and the risks of serious mistakes played down or ignored. Brown (1975, p. 174) cites a prominent American lawyer's claim in 1890 that 'very few innocent men are lynched, and, of those who have not committed the past offence for which they suffer, a still smaller proportion are decent members of society' while the official legal system is 'habitually duped and evaded by means formally lawful'.[12] Although there may exist a varying degree of truth behind such emphases and claims, I need scarcely say that one can rarely take them sensibly at face value, especially when they become a passionate focus of media attention and a vehicle of political ambition.

A similar caveat can, of course, also be issued about much of the language of anti-vigilante criticism. One major strand of this has always been a stress on the imperative value of the state and its formal legal institutions, however flawed these may be in practice. Vested interests in state hegemony and formal bureaucratic control are likely to be present among those who wield them, and criticism of vigilantism is likely to reflect the fact that it typically constitutes an uncomfortable criticism of the efficiency of police and courts and of the failure of government to command widespread legitimacy and be attuned to popular concerns. This was clear when Sungusungu village vigilantism began in Tanzania in the early 1980s among the Nyamwezi and Sukuma people. Bureaucrats, police and some local officials immediately branded it as a dangerous illegitimate threat to the formal political and legal order that had to be repressed at once. It was only when some ruling party officials and President Nyerere himself supported it as a genuine grass-roots effort to bring law and order back into the countryside, that repression of the movement ceased and an attempt was made to accommodate it within the constitutional framework (Abrahams and Bukurura, 1993).

One issue, which the movement's critics saw or at least claimed to see as worrying, was some of the labels that the groups adopted. A key point here was the groups' description of themselves as a *chama*. This was in fact a perfectly defensible usage – since this Swahili word can legitimately be used to refer to any sort of voluntary association. However, it is also the word used for a political party, and Tanzania was at that time a one-party state under the rule of the Revolutionary Party (*Chama cha Mapinduzi*). Local and other party bureaucrats anxious to suppress the groups therefore read their choice of the term as at worst a challenge to their own hegemony and at least a confusing and unwarranted claim to political legitimacy. Similar criticisms were also levelled at the groups' use of the word *mtemi* (the standard local term for the 'chief' of a traditional chiefdom) for their village level leaders. This again was a legitimate form of usage in the area – the term had also customarily been applied to leaders of a wide range of voluntary associations there over a long period. Chiefship itself, however, had been formally abolished as a political office after Independence in 1961, and Sungusungu's critics were again quick to try to claim that the movement sought to reintegrate the former hereditary chiefs into the political system.

Differing characterizations of the activities of Northern Ireland 'punishment' groups, or 'squads', as they are often referred to more pejoratively by critics, also throw light on these issues. Some claim that the groups are satisfying local community needs to control activities such as drug and alcohol abuse, joy-riding, theft and vandalism among young offenders, while others tend to emphasize the illegitimacy of their often brutal violence as they seek to gain and maintain political control of 'the streets'.[13] As Knox (2001) clearly shows, 'victim' is one of an interesting set of strongly contested concepts here. The opponents of the groups' activities see the recipients of 'punishment' as key 'victims' in this situation. For some supporters, however, these targets are unacceptable 'perpetrators' of offences and at best 'deserving' victims of just retribution, while the true victims are the communities they have disrupted. Many actors and some commentators would extend this to explain or justify these 'punishment' activities and also more overtly political sectarian violence by casting their 'perpetrators' as 'victims' of sectarian violence and, for some, of state repression. It has also been suggested that everyone in Northern Ireland may be seen to some degree as 'victims' or as 'perpetrators' of 'the troubles'.[14]

Again, as the liberal use of inverted commas in my own and other texts suggests, the term 'punishment' itself is similarly and relatedly contested. Knox (*loc cit*) has commented that the 'use of the term "punishment", as Kennedy (1995) suggests, is value-laden in that it carries a presumption that the victim somehow deserves what is meted out by the paramilitaries. Moreover, it can conjure up an image of chastisement, threatening behaviour and minor physical violence' (p. 190). He notes, too, that the same point has been made more forcefully by critics, such as the Conservative spokesman, Andrew Mackay, who told Parliament in 1999 that the 'term "punishment beating" sounds like a modest extension of neighbourhood watch – at the very worst some vigilante group modestly beating up drug dealers or vandals. (Yet) what is going on in Northern Ireland (is) mutilation, and...beatings in which every bone in the victim's body is deliberately broken. It is intimidation of the very worst sort, and often leads to exile' (*ibid,* p. 190). As I suggested earlier, and as Knox himself rightly remarks, such emotive language must be understood within its special historical and political context as something rather more than the simple statement of fact that it claims to be.

Committees, Mobs, and Lynchings

Particularly in America, where vigilante violence has a long and varied history, one powerful but, again, contested weapon in critiques of vigilantism has been the label 'mob' and derived terms like 'mobocracy'. The use of the term 'mob', as an English abbreviation of the Latin 'mobile vulgus' ('unstable or excitable crowd'), apparently dates back to the late seventeenth century. With the main exception of nineteenth and twentieth century antipodean usage, it has mainly had pejorative connotations.[15] The Oxford English Dictionary glosses it as 'the disorderly and riotous part of the population, the roughs, the rabble'; 'the common mass of the people; the lower orders; the uncultured or illiterate as a class; the populace, the masses'; and as 'disorderly or lower class people forming a crowd'. The term 'mobocracy', for 'mob rule', is less widely used but also goes back some 250 years.

Often combined with the word 'mob' in this context, 'lynch' and 'lynching' are slightly younger terms which appear to derive from the late eighteenth century activities of a Colonel Lynch of Bedford County, Virginia (some early accounts also locate him in Carolina), who decided with some of his fellow leading citizens to take the law into their own hands in the absence of locally satisfactory formal mechanisms for dealing with offenders.[16] Although lynching typically implies hanging nowadays, 'Lynch's law', as it was also known, seems to have included flogging and tarring and feathering in its repertoire of punishments.

While it would be pointless to deny that such terms provide an apt characterization of much vigilante behaviour, their use in criticism of all such activity is much more contentious. An example is the work of John Caughey, who, in 1960, published a volume of accounts of vigilantism over the previous century. The phrase used as the title of the book, *Their Majesties the Mob,* was drawn from an early 1850s account of a harsh and partly drunken vigilante hanging in Indian Bars, California. Caughey was well aware that not all vigilantism was of this sort, but he was opposed to it in all its forms, and his choice of title reflects this. In his Introduction, he writes as follows. 'Whatever else is said about vigilantism, it must be remarked that it is a subject afflicted with a sliding scale of labels. At the outset, therefore, it is advisable to pin down one basic definition. Vigilantism, lynch law, mobocracy – these are some of the variant terms. Each has an emphasis of its own, but in all of them the essence is the same. That essence is a group action in lieu of regular justice. Whichever synonym is used, that is the identifying character'. In quoting this passage, I have relatively little to quarrel with in the actual definitional discussion that Caughey begins here and goes on to develop, and I would not disagree with his assessment that much vigilantism is driven by forces additional to or other than a genuinely simple search for the control of crime in the absence of effective state institutions. It does, however, seem worthwhile to highlight how his choice of an emotive title and his use of the word 'synonym' go well beyond a straightforwardly analytical approach to vigilante behaviour.

This point was in fact anticipated in a much earlier discussion by the American historian Hubert Howe Bancroft who devoted much of his life as a scholar to the documentation of vigilantism in all parts of the American West, and especially to the large-scale movements, which arose in San Francisco in the 1850s. Unlike Caughey, Bancroft was favourably disposed to much vigilante activity, which he saw as filling a gap commonly left by the absence of effective state crime control in frontier conditions such as those of the mid-nineteenth century American West. His monumental two-volume work of 1887, has the significantly mild title 'Popular Tribunals', and he argues passionately there against a mindless worship of the law, which dismisses vigilantism simply as 'illegal'. 'Law is the voice of the people' he tells us (Vol. I, p. 9), and 'Law is the servant and not the master of men' (Vol. I, p. 43). He also claims (Vol. I, p. 36) that 'Law we must have...But to talk of the sacredness of law...is to clothe rules and prescriptions with the superstitious veneration which enshrouded them of old'. He goes on interestingly to discuss the influence of 'words and symbols of authority, such as legal verbiage, red tapes and seals, and all that claptrap of justice of which wigs, gowns, and divers hollow ceremonies are a part' (Vol. I, p. 37). He stresses the uselessness of law if effective courts are unavailable to people, and he also colourfully questions the integrity of many of those he calls the 'law and order party' (Vol. II, pp. 141 and *passim*). 'Crime fattens on the fruits of industry, and lawyers fatten on crime' he tells us, and he describes those concerned as 'office-holders, judges, lawyers, sheriffs, policemen, jail-keepers, politicians, law-makers, and such nondescript subalterns, contractors, demagogues, manipulators of elections and hangers-on as found food or profit in the law' (Vol. II, p. 142).

As Bancroft's title suggests, this position emphasizes that law, society, and the state exist for 'the people', and that the people must and will fend for themselves when necessary. This idea is of course enshrined in the United States constitutional doctrine of 'popular sovereignty', but its attraction extends more widely to all critics of the 'dead hand' of bureaucracy and other pathological conditions of the state.[17] As usual, however, with such rhetoric, the problem is what lies behind it. When one enquires who 'the people' are, the answer varies from one case and context to another, and there may well be different answers from within the same 'community'. Bancroft, like several other nineteenth century American commentators, is in fact self-consciously elitist on this point, especially in his case with regard to San Francisco.[18] He is particularly keen to emphasize the difference between the disciplined activities of the leading members of the city's vigilance committees and the undisciplined tendencies to 'mobocracy' of the populace at large, and he devotes several pages to this question (Vol. I, pp. 8-15). In direct confrontation to Caughey's later comment, he argues that the 'terms vigilance committee, mob-law, lynch-law, are not, as many suppose, synonymous...The vigilance committee is not a mob...Indeed prominent among its other functions is that of holding brute force and vulgar sentiment in wholesome fear. The vigilance committee will itself break the law, but it does not allow others to do so. It has the highest respect for law...yet it has a higher respect for itself than for ill-administered law' (Vol. I, p. 8). He admits to superficial similarities with mob-violence – they emerge in similar conditions and 'become a law unto themselves' but 'One is an organization officered by its most efficient members, aiming at public well-being, and acting under fixed rules of its own making; the other is an unorganized rabble, acting under momentary delirium, the tool, it may be, of political demagogues, the victim of its own intemperance. Underlying the actions of the one is justice; of the other revenge' (*ibid*). One need scarcely say that such distinctions are more easily sustained on paper than in hangings. Nor are one's anxieties about them necessarily allayed by learning that many of the elite in question were businessmen or freemasons, however proud of this they were themselves, or that the 1856 Committee in San Francisco was largely concerned with the destruction of its political opponents, however corrupt their political machine.[19]

The issue of reality and rhetoric looms much larger when one shifts attention from such cases to the covert operations of the state's own personnel in the asserted vigilantism of death squads and 'counter-insurgency' groups in Central and South America and the Philippines, and in so-called 'black-on-black' conflicts of pre-apartheid South Africa. In such cases, what Rosenbaum and Sederberg (1976) have called regime-support and control, plus elite economic interests, may be disguised by specious claims that such activities essentially constitute a popular grass-roots reaction to problems of personal and national security.

The material I have considered makes it clear that vigilantism is rarely simply a popular response to the failure of due legal process to deal with breaches of the law. 'The people' and 'the community' are, on inspection, complex concepts, and the populism of much vigilante rhetoric conceals, or in Bancroft's case goes hand in hand with, a self-satisfied elitism. Indeed, as Smurr (1958, p. 15) argued for 1860s Montana, this may also be accompanied by a contempt for more populist forms of 'trial by jury' and 'miners' courts', which the vigilantes in question chose, in his view, to neglect rather than support and protect.

Sticks and Stones, and Lethal Labels

My own first studies of vigilantism focused on the emergence in the 1980s of the widespread village movement of so-called Sungusungu vigilantes among the Nyamwezi and closely related Sukuma people of Tanzania (Abrahams 1987; 1989). I first studied Nyamwezi society in depth during the late 1950s, and I have revisited the area several times. As my several books and many papers amply show (*cf* Abrahams 1967; 1981; 1994), I have had and still have enormous admiration for the mutual aid and spirit of good company that I encountered among the Nyamwezi, and I felt considerable sympathy for their attempts to quell increasingly troublesome cattle rustling and highway robbery through Sungusungu vigilante action in the undoubted absence of effective policing in the rural areas. At the same time, however, some of the groups started to hunt out and occasionally kill witches.[20] I have no doubt of the good faith of most of those involved. They believe that witchcraft is a genuinely lethal danger that should be eradicated. However, as one who does not share this view, I find it little comfort to know that such eradication is perceived as some sort of public hygiene.

Such targeting of alleged 'witches' recurs in a variety of guises in much vigilante activity, and it points to a more general issue, which is implicit in much of my earlier discussion and is of deep importance both in academic and in practical terms. This is the question of the negative implications of the human capacity for classification and labelling. Let me acknowledge here my debt to the distinguished social anthropologist Edmund Leach, who was my own first teacher in the subject. For as Michael Herzfeld (1992) has also noted, in the context of his study of bureaucratic stereotyping and 'indifference', Leach's work in this particular area has been enormously insightful.[21]

The basic argument is by now well known. One part of it is the way in which the plethora of human languages – vividly recognized in the story of the tower of Babel – provides one of a number of bases on which people sometimes find it possible to decide to treat others not so much as fellow humans but as members of an alien species. More central to the present context, however, is the general fact that human beings are fundamentally linguistic, and as such classifying, animals. Language and its labels are both the key way we comprehend the world, and even put it to good use, and the way in which we contrive either accidentally or, as John Barnes has pointed out in his book *A Pack of Lies*, often enough deliberately, to distort and misrepresent it. One does not need to take a hard-line Whorfian position on the influence of language upon thought to accept that we relate in highly significant ways both to the world in general, and to other people in particular, through the labels we attach to them. Herein arguably lies a great deal of our peculiarly human capacity for both good and evil and, of course, for argument between and about them.

It is so natural to us to relate to the world in this way that we can easily be led or misled to mistake the label for the labelled. And a key point here is that labels often have a lethal quality – they provide us all in different times and places with a Bond-like licence to kill. It was an optimist or a fool who coined the children's chant that sticks and stones could break our bones but names will never hurt us, if only because the two are all too often intimately connected.

This is perhaps especially important in the present context in the identification and characterization of some of the targets and 'victims' of vigilante groups. For in addition to the stereotyping of individuals through the use of superficially descriptive labels such as sex-offender, 'bummer' (in nineteenth century Montana), street-children, Black or Jew, or Australian (as main targets in the first large San Francisco movement of the 1850s), or independent-minded woman, the world is littered with examples of potentially deadly slippage which assumes that such terms are synonymous with others such as murderer or witch or other not quite human 'enemy within'. And as I have noted, such labels can be lethally accompanied by beatings, torturings and lynchings whose victims might well have preferred the odd stick or stone. Of course, it is not only vigilantes who in varying contexts and to varying degree perform this kind of linguistic black magic. As various forms of death squads make clear, and as political propaganda of all sorts also demonstrates, the state itself is no sluggard in this field, either through direct action or through varyingly successful attempts to lead others into doing its political dirty work. Similarly, one can see the deadly costs of labelling, and much worse of believing in the more dehumanizing forms of label, in more directly oppositional politics at sub-state level in Northern Ireland, the Middle East and most parts of the former Yugoslavia in which anything from residential ethnic cleansing to bombing, military rape and attempted genocide of their harshly labelled and 'dehumanized' enemies appears to be justified to their performers at the time.

The lethal potential of such stereotypes starkly highlights the need to treat all labels with quite suspicious care. To a modern Western observer, this may seem obvious enough with accusations of witchcraft, but some other cases may be rather less clear at first sight. Martha Huggins and others have clearly illustrated this with respect to so-called 'street children' in Brazil (*cf.* Huggins and Mesquita, 1996), where more than 7000 poor children and adolescents are said to have been murdered in increasing numbers between 1988 and 1991, with further increases in subsequent years. The very large majority of these murder victims (almost 90 per cent) have been teenage males who are also typically extremely poor and black. Huggins and Mesquita, and also Penglase (1994), have seriously questioned the common designation of such victims as 'street children', with its implications of living permanently as strays on the streets. Although a minority clearly fit the stereotypes of young criminals living off theft and peddling drugs, and often being drug addicts themselves, most of them do not. While they often pass their daylight hours '*on* the street', a majority live with their families, often in makeshift homes, in the poorest areas of the city, and many of them work as best they can in extremely low-income occupations. Moreover, despite many claims that they are dangerous as well as criminal, even those involved in crime are relatively rarely violent — unlike the military and civil police who often engage in common criminal activities themselves. As the authors note, however, such stereotypes are used to dehumanize *all* the children concerned and to classify them more or less as social vermin and 'feral discards' whose destruction is essential for the survival of respectable society. They also argue plausibly that such labelling, combined with their high degree of public visibility, renders poor black youths on the streets especially vulnerable to violence from more 'respectable' citizens who fear or resent their presence.

Unlike most other murder victims, who are killed by members of their families or some other close associate, these young males are typically killed by strangers. Homicide data on 15-17 year olds in São Paolo for 1990 shows that in cases where the perpetrator was identified, public police accounted for almost half of the killings and so-called 'extermination groups' for almost a third. Although most of the perpetrators remained unidentified, there are reasons to believe that 'extermination groups' (*grupos de extermínio*) with connections to the police – either on or off duty – were often involved. Death squad members and other killers of such children are in fact often known to the police, but few have been prosecuted. The large majority of the victims were shot, and many of them were also badly mutilated and tortured.

There appear to be several reasons for general police inability and reluctance to pursue the guilty parties in such cases, including the cumbersome nature of the judicial process, intimidation, and a lack of enthusiasm to hunt out the killers who are known or suspected to be police themselves or their associates. At the same time, as Huggins and Mesquita comment, such reluctance and, indeed, the killings themselves are only understandable in the broader context of a society whose more 'respectable' members are generally little concerned with the fate of the young people in question. In fact, many citizens are critical of the apparent inability of police and courts to keep such undesirable 'animal' elements off the streets, and their attitudes often range between acquiescence in and positive support for the killings which are seen as necessary if 'decent' society is to be protected. Such citizens are also willing to connive in and help foster the claims that the young people in question are often victims of each other's violence or of individual 'lone wolves' rather than organized groups of police and others.

Huggins and Mesquita interestingly contrast such blinkered attitudes and lethal stereotyping in a 'democratizing' Brazil with the more widespread hostility towards the violence directed against 'enemies' of the previous military regime (1964-85). They describe such earlier Brazilian violence as more 'visible', partly because much of it was perpetrated by armed and uniformed police and military personnel, and partly because of the social standing of the victims. They comment that at that time 'the primary victims of murder were middle- and upper-middle-class political dissidents whose alleged transgressions were challenging the military regime', and they note that the visibility of victims was increased by 'the fact that they were young adults with indisputable civic status as university students, or priests, nuns, or professional people, children or adolescents being much less likely to be direct victims of this political repression' (1996, p. 94). They also comment that the social class of many of the victims of violence at that time was higher than that of its perpetrators.

Making Monsters

In Britain recent outbreaks of popular protest and vigilante-style harassment of alleged paedophiles in Portsmouth and elsewhere also illustrate some of the problems of 'dehumanizing' stereotypes, while at the same time bringing into high relief the powerful role which is often played by the popular press in such contexts of extreme 'moral panic' (Cohen, 1972; Goode and Ben-Yahuda, 1994) and other situations of heightened popular anxiety. This was, for instance, a significant feature of the 1856 San Francisco outbreak of vigilantism against an asserted wave of crime and political corruption, as it also was in another well-documented case of the late 1880s from Tampa, Florida.[22] There the targets were mainly Cuban trade unionists who were denounced as 'evil...agitators, revolutionists and agitated patriots' whose 'terrorism would be dealt with promptly by whatever means were necessary'. In the present context, provocative British tabloid media attention to paedophiles has been noticeably strong during the last decade, and a recent survey of articles on the subject in six popular newspapers (Soothill *et al*, 1998 quoted in Thomas, 2000, p. 18) found many examples of the use of violent language there, including liberal resort to such terms as 'sex monster', 'beasts', and 'sex fiends'.

The Portsmouth protests arose in July and August 2000 as a local reaction to the murder of an eight-year-old girl, Sarah Payne, in Sussex. One consequence of the widespread revulsion which the murder generated was a revival of popular anxiety about paedophiles and interest in the provision of information to local communities about them and other sexual offenders through the introduction of a 'Megan's Law' in Britain, along the lines of the legislation enacted some years ago in New Jersey, and subsequently in other US states, after the murder of a young girl, Megan Kanka. The popular tabloid newspaper, *The News of the World*, took a leading stance in supporting this demand in Britain, and it began its own campaign of 'naming and shaming' paedophiles said to be living in various communities after their sentences. A number of families on the Paulsgrove estate in Portsmouth, and in some other parts of Britain, began to hold protests and vigils, accompanied by threats and some acts of violence against suspects, aimed at driving out all paedophiles from their own locality. Whole families, including young children, took part in the Portsmouth protests and posters were carried, and even attached to babies' push-chairs, with such slogans as   'DON'T HOUSE THEM, HANG THEM!!', and 'KILL THE PAEDOPHILES', while a photograph shows one child wearing a T-shirt inscribed with the message 'PROTECT ME!'. The Paulsgrove protesters claimed to know who the alleged paedophiles were, though a variety of less sensationalist media discussion at the time suggested that this claimed knowledge was at best imperfect. At least one case of mistaken identity led to the evacuation of a harassed family, and there were violent attacks on some suspects' homes.

Although it is often said to be counter-productive, since it risks driving offenders underground, this kind of reaction to the presence of convicted and suspected paedophiles in local areas is not uncommon. As in many other emotionally charged situations, fact, theory and fantasy are not easily disentangled on this issue. The anger, hatred, protests and harassment clearly share some features of a 'witch craze'. At the same time, however, it has been remarked in a study of the 'anthropology of evil', that in some societies 'evil is attributed to monsters that cannot exist', whereas in modern Britain and the West it is attributed to monsters that do (Pocock, 1985, p. 56). It is in fact quite hard to know how accurate this contrast is, and which, in any case, of these conditions should be thought the more regrettable. Nonetheless, the realities of the Holocaust and other forms of genocide, along with different patterns of humiliating and often enough deadly violence mentioned earlier, certainly testify to the reality in the West and elsewhere of the extraordinary depths of behaviour which human nature sometimes plumbs. The sexual assault and murder of young children not surprisingly arouses a great deal of horror, and once again there is clear evidence from recent cases, including the discovery of organized paedophile rings engaged in such activity, that attests to the actual occurrence of such killings.

On the other hand, it appears that the murder of young children is relatively rare – in England and Wales there are about 50 homicides per year of children under 16 years of age, excluding babies under one year old. Moreover, along with a majority of sexual and other assaults on them, such murders are mostly committed by a child's own parents or someone otherwise close to them. The annual number of sex-related murders attributable to strangers is usually in single figures, and serial sex-killers of children appear to be extremely rare.[23] At the same time, recently quoted figures suggest that as many as one in one hundred and thirty men have a conviction for a sexual offence against a child by the age of forty, and up to 3,000 convicted paedophiles are said to be released from prison each year. This suggests that, however repugnant their behaviour may appear to most people, the vast majority of paedophiles are not homicidal, and that the idea of the monstrous, murderous paedophile as the archetypal child-sex offender preying in large numbers on other people's children is a nightmare myth rather than an image of reality.[24]

Conclusion

My aim in this paper has been to explore the role of language, and especially rhetoric, in different areas of vigilante activity and reactions to it. It seems clear, in a variety of contexts ranging from relatively simple choices of vocabulary and disagreements over the correct gloss of a term to the more emotive language of inflammatory press outbursts and campaigns, that this role is considerable both in criticism and in support of vigilantism. I commented earlier that my airing of this issue was not meant to serve as a diversion from the facts of vigilantism themselves, though my discussion does, I hope, bring out some of the problems of extracting these facts from the welter of value laden terms and propaganda which many commentaries contain. Rather, my hope is that my discussion reveals clearly the double-sided nature of the phenomena in question. Forms of vigilante activity vary greatly, as do their various characterizations. Both too can affect the perceptions of actors and observers, yet neither is a reliable guide in itself to the other. The relation between them is complex, if only because vigilantism itself is full of paradox and ambivalence. Although, in my own view, what people actually do is ultimately more significant than what they say they do, it will I hope be clear that what they say also deserves careful study since it may exercise potentially powerful supporting and inhibiting influence upon their own and others' actions.

Notes

1   I use the term 'informal criminal justice' here in the loose sense of non-state interventions by individuals and groups in dealing with alleged offences, although the word 'informal' might be considered problematic in this sense because some forms of such activity are in fact highly 'formalized'. My aim in using the term is, however, to avoid rather than create definitional wrangles which might unduly limit the scope of my discussion. It will be clear from my 'ideal type' definitional approach to vigilantism

itself in the text, that I consider tightly bounded 'pigeon-holing' definitions less helpful than they might appear to be at first sight.

2   There is broad agreement on this among students of society, though they differ in their explanations of the situation and in their readiness to extend the argument to their own and others' analyses.

3   As I mention later, my focus here should not be taken to imply that the State itself in its various guises does not engage in many forms of linguistic propaganda and manipulation.

4   For other useful definitional discussions see Johnston (1996) and also Brown (1975, pp. 118-21). For an example of problems of handling phenomena on the edges of such definitions, see Sharp and Wilson (2000).

5   *Cf.* Brown's use (1975, p. 94) of the term 'conservative mob' here.

6   *Cf.* Abrahams (1998) for a detailed comparative analysis of vigilantism and related forms of activity in a wide range of contemporary and historical settings.

7   There is valuable discussion of, and bibliographical reference to, this issue in Knox (2001). I am grateful to Professor Knox for permission to make use of this paper and to cite some of its contents prior to publication. I am also grateful to Dermot Feenan for advice, and to Jade Moran for helpful discussion on this subject.

8   I use 'emic' here to refer to the 'subjective' status of a term as part of cultural (or sub-cultural) usage, rather than constituting an 'etic' part of an 'objective' view of the world. The two terms are derived by foreshortening from the distinction between 'phonemics' and 'phonetics' in linguistic studies of phonology.

9   *Cf.* Abrahams (1998, *passim*).

10 BBC, *World at One*, 30 August, 1993 (reported by Michael White, *The Guardian*, p. 2, 31 August, 1993).

11 See Haysom (1986) and essays by Harris and by Phillips in Kirkwood (ed.) (1989). I am grateful for information from Rachel Monaghan on the current situation.

12 As Brown (1975, pp. 155-6) and others have noted, the relative low cost of vigilante 'justice' was also often cited as a valuable virtue in nineteenth century North America.

13 Such groups' activities arguably fall within the 'related forms of informal criminal justice' in my title because their members are not 'ordinary citizens'. The aim of my discussion is to note the contested language which describes and surrounds their activities in a similar way to that often found with 'mainstream' vigilantism, including common claims from their supporters that they serve the communities within which they operate in the absence of satisfactory State intervention.

14 For a useful discussion of such assertions see Smyth (1998, p. 34 and *passim*).

15 Brown (1975, p. 97) notes that the term 'mob' was also in apparently standard use for vigilante groups in Central Texas.

16 For the origins of 'Lynch Law' *cf.* Brown (1975, p. 59) and Stuart (1833, Vol. II, p. 178 *ff.*).

17 For discussion of the significance of 'popular sovereignty' and other special factors in the American vigilante tradition, see Brown (1975, pp. 112-17).

18 Brown (1975, pp. 111 *ff.*) has interestingly stressed the significance of elitism in the American vigilante tradition.

19 For a revisionist discussion, which highlights the influence of sectional business and political interests on San Francisco vigilantism, and questions the reality of the high levels of crime and corruption cited as its justification, see Senkewicz (1985).

20 *Cf.* Bukurura (1994) and my own discussion in Abrahams (1998).

21 Herzfeld refers to Leach (1965) and I have found Leach (1977) especially useful.

22 On Tampa, see Ingalls (1988). For a critical view of press activity in San Francisco at this time, see Senkewicz (1985).

23 I draw here upon West (2000a) and on his aptly titled paper 'Paedophilia, Plague or Panic?' (2000b), which provide excellent overviews of the realities of sex offenders and offences against children. I am very grateful to Professor West for the opportunity to discuss some of these issues with him. I am also grateful to Loraine Gelsthorpe for drawing my attention to Thomas (2000) and other material on 'moral panics'.

24 West's material also shows that the common assumption that all or even most sex offences against children are likely to leave lasting damage is not well supported by the facts. Similarly, although recidivism in paedophiles is likely to persist into old age, the recorded rate of recidivism among them within a period of 2 years after their release is quite low (2 per cent) as compared to criminals in general (56 per cent).

References

Abrahams, R. (1967), *The Political Organization of Unyamwezi*, Cambridge University Press, Cambridge.
Abrahams, R. (1981), *The Nyamwezi Today*, Cambridge University Press, Cambridge.
Abrahams, R. (1987), 'Sungusungu: Village Vigilante Groups in Tanzania', *African Affairs*, Vol. 86, pp. 179-96.
Abrahams, R. (1989), 'Law and Order and the State in the Nyamwezi and Sukuma Area of Tanzania', *Africa*, Vol. 59(3), pp. 354-68.
Abrahams, R. (ed.) (1994), *Witchcraft in Contemporary Tanzania*, African Studies Centre, Cambridge.
Abrahams, R. (1998), *Vigilant Citizens: Vigilantism and the State*, Polity Press, Cambridge and Malden.
Abrahams, R. and Bukurura, S. (1993), 'Party, Bureaucracy and Grass Roots Initiatives in a Socialist State: the Case of Sungusungu Vigilantes in Tanzania', in Hann, C. (ed.), *Socialism: Ideals, Ideologies and Local Practices*, Routledge, London, pp. 92-101.
Bancroft, H. (1887), *Popular Tribunals* (2 Volumes), History Company, San Francisco.
Barnes, J. A. (1994), *A Pack of Lies*, Cambridge University Press, Cambridge.
Brown, R. M. (1975), *Strain of Violence*, Oxford University Press, Oxford.
Bukurura, S. (1994), 'Sungusungu and the Banishment of Witches in Kahama Tanzania', in Abrahams, R. (ed.), *Witchcraft in Contemporary Tanzania*, African Studies Centre, Cambridge, pp. 61-9.
Caughey, J. (1957), *Their Majesties the Mob*, University of Chicago Press, Illinois.
Cohen, S. (1972), *Folk Devils and Moral Panics*, McGibbon and Kee, London.
Dimsdale, T. (1866, New Edition 1953), *The Vigilantes of Montana*, Oklahoma University Press, Norman and London.
Goode, E. and Ben-Yahuda, N. (1994), *Moral Panics: The Social Construction of Deviance*, Blackwells, Oxford.
Harris, P. (1989), 'The Role of Right-wing Vigilantes in South Africa', in Kirkwood, M. (ed.), *States of Terror*, Catholic Institute for International Relations, London, pp. 1-13.
Haysom, N. (1986), *Apartheid's Private Army: The Rise of Right-wing Vigilantes in South Africa*, Catholic Institute for International Relations, London.
Herzfeld, M. (1992), *The Social Production of Indifference: Exploring the Symbolic Roots of Western Bureaucracy*, Berg, New York.
Huggins, M. and Mesquita, M. (1996), 'Exclusion, Civil Invisibility and Impunity as Explanations for Youth Murders in Brazil', *Childhood*, Vol. 3, pp. 77-98.
Ingalls, R. (1988), *Urban Vigilantes in the New South: Tampa 1882-1936*, University of Tennessee Press, Knoxville.
Johnston, L. (1996), 'What is Vigilantism?', *British Journal of Criminology*, Vol. 36(2), pp. 220-36.

Kennedy, L. (1995), 'Nightmares within Nightmares: Paramilitary Repression within Working-class Communities', in Kennedy, L. (ed.) *Crime and Punishment in West Belfast*, The Summer School, West Belfast, Belfast, pp. 67-80.

Knox, C. (2001), 'The "Deserving" Victims of Political Violence: "Punishment" Attacks in Northern Ireland', *Criminal Justice*, Vol. 1(2), pp. 181-99.

Leach, E. (1965), 'The Nature of War', *Disarmament and Arms Control*, Vol. 3, pp. 165-83.

Leach, E. (1977), *Custom, Law and Terrorist Violence*, Edinburgh University Press, Edinburgh.

Penglase, B. (1994), *Final Justice: Police and Death Squad Homicides of Adolescents in Brazil*, Human Rights Watch/Americas, New York.

Phillips, M. (1989) 'Divide and Repress: Vigilantes and State Objectives in Crossroads', in Kirkwood, M. (ed.), *States of Terror*, Catholic Institute for International Relations, London, pp. 15-36.

Pocock, D. (1985), 'Unruly Evil', in D. Parkin (ed.), *The Anthropology of Evil*, Blackwell, Oxford, pp. 42-56.

Rosenbaum, H. and Sederberg, P. (eds)   (1976), *Vigilante Politics*, University of Pennsylvania Press, Philadelphia.

Senkewicz, R. (1985), *Vigilantes in Goldrush San Francisco*, Stanford University Press, Stanford.

Sharp, S. and Wilson, D. (2000), '"Household Security": Private Policing and Vigilantism in Doncaster', *The Howard Journal*, Vol. 39(2), pp. 113-31.

Smurr, J. (1958), 'Afterthoughts on the Vigilantes', *Montana Magazine of Western History*, Vol. 8 (2), pp. 8-20.

Smyth, M. (1998), 'Remembering in Northern Ireland: Victims, Perpetrators and Hierarchies of Pain and Responsibility', in Hamber, B. (ed.), *Past Imperfect: Dealing with the Past in Northern Ireland and Societies in Transition*, Derry/ Londonderry, INCORE, pp. 31-49.

Soothill, K., Francis, B. and Ackerley, E. (1998), 'Paedophilia and Paedophiles', *New Law Journal*, Vol. 148 (6844), pp. 882-3.

Stuart, J. (1833), *Three Years in North America*, Robert Cadell, Edinburgh.

Thomas, T. (2000), *Sex Crime: Sex Offending and Society*, Willan, Portland.

West, D. (2000a), 'The Sex Crime Situation: Deterioration More Apparent than Real?', *European Journal on Criminal Policy and Research*, Vol. 8, pp. 399-422.

West, D. (2000b), 'Paedophilia: Plague or Panic?', *Journal of Forensic Psychology*, Vol. 11, pp. 511-31.

4 Community Justice in Conflict: Paramilitary Punishment in Northern Ireland

Dermot Feenan

Introduction

Paramilitary punishment in Northern Ireland represents, in part, a contest over the legitimacy of community justice within a society deeply divided along ethno-national lines, large parts of which experience alienation from the formal state system, particularly in the recent thirty-three years of political violence. This contest over the legitimacy of community justice is not unique to Northern Ireland. It is a theme that is explored elsewhere in the context of popular justice (Merry and Milner, 1993), revolutionary justice (Santos, 1982, 1979), and informal justice (Abel, 1982; Matthews, 1988). It has resonance for examination of the relations between the state and diverse areas or communities within the jurisdictional borders of the state. It questions the insistence on the universality of a notion of a singular, total 'rule of law'. The unruly nature of community justice, one that does not necessarily seek accommodation with the state poses problems for those who would support the idea that legal pluralism is an achievable goal.

The contest over the legitimacy of paramilitary punishment is reflected in the gamut of academic literature on the phenomenon, ranging from purely condemnatory indictment of 'surrogate terrorism' (Silke and Taylor, 2000) to sympathetic treatment (Munck, 1984, 1988). It is in the justifications by the paramilitaries themselves, the communities from which they come and in the responses of the state apparatus that the contest over legitimacy is most keenly fought. This chapter seeks to describe the paramilitary punishment practised by Republican (and Loyalist) paramilitaries and argues that it is largely a form of community justice. It argues that, in general, previous attempts at understanding such practices have foundered on simplistic and/or moralistic perspectives about the relationship between paramilitaries, communities and the state in relation to policing and crime management. Effective, non-violent alternatives to paramilitary punishment, which find favour among many paramilitaries and their communities can only be understood and delivered through such a nuanced appreciation. It is suggested that the long legacy of community criminal justice is unlikely to change radically in the near future, even with the recent changes to state policing and the proposed reforms of the formal criminal justice system pursuant to the Belfast (or 'Good Friday') Agreement of 1998.

Punishing Practices

Punishment by Republican and Loyalist paramilitary groups is a practice that has gained greatest attention during the recent three decades of political conflict in Northern Ireland. However, at least on the Republican side, the antecedents of IRA activity can be traced to the separatist actions of Dáil Éireann and the original Irish Republican Army in the War of Independence, 1919-1921. Then, the government set-up in opposition to British rule established an alternative system of justice comprising land arbitration courts and, soon after, general Dáil courts (Kotsonouris, 1984; Macardle, 1951; Bell, 1996; Casey, 1974, 1970; Davitt, 1968). The IRA was called upon occasionally to enforce the orders of the courts. The tradition of anti-state popular justice characterized many challenges historically against British rule in Ireland (Hillyard, 1985), including the precursors of the IRA – the Irish Republican Brotherhood (Coogan, 1980). Often these were emancipatory or alternative attacks on the state. They survived partially in the North following the partition of Ireland in 1922, with Republican policing reported occasionally throughout the early years of the Northern state (Ryder, 2000). With the riots of 1969 in the North that started the most recent phase of political violence, a new framework for alternative justice developed in both Loyalist and Republican urban, working-class areas. This new framework was based on defensiveness from threats outside the geographic boundaries of ethno-national communities, which later justified claims to protect the community from internal threats.

Following the civil rights protests on behalf of the minority Catholic population, militant Protestants attacked Catholic homes in the predominantly working-class areas of west Belfast in the summer of 1969 through 1970. In the absence of the IRA, Nationalist residents established Citizen Defence Committees whose primary aim was to provide security for the area by organizing constant foot patrols and supervising barricades (Hillyard, 1985). The Catholic Ex-Servicemen's Association contributed to the patrolling following the incursions of the state forces into Nationalist areas in 1971 and attempted to control and stop riots (Burton, 1978). Similarly, in Protestant areas local people organized vigilante groups to patrol boundaries and staff barricades against retaliatory attacks (Nelson, 1984). These groups formed the basis of the Ulster Defence Association, the largest Loyalist paramilitary organization in Northern Ireland. Here, too, Loyalist policing had its precursors in the violent circumstances surrounding the creation of the Northern state. During clashes between Protestants and Catholics in Belfast in 1920, leading members of the Ulster Unionist Labour Association created an unofficial special constabulary, drawn mainly from shipyard workers, with the task of policing Protestant areas (Bew *et al*, 1996). Following partition, Loyalist vigilante groups operated along parts of the border that were populated predominantly by Protestants in order to thwart any feared attack by the IRA from the South (Ryder, 2000).

The defensive aspect of these groups was augmented in Republican areas by systems of alternative justice. Following the riots of 1969, when the Royal Ulster Constabulary (RUC) effectively abdicated its policing role in areas of west Belfast, community councils were established from local elected members. These comprised justice, development and welfare committees. In one area of Belfast, the justice committee was largely concerned with hearing complaints against the British Army and IRA (Burton, 1978). More radically, in mainly urban, Nationalist areas following internment People's Courts were created as part of a wider experiment of non-co-operation with the state (Morrissey and Pease, 1982). The Courts comprised panels elected from each local area. Cases brought before the courts involved minor offences, such as vandalism and petty theft, and often resulted in community service-type sentences, including restitution (Morrissey, 1980). In some areas there were rudimentary people's prisons (Munck, 1984). Yet, while the courts aimed at less severe punishments than those meted out by the paramilitaries, the IRA retained the ultimate sanction. While the courts evaporated within a short time some mechanisms of community control were still exercised over the IRA's systems. After the breakdown of the 1975 IRA truce, the IRA called upon local people such as teachers, doctors or shopkeepers to ensure the 'impartiality of republican judicial procedures' (Munck, 1988, p. 45).

During the conflict paramilitaries contributed to crime management in local areas through systems of justice that paralleled to some extent but differed in key respects from the state system. These hybrid forms of paramilitary justice fed upon other local means of informal crime management in Belfast, such as kinship networks and close-knit neighbourhood structures (Brewer *et al*, 1998). This paramilitary punishment developed characteristic features of rudimentary justice systems, including: organized structure and personnel; clearly delineated 'crimes'; crime prevention; procedures, including investigation, adjudication of guilt or innocence, sentence and punishment; tariffs; and mitigating circumstances. As with the formal system, the systems have produced mistakes and abuses and were subject to broader political pressures. Given the nature of paramilitary punishment, there are obvious deficiencies in due process when compared to the formal state system. For instance, while alleged offenders before Republican paramilitaries have had a theoretical right for an advocate to present a case on their behalf, this is rarely applied and the accused have no right to appeal once punishment has been administered (Silke, 1999a). And despite some differences in ideology, motivations and practices (Silke and Taylor, 2000) Loyalist and Republican punishments bear remarkable similarities.

The punishments can range from warnings to violent physical assaults or shootings. They include: warnings, curfews, fines/victim restitution, acts of public humiliation, assaults, shootings, expulsions, assassination (Silke, 1999b), and property damage and intimidation. As part of my research, I compiled a database of all 'punishment' activity reported in the three Belfast-based daily newspapers (*Belfast Telegraph, Irish News, News Letter*). In the period July 1998 through June

1999, reported assaults (or 'beatings') often involved forced entry into the target's residence where he or she was beaten with blunt instruments. These instruments have in the past included baseball bats, hurley sticks, clubs, batons, bars or hammers. The resulting physical damage ranges from bruising to severe laceration and fracturing of bones. Shootings can be through the soft tissue on the legs, but includes bone shattering in the ankles, knees and wrists. The beatings, often committed by several assailants at a time, can lead to substantial, long-term psychological injuries (Anderson, 1998). If, as is arguable, these armed groups are subject to international human rights and humanitarian law such punishment amounts to torture, inhuman or degrading treatment (Human Rights Watch 1991, 1992).

The severity of such punishment is not unique to Northern Ireland – violent punishment being historically pervasive (Adams, 1998, Andrews, 1997) – and taking its place alongside violent punishments in recent popular justice as widespread as South Africa (Minnaar, 2002) and Peru (Starn, 1999). Conversely, not all paramilitary punishment is violent, echoing the complex mix of brutal and peaceful popular street justice in other countries, such as South Africa (Lee and Seekings, 2002). Merry's (1993, p. 63) view that popular justice 'introduces a new ideology of conflict resolution based on non-violence and opposition to the violence of law' rests, therefore, on a limited view of popular justice. Nor is violent punishment limited to popular or informal mechanisms, or to physical injury. Arguably, states are both the most influential and the most prodigious participants in violent punishment, including psychological torture (Amnesty International, 2000). Moreover, violent punishment by the state can set a precedent for popular justice (Starn, 1999).

Explaining Paramilitary Punishment

The contest over the legitimacy of community justice has been particularly acute in Northern Ireland due to the nature of the broader political conflict. Both the British government and the Northern state have, variously, faced sustained operations by effective, marxist, revolutionary guerilla activity intended to bring about a re-united Ireland. The state has engaged in responsive military and propaganda campaigns to undermine the threat by criminalizing political militants and, through internment, large sections of the population perceived to be part of the Republican movement. The existing illegitimacy of the Northern state in the eyes of Nationalists and Republicans, was further damaged by sectarian policing and major abuses of human rights by the security forces. In this context the state and its supporters have failed to acknowledge the justice needs of distinctive communities in primarily urban, working class areas.

It is in the context of community demand that paramilitary punishment can be best, even if not sufficiently explained. Before proceeding to explore this context, including a critical exegesis of the concept of 'community', it is essential to correct the sometimes mistaken perception that paramilitaries operate independently of, or abstracted from, their communities. Loyalist and Republican paramilitaries arise from, live within and depend upon the communities in which they are based. As Jeff Sluka (1989) suggests in the title of his ethnographic account of the IRA and Irish Nationalist Liberation Army in nationalist west Belfast in the 1980s, the paramilitaries are 'fish' in the community 'water'. While the metaphor underlines the dependent nature of the paramilitaries on their respective communities, it does not adequately convey the fact that military operations are conducted almost exclusively to an organizational agenda and that the paramilitaries are active agents in broader political and community developments. Communities, too, are neither mere environments in which paramilitaries operate. As pointed out by McEvoy and Mika (2002), they may become over-reliant on paramilitaries to engage in policing roles. The relationship might be viewed at times as co-dependent, or when less bound, transactional. Thus, Cavanaugh (1997) notes that '[p]aramilitants depend on their community for protection, discretion and financial support...In turn, the community members demand defense and protection – from loyalists, security forces and the hoods' (p. 39).

The concept of community is clearly a contested one (Abel, 1995; Lacey and Zedner, 1995), no more so than in Northern Ireland, where the very naming of the state is contested. For Republicans and Nationalists the preferred term is 'the North of Ireland', thus disqualifying the name 'Northern Ireland' which is seen as the product of an illegitimate treaty between the Free State and Britain. For Loyalists, the term 'Ulster' (though still one of the four ancient provinces of Ireland) ideates a symbolic territory of Protestant Unionist supremacy, whose identity was cast in the anti-Home Rule campaigns of the late-nineteenth and early-twentieth centuries. In this context, 'community' is politically pregnant in Northern Ireland. Belfast proliferates with community-based organizations, staffed by community workers who work for 'their community'. Certainly, these communities meet the objective measures of what Willmott (1987) sees as communities characterized by territoriality, a shared sense of ethnicity, religious background and occupational or leisure pursuits. In the Northern Irish context one might add 'kin' and 'social traits', means by which the insider and outsider are, in part, distinguished (Burton, 1978). Part of this homogeneity of distinct communities has been shaped by sustained attacks upon the identity and territory of the populations from opposing paramilitary groups or the security forces. The role of local paramilitaries in defending their own people, means that communities have developed in Northern Ireland in a way which equates with Weber's concept of the 'political community'. According to Weber, this is 'a community whose social action is aimed at subordinating to orderly domination by the participants a "territory" and the conduct of persons within it, through readiness to resort to physical force, including normally the force of arms' (Weber, 1978, p. 901). Though Weber used this concept in relation to the distinctive features of the modern state, his definition can equally be applied to Loyalist and Republican communities. However, these communities are also, to adopt Anderson's reference to nations, 'imagined communities'; by which '[c]ommunities are to be distinguished, not by their falsity and genuineness, but by the style in which they are imagined' (Anderson, 1983, p. 15). The urban communities of 'west Belfast' or the 'Shankill' represent political communities, where the diversity of racial minorities, sexual orientations and political beliefs are often sublimated within an imagined polity. However, as Crawford (1998) points out, the definition of social identity based on state of mind 'fails sufficiently to explain the nature of the community's capacity for informal social control or its ability to address and organise around issues of crime and its prevention' (p. 157). Thus, while problematizing the notion of community and identifying its boundary-defining functions (Cohen, 1985) the prevalence of paramilitary punishment in urban, working class areas owes much to demand within the community.

Community Demand

The demand within communities is widely regarded by authoritative observers as a key factor in the paramilitaries assuming a justice role within their communities (Sluka, 1989; McEvoy and Mika, 2002; Winstone, 1997; Brewer *et al*, 1998). The purported extent of community demand varies depending on the position of the observer. David Irvine, leader of the Progressive Unionist Party which is closely associated with the loyalist paramilitary Ulster Volunteer Force, describes paramilitary punishment as 'populist' (Channel 4 News, 2000). Some paramilitaries suggest overwhelming pressure from within their communities. Winstone (1997) reports that senior Loyalist figures were 'not very enthusiastic about their role in dispensing this form of justice' but 'felt under pressure from the community to do so' (p. 125). Another paramilitary commander comments: 'A UFF [Ulster Freedom Fighter] or a UDA [Ulster Defence Association] commander just doesn't wake up some morning and says, "I think I'll go and beat wee Billy"...It's because the community has asked for it, or some members of the community have asked for it. Somebody has done some anti-social deed against the community, and they're being punished' (Taylor, 1999, p. 260). The acknowledgement in the latter view that the pressure comes from some members of the community is closer to what happens on the ground. Within communities that might be broadly termed 'Nationalist', 'Republican', or 'Loyalist' there exists a range of allegiances, political views and beliefs about appropriate crime management, which can fluctuate over time (Auld *et al*, 1997). In the Divis area of west Belfast – a poor, Nationalist working class district – public opinion about the IRA's policing role was mixed. The area comprised, at one time, several high rise residential blocks which were often invaded in the 1970s and 1980s by the security forces and opposition to the RUC was strong. 'There are those in Divis who completely approve of the IRA's law and order role, and those who completely disapprove of it, but most people accept the basic necessity of the [sic] their filling the role' (Sluka, 1989, p. 90). Thus, when the IRA made a statement in 1981 that they were not going to do any more kneecappings, one observer notes that 'ordinary people went to the IRA and said "you've got to start doing something about this crime". It's not the answer but there is still no solution' (Brewer *et al*, 1997, p. 193).

The undoubted support within sections of the community is complex. It can vary according to the nature of the offence, and if the offender or victim was known (Morrissey and Pease, 1982; Sluka, 1989). The dynamic nature of the relationship between the broader community and the paramilitaries is reflected also in the responsiveness of the latter to perceived excesses or deficiencies in punishment. In the early 1980s the IRA explored ways to engage in less physically violent forms of punishment. Addressing its readership in 1980, the IRA wrote in the newspaper of the Republican movement; 'We have canvassed opinion and are happy that you realise the necessity for this short-term, though imperfect policy of dealing with criminals. Ideas from you for a less arbitrary method of adjudication...will be studied' (*An Phoblacht*, 18th February 1980). In 1982 the IRA developed a new approach; involving discussion with young people accused of anti-social behaviour, in which the context of their actions were explained. The young person was required to give a public undertaking and a written statement that they would desist from those actions (Munck, 1984; McCorry and Morrissey, 1989). At Easter 1983, partly as a result of public pressure, the IRA announced that it would stop kneecappings (Hillyard, 1985; Brewer *et al*, 1997). Both beatings and shootings by Republican paramilitaries declined dramatically in the period 1980-1983. But letters appeared in the Republican press in early 1984, following a series of brutal rapes, urging the IRA to reconsider its policy.

The relationship between on the one hand the paramilitaries and on the other hand sections of their communities is at times dialectical, what Burton terms a 'see-saw' relationship (Burton, 1978). At certain times in the recent conflict, such as following internment, the IRA gained increasing legitimacy for its policing role. At other times, it is suggested that the demand from the community engages the IRA in a co-dependent relationship (Cavanaugh, 1997). In certain quarters, a culture of dependence upon the IRA to deal with anti-social crime has developed (McEvoy and Mika, 2002). In turn, the IRA need to remain responsive to the demands of the community. The late Eamon Collins, a one-time volunteer with the IRA, placed this responsiveness in the context of the organization's military operations generally; 'The IRA...tried to act in a way that would avoid severe censure from within the nationalist community; they knew they were operating within a sophisticated set of informal restrictions on their behaviour' (Collins, 1997, p. 296). As with Loyalist paramilitaries, the community is its lifeblood. In addition to acting as supra-communal militants, the paramilitary organization acts as defender from attacks by opposing paramilitaries. The communities have sustained their military campaigns, including supply of recruits, provision of safe-houses, and turning a blind eye when operations became visible. If paramilitaries depend on a close-knitted community, it follows that they also have an interest in preserving the 'imagined community' for broader strategic purposes.

Grass-roots objections within communities to paramilitary policing exist, however, though the survey research is sketchy. Political parties universally condemn the practice, while varying in degrees of understanding of the phenomenon. Kennedy (2000) found that 79 per cent of respondents on a Nationalist estate near Lurgan, outside Belfast, responded 'no' to the question 'Are you in favour of punishment beatings?' in the immediate aftermath of the shooting of a 15-year-old male. Eighty-eight per cent responded 'no' to a similar question regarding shootings. Significantly, 16 per cent responded affirmatively to the first question, with 9 per cent answering 'yes' to the second. A vague report of an opinion poll of residents on a Nationalist estate in Portadown following an IRA expulsion of two men from the estate revealed a 'resounding "no"' to the issue of whether the IRA had the right to expel the men (Lee, 1990). That punishments are viewed as problematic within the urban heartland of paramilitaries, was revealed by the first Northern Ireland Communities Crime Survey. It found that 17 per cent of respondents in Catholic lower working class urban areas saw punishment beatings as a 'big' problem in their area, after joyriding (37.7 per cent), vehicle theft (30.5 per cent) and drug abuse and dealing (24.4 per cent) (O'Mahony *et al*, 2000). However, these findings are based on narrow questions that do not allow for complex responses to, for instance, issues about the appropriateness of different levels of punishment. Nor do they seek to contextualize the responses with reference to whether the respondents had any experience of crime by those punished, local crime management and policing in the area.

In addition, there are anecdotal critical responses within the communities to the paramilitaries which give a flavour of the broader opposition. The most likely, though by no means automatic, criticism of the paramilitaries comes from the parents of young people targeted. A mother whose son was executed described the IRA as 'snakes and worms', adding 'God help us if these are our protectors' (Morrissey and Pease, 1982). The opposition can be mobilized against particularly severe punishments. In 1984, following the execution of one man, described by the IRA as involved in 'criminal activities', the man's widow organized a petition with over one thousand signatures demanding an investigation into the IRA's action (Hillyard, 1985). One resident of a Loyalist area thought that 'innocents could get a hammering', with the overwhelming objection across communities being the opposition to violent punishment (Brewer *et al*, 1997, p. 163 *ff.*). Nonetheless, support for such violent punishment exists, as shown in Kennedy's survey, above. Occasional public meetings in, mainly Nationalist, areas demonstrated that some participants were in total support of a popular system that included kneecappings (Hillyard, 1985).

The variation in community support for paramilitary punishment makes this a site of struggle over crime management within communities. Within the broader political conflict, where the military aims of the organizations are tied up to some extent with internal policing, the legitimacy of community justice becomes part of the wider struggle. And it is here that the state contests such legitimacy.

Contesting Community Justice

Chief among the objections to the formal criminal justice system in Nationalist and Republican areas is the illegitimacy of the British state. This extended not only to the RUC — prior to its reform as the Police Service of Northern Ireland (PSNI) — but also to a rejection of the institutions which structured police-community relations: the former Police Authority of Northern Ireland, the Police Liaison Committees and the Lay Visitor scheme (Brogden, 1995). The refusal to co-operate with the security arm of the British state has been a part of republican strategy since its inception (McEvoy, 2000), with the RUC in particular regarded as lacking legitimacy due to its historically oppressive treatment of Republicans and Nationalists. The recent 'peace process' between the protagonists, culminating in the Belfast Agreement, has seen no sustained cessation in paramilitary punishment. While the Agreement led to the creation of the new PSNI in November 2001 and an independent review of parts of the criminal justice system, suspicion remains among sections of Nationalist and

Republican communities towards the criminal justice system. This is due in part to the failure of the state to dismiss police officers responsible for human rights abuses and to require remaining officers to affirm an oath to uphold human rights. Although the continuing reforms of the police service and the proposals for the criminal justice system promise more accountable, community-responsive measures, the decision of the leading Republican party, Sinn Féin, not to take up seats on the new Policing Board indicates that Republicans will continue for some time to regard the police with caution.

During the conflict, the IRA was ideologically bound as a revolutionary organization to ensure a level of law and order in areas where it exercised influence. Moreover, the formal criminal justice system has been degraded through successive draconian measures, such as police brutality, internment without trial, non-jury courts, the 'supergrass' system, and alleged 'shoot to kill' practices. Confidence in British justice generally has been further undermined by this effective abrogation of the rule of law (Hillyard, 1985). Moreover, as Burton points out in relation to the lived experience of justice degraded; '[t]he community repression as well as its experience of the social consequences of the suspension of due process have seriously damaged the legitimacy of the law in the Catholic districts' (Burton, 1978, p. 85). Confidence in the courts has oscillated, particularly within the Nationalist and Republican communities between low and zero following clear instances of double standards. For instance, following the prosecution of four RUC officers for the unlawful killing of individuals in what was deemed to be part of a 'shoot-to-kill' policy against Republicans, the judge at one of the trials congratulated the police on despatching the individuals to what he called the 'final court of justice' (Ryder, 2000, p. 346). The friable nature of indigenous respect for notions of law and order can also be set alongside the precarious governance of the state. The Stormont Assembly was suspended in 1972 following the inability of the Unionist government to properly manage the affairs of Northern Ireland, with the British government instituting direct rule. Again, in 1974, the short-lived Northern Ireland Executive collapsed in the face of the government's inability to deal with Loyalist strikes. Since the Belfast Agreement, the Assembly has been suspended on a number of occasions following attempts by the Ulster Unionist Party to expel Sinn Féin from the Executive.

Many within the Catholic communities were also unwilling to contact the RUC when incidents occurred 'because they [did not] trust them, seeing them as representatives only of the Unionist community' (Human Rights Watch, 1992). A number of surveys showed low levels of trust and confidence amongst Nationalist and Republican or Catholic respondents towards the RUC. A community survey of Nationalist residents' views of crime, the police and courts found that only two out of 264 respondents said they would give general support to the armed RUC, and only eleven per cent to an unarmed RUC (Hillyard, 1985). Social attitudes surveys in the late 1980s and early 1990s found that only fifty per cent of Catholics were satisfied with the police, with less than half of the Catholic population believing that the RUC did a good job in controlling sectarian crime or in treating them equally to Protestants (Breen, 1995; Gallagher, 1995).

The role of the RUC in the front line of security strategy from the mid-1970s ruptured their ability to develop trust and confidence within communities. In the context of paramilitary punishment and policing, this point is vividly illuminated by the former chief probation officer for Northern Ireland:

> The main reason punishment beatings take place is that you move a civilian police force into being the frontline fighters of terrorism, and if that terrorism is endemic in certain communities as in Northern Ireland, it is obvious that you will lose the confidence of those communities in the civilian police force. You can't have both in the Force. One day, the police are kicking down your door, taking the house apart and treating you like a terrorist. The next morning, you can't call the police to report a burglary. Even though the RUC may be able to change roles, the local community aren't as trusting nor is it that easy for them to solve their ambivalences. Until there is a resolution between the police and their communities most affected by crime and terrorism, there will continue to be punishment beatings. (Quoted in Human Rights Watch, 1997, pp. 104-5)

The use by the RUC of investigation of minor offences to further a broader security strategy has further alienated many within local communities. Members of both the Nationalist and Republican communities reported not calling the police when crime occurred because they suspected that the RUC would not respond or would respond inappropriately, for example by ignoring their call for assistance and attempting solely to employ the complainant or the alleged perpetrator as a political informer (Human Rights Watch, 1997). This accounted for the widespread practice in Republican areas of individuals publicly announcing, often in the company of Sinn Féin representatives, that they resisted attempts by the RUC to employ them as informers. Any failure to clear suspicion of informing could lead to execution by the paramilitaries.

While the absence of state legitimacy has no relevance amongst Loyalists, successive political developments compromised the legitimacy of the RUC in the eyes of many Loyalists. Following the Anglo-Irish Agreement of 1985, in which the Irish government was given a consultative role, and base near Belfast, in Northern Irish affairs, Loyalist protests were thwarted by the RUC. This gave rise to opposition among Loyalists, which spiralled in 1995 when the RUC prevented Orangemen from marching down the Garvaghy Road near Portadown. The alienation from the state sector runs deeper in some Loyalist communities, where there is a breakdown in relationships due to the perceived failure of many local statutory organizations to understand local community issues (Winstone, Watters and Drummond, 1999).

The lack of RUC legitimacy was compounded by its inability or unwillingness to undertake 'normal' policing roles in certain areas. During late 1969 and the early 1970s some areas of west Belfast and Derry were 'no-go' areas to the RUC and British army, leaving the IRA to maintain order within the areas (Hillyard, 1985). Responses to calls in Republican areas could also place the security forces under paramilitary attack. Rapid response was precluded by the need to ensure that police officers entered in armoured vehicles, often accompanied by the British army. Both the delay and high visibility of security presence could also deter routine calls for assistance. In part, this contributed to a view that the RUC were ineffective in dealing with crime, a broad critique that has allowed Republican (and Loyalist) paramilitaries to step into the breach.

The Northern Ireland Community Crime Survey (O'Mahony *et al*, 2000) found that Protestant, lower working class urban areas had the highest rate (41.2 per cent) of respondents who did not report incidents to the police because they believed that the police could do nothing. Winstone (1998) reported an RUC clear-up rate of 2 per cent in the division comprising the Loyalist Woodvale area of Belfast. The view among many individuals bears out the frustration with the police. One woman who faced stalking and harassment by an ex-partner stated that 'the police were getting nowhere. I was desperate, so I went to the boys. They had a word with him and there was no more trouble after that' (Interview, June 2001). In the words of other residents in east Belfast; 'The paras get things done, things are done'; and, 'they have been effective. Within twenty-four hours they get your money back, every penny that has been stolen. Now the police haven't the power to do that' (Brewer *et al*, 1997, pp. 162-3). The frustration extends to the wider criminal justice system, with the courts being perceived as too lenient and paramilitary punishment providing a more tangible, visible and immediate form of retribution (Winstone, 1997).

How one measures effectiveness is of course a function of perspective and values. In the previous paragraph effectiveness is measured from the victim's perspective in terms of recovering money or preventing harassing behaviour. Paramilitary punishment is often perceived more generally as acting as a deterrent through its severe sanctions. In the words of one resident: '...the paras will blow their knees off. It will frighten them more. I mean, you can go to court and they get a fine, but if they think they are going to get shot, they will stop more quickly (Brewer *et al*, 1997, pp. 162-3). While the deterrent effect is doubted, even among the paramilitaries, this perception amongst other community members exists and helps sustain the legitimacy of paramilitary punishment over that of the formal criminal justice system. The attraction of paramilitary punishment is maintained through its swiftness, a feature of the formal justice system that resonates with the public (Travis, 1998). One youth worker in a Republican area refers to the desire for immediate sanction; 'people want punishment the next day rather than months later through the courts' (Brewer *et al*, 1997, p. 163). Such violent, swift punishment also satisfies a wish for retribution, often of a vengeful nature, within communities.

> Petty criminals think they can get away with things...challenging authority and causing crime in the community. People go to the organisations and say, 'Sort him out'. Contrary to popular belief, some people want revenge. (Interview with Loyalist ex-prisoner, November 1998)

Similar sentiments are expressed among individuals in Republican areas (Human Rights Watch, 1997; Moriarty, 1995).

Other Explanations

Other explanations are offered for paramilitary punishment. These range from the plausible, sociologically informed explanation to the sensationalist and critical. At the former end of the spectrum are those that place paramilitary punishment within a broader historical context of protecting distinct communities. This has already been mentioned in relation to the development of community policing and vigilantism in

Nationalist and Loyalist areas. Here, paramilitary policing evolved from managing external threats. Republican paramilitaries have described a strong sense of communal responsibility to defend and protect, which underpinned their broader military commitments (Cavanaugh, 1997). In the absence of any, or effective policing, some believe that the paramilitaries have an obligation to intervene. For example, during one public meeting in a Republican part of west Belfast to discuss joyriding one speaker stated that 'it was the duty of the IRA to be the law in the area' (Darby, 1986, p. 107).

The importance of safe communities to paramilitaries as a means of both protecting kin and maintaining the imagined community, has contributed to a strong sense among paramilitaries that they should also protect the community from internal threats. According to Jackie McDonald, the UDA's South Belfast Commander; '[s]omebody has done some anti-social deed against the community, and they're being punished...the whole reason for the UFF and the UDA being here is to protect the people, should it be from members of their own community or from republicans' (Taylor, 1999, p. 260). The community support for paramilitaries is based in part on a NIMBY (Not-In-My-Back-Yard) concern about crime. This is illustrated in the response of one middle-aged man, otherwise deeply critical of the IRA, who approved of sanctions against local delinquents. He concluded that 'they were fair game to be shot, but if they were outside the area they weren't hurting their own people, and that was OK' (Brewer *et al*, 1998, p. 581). Such a view has antecedents in Republican strategy. During the War of Independence the republican police were keen to ensure that petty criminals did not take advantage of the guerrilla war for their own ends (Macardle, 1951). This concern for community extended to the IRA's unusual step of involving itself during the 1970s (momentarily) with the cleanliness of their communities. Burton (1978) reports the following notice: 'The condition of our streets and entries leaves much to be desired. To facilitate their cleansing, provision is being made for ten skips to be placed at strategic points...it will be an offence to dump rubbish other than in the skips...Na Fianna Éireann will assist you in this work' (p. 105).

Paramilitary punishment has also reflected in certain respects the broader military objectives of the organizations. A number of observers support the position of, at least, Republican paramilitaries that one of the reasons for punishing violently young offenders was that they placed other paramilitary operations and activity under threat. The IRA's position was set-out starkly in the weekly newspaper of the Republican Movement:

> The IRA has, in 100s of cases, been called in as arbiters in disputes where people are loathe to involve the Northern administration...We make no bones about it — our justice is a rough form of justice, forced upon us in the circumstances...The hoods have a choice. Give it up. The concentration of resources against the hoods is a major distraction from the war effort. (*An Phoblacht*, 5 May 1982)

A similar view is expressed by a member of the INLA, opining the fact that 'the hoods' were bringing the police into the area (Feldman, 1999). This concern is reflected partially in the most recent crackdown by the IRA against drug dealers, often under the cover name of DAAD (Direct Action Against Drugs). Here, part of the motivation also reflects a concern about drugs being supplied by Loyalists, with the Irish People's Liberation Army (IPLO) as a conduit, and a broader fear that suspects will be used as informers by the RUC (Conway, 1997; McEvoy *et al*, 1998). However, it may also reflect a conservatism within Catholic, Nationalist and Republican communities against certain types of deviance.

A further, though proportionately small, number of punishments are carried out as part of internal discipline within the organizations. It is believed that a higher proportion of punishments by Loyalists are done for this reason (Silke, 1999c). In the IRA the ultimate punishment for a volunteer informing is execution with a bullet in the back of the head (Toolis, 1995). It is also claimed, without evidence, that punishment serves broader military objectives by 'blooding' new recruits and, during the recent 'ceasefires', providing a substitute channel for military activity (Kennedy, 1994; Silke, 1999a). The broader political goals of the paramilitaries, particularly Republicans, are sometimes achieved by targeting political opponents within the community (Silke, 1999b). Thus, the IRA assaulted Kevin McQuillan of the Irish Republican Socialist Party and Mickey Donnelly, chair of Republican Sinn Féin – organizations that remain critical of the IRA/Sinn Féin strategy in the recent political negotiations. Such individual punishments can sometimes escalate into intra-communal feuds, as has occurred most commonly between the Provisional IRA and the Official IRA. Sometimes the attacks can be aimed at silencing critics of punishment attacks generally, as in the assaults on two Social Democratic and Labour Party councillors who condemned the IRA in the 1990s.

It is speculated that some of these punishments also arise from personal grudges (Munck, 1988; Silke, 1999a). While there is no hard evidence of this, it is suggested that the fatal shooting of Andy Kearney in 1998 resulted from his crossing a leading member of the IRA (interview with Mrs. Maureen Kearney, February 1999, now deceased). Again without hard evidence, some commentators explain attacks in terms of personal pleasure and excitement (Kennedy, 1995), furthering personal interests (Knox, 2001), personal pathology (Silke, 1999a) or keeping newly idle members occupied during ceasefires (Silke and Taylor, 2000). More plausibly, some critics of paramilitaries regard punishment activity, in part, as an opportunity to consolidate their power within communities. The influence of the IRA within the wider community was vital to its military strategy. Following the policing vacuum between 1969 and 1972, the paramilitaries were well aware that by assuming internal policing functions they were forging an additional mechanism for consolidating power in their communities (Feldman, 1999). The preservation of IRA authority to police, alongside Sinn Féin's management of social, economic and welfare issues within Republican communities became an important part of republican strategy from the late 1970s onwards. One well-placed source on paramilitary punishment has stated that '[a] lot of it's about the paramilitaries making themselves indispensable within the community' (Human Rights Watch, 1997, p. 109). However, the thesis that paramilitary punishment is all about social control is vastly overstated. A number of authors support this thesis (Knox, 2001; Report of the Chief Constable, 2000-2001; Silke, 1999b; Kennedy, 1995; O'Shea, 1994). Scholars who have taken a more grounded, ethnographically informed approach reject the reductionist arguments of counter-insurgency theorists that national liberation or guerrilla movements achieve order and control through intimidation and coercion (Cavanaugh, 1997; Burton, 1978). Breidge Gadd, former chief probation officer for Northern Ireland, reported in 1997: '[t]hese are not crazy men exerting control. If they stopped tomorrow and there was no agreement with the state police force to come back and start policing, there would be anarchy' (Human Rights Watch, 1997, p. 108). It is undoubtedly true, however, that the violent targeting of some political opponents has contributed to some fear about speaking out publicly in communities (Brewer *et al*, 1997; Kennedy, 2000; Human Rights Watch, 1997).

Contesting Crime and Deviance

The construction of crime is a function of power in society. In the North of Ireland the definition of crime has become a struggle also about the legitimacy of the combatants. This is exemplified in the contest over the status of political prisoners, the ascription of 'terrorism' and the ownership of 'victim' status. As with the formal criminal justice system, the system of community justice policed primarily by paramilitaries reveals its own concerns in the regulation of the moral economy and social order. Perhaps unsurprisingly, young people are demonized within the local moral economy. Young males make up the majority of victims (Feenan, 1999; Kennedy, 2001), with a forty per cent increase in the number of males under twenty years of age targeted by Republicans since the cessation of military operations in 1994 (Silke and Taylor, 2000). The construction of the 'hood', a juvenile delinquent, provides a classic anti-social *bête noir*, particularly in Republican communities. The 'hood' slips capture, at times apparently coming from a coherent group, at other times representing any young person who resists authority (McCorry and Morrissey, 1989). In the wake of punishment shootings in 1984, Sinn Féin responded to criticism from the SDLP and Alliance Party by claiming that it was under pressure from the Nationalist community to take more action against the 'hoods' (Hillyard, 1985, p. 262). During the late 1970s and throughout the 1980s Republican newspapers were replete with condemnations, warnings and punishment reports about the 'hoods', and many observers have virtually collapsed the victim of such punishment into the young offender (Bell, 1996). This demonization of the young is part of a traditionally conservative trend in perspectives about crime in Ireland, which sees young men as pre-eminently responsible for crime (Tomlinson *et al*, 1988). In the context of the political conflict, the ascription of 'hooding' during the 1970s provided the paramilitaries with the means to develop community policing alongside propagation of 'a counter-iconography to the law-and-order image of state counter-insurgency' (Feldman, 1999, p. 211). The construction of joyriders as deviants occurred as the British government started its criminalization policy towards political combatants. '[I]n turn the IRA re-appropriated the stigma of criminality and theatrically re-imposed it on the hoods and joyriders' (Feldman, 1999, p. 224). In turn, the young deviant, ostracized from a socially conservative community adopts the counter-insurgent status of 'hood' as a badge of honour and defiance of the IRA, in much the same way as marginalized black youth in urban America chose the 'hoodlum' status of drug dealing in order to assert their dignity by refusing to '"sling a mop for the white man" for "chump money"' (Bourgois, 1989, p. 639).

If the young male delinquent was seen as a threat to the body politic, the young male also needed to be protected from himself and contained as the symbolic threat posed to the community's moral integrity occasioned by young people's use of non-medical drugs. In the late 1970s the then commander of the IRA's Belfast Brigade spoke of drug-taking as the 'poison of our community' and in a public notice, headed 'CRIMES AGAINST HUMANITY', cautioned: 'We warn everyone, especially parents, to be on their guard lest this evil embraces our youth in its tentacles' (Burton, 1978, p. 105). In May 1982 the IRA warned that they would close down premises selling alcohol to those under the legal age for drinking, and shortly after closed an off-licence for two weeks. These interventions reflected more conservative views within Republicanism, with similar attempts to reduce truancy (Munck, 1984) and gambling (Sluka, 1989). Part of that conservatism, is tied to a homophobic strand within Republicanism and Loyalism that has led to the targeting of gay men (Burton, 1978; Silke, 1999c). Individuals suspected of sexual offences against children are particularly likely to be targeted, though this, too, is not unique to Northern Ireland.

State 'Community' versus Local 'Community'

The justification of paramilitary punishment in terms of protecting 'the community' spawned a counter-insurgent discourse in the RUC's portrayal of such activity, making it difficult to penetrate the well-resourced propaganda of the state. Traditionally in police pronouncements, 'community' embraced all groups in a seemingly prelapsarian state of harmony, irrespective of the incommensurable differences in political ideology, ethnicity or class. Often, this idyll was imagined alongside the equally fictive 'decent citizen'. Thus, in an editorial in the *Constabulary Gazette* in April 1973, it is stated that '[i]t is the wish of every good citizen that the Royal Ulster Constabulary should, without fear or favour, continue to provide for all members of the community the same exemplary service it has always rendered' (quoted in Boehringer, 1973, p. 25). During the 1980s the RUC tackled the IRA's claim as community protector head-on. In a landmark press release titled 'Paramilitary Thuggery' (RUC, 1987), it opined that 'sometimes these people...will pose as "protectors" of the community in dealing with petty criminals. That is hypocrisy. The fact is that they are determined to have a monopoly on crime for themselves in their areas' (p. 3). The conflation of homogenous community and decency continued: '[t]hey are a menace to all decent people in this community. We and the community must rid ourselves of them' (p. 1). The inability of the police to acknowledge the unruly nature of the communities it attempts to police, is linked to its refusal to accept explicitly its responsibility for systemic human rights abuses and its lack of legitimacy in the eyes of many Nationalists and Republicans. The resulting erasure of community opposition has accompanied a claim to a neutralized concept of community. While the post-Belfast Agreement era of the late 1990s heralded an acknowledgement of the 'communities' the RUC existed to serve (Report of the Chief Constable, 1998/99), the final report of the RUC Chief Constable still oscillates ambiguously between 'the entire community', 'communities' and 'both communities' (Report of the Chief Constable 2000-2001). Nonetheless, steadfast opposition to community justice reinstates a latent, transcendent idea of 'community', existing beyond sectarian cleavages and alienation, over which the RUC alone had authority to police. 'Paramilitary justice is a contradiction in terms. It cannot be allowed to succeed, for the entire community is a loser' (Chief Constable's Annual Report, 1997/98, p. 13).

State resistance to the idea of community justice has extended, even in the contemporary era of 'community policing', to locally-based restorative justice projects in Republican and Loyalist areas. A state-centred reaction followed the emergence in the late 1990s of the Community Restorative Justice project in Nationalist areas and the Alternatives project in the Loyalist Greater Shankill area. The Community Restorative Justice project set its face against co-operating with the RUC, while promising to enter into dialogue with a replacement 'acceptable police service on how the two organisations could co-operate independently of each other for the benefit of all' (Auld, 1999, p. 20). The RUC responded initially to the project by threatening to prosecute any member who withheld information about criminal offences. While the Alternatives project engaged with the RUC, it is still, according to one member, viewed with suspicion (Interview, November 1998) and mistrust (Drummond, 1998). The RUC made explicit its view that such initiatives should be state-centred (McDonald, 1998). This has resulted in the production of protocols from the British government's Northern Ireland Office that are drafted without community involvement (Watters, 1999). The opposition to 'alternative' structures by the British government leads to a statist determination of local needs. During the political talks process the then Minister of Security presaged his position in relation to the crime and restorative justice papers to be tabled, noting that '[d]ecisions on the provision of services for which [such initiatives] are accountable need to remain matters for the agencies with the relevant statutory responsibilities. They have the expertise and they can provide safeguards against abuse' (Ingram, 1997, p. 7; 1998a; 1998b). The potential for effective, locally-based independent systems was smothered in the contemporary discourse of 'partnership' with 'official systems' (Ingram, 1998b). State opposition to community restorative justice in Nationalist and Republican areas ensures also that the British identity of Northern Ireland is consolidated through links to sovereignty, state, and state-like institutions rather than potentially endangered through diffusion within alternative sites of dispute processing (*cf.* Shamir, 2000).

Conclusion

The development of paramilitary punishment in Northern Ireland arises in part from community demand for locally-based responses to crime within predominantly urban working class areas alienated from the formal criminal justice system, and in the case of Republicans and Nationalists, from the British state more generally. The unlawful nature of paramilitary punishment, has led to an abbreviated form of justice that often reflects the wishes of certain sections of the community for swift, visible and violent punishment. This form of community justice challenges the state's ability to maintain control, and leads to a contest over the legitimacy of local crime management. The contest is inflected especially in the attempts to control the privileged concept of 'community' in Northern Irish politics. The contest over the legitimacy of community justice is not only about practices opposed to the state (and in the case of Republican punishment, opposed to the British state). It is about ownership over a responsive, community-owned form of justice that reflects particular concerns about crime, and ideas of prevention and punishment. Thus, the explanations of paramilitary punishment can be partly understood with reference to the political objectives and context of paramilitary organizations. However, they must also be understood in relation to the lived experiences and needs of the predominantly urban, working class areas where indigenous practices of justice have developed both independently of and in opposition to the state system. The failure of commentators and the state to acknowledge the complexity of explanations for paramilitary punishment has stultified the development of broader based community justice that can, in parallel with the unfolding peace process in Northern Ireland, move beyond reliance on statist and violent methods of crime control.

Acknowledgement

I wish to thank Paddy Hillyard for comments on a draft of this chapter.

References

Abel, R. (ed.) (1982), *The Politics of Informal Justice: Volumes 1 and 2*, Academic Press, New York.

Abel, R. (1995), 'Contested Communities', *Journal of Law and Society*, Vol. 22(1), pp. 113-26.

Adams, R. (1998), *The Abuses of Punishment*, Macmillan, Basingstoke.

Amnesty International (2000), *Stamp Out Torture*, Amnesty International, London.

Anderson, B. (1983), *Imagined Communities: Reflections on the Origin and Spread of Nationalism*, Verso, London.

Anderson, B. (1998), '"Punishment" Victims' Torment Lasts Longest', *Irish News*, 22 July, 7.

Andrews, R. M. (ed.) (1997), *Perspectives on Punishment: An Interdisciplinary Exploration*, Peter Lang, New York.

Auld, J. (1999), 'Community Justice', *Fortnight*, September, pp. 19-20.

Auld, J., Gormally, B., McEvoy, K. and Ritchie, M. (1997), *Designing a System of Restorative Community Justice in Northern Ireland*, Belfast, The Authors.

Bell, C. (1996), 'Alternative Justice in Ireland', in Dawson, N., Greer, D., and Ingram, P. (eds), *One Hundred and Fifty Years of Irish Law*, SLS Legal Publications, Belfast, pp. 144-67.

Bew, P., Gibbon, P. and Patterson, H. (1996), *Northern Ireland 1921-1996: Political Forces and Social Classes* (Revised and updated), Serif, London.

Boehringer, G. (1973), 'The Future of Policing in Northern Ireland', *Community Forum*, Vol. 3(2), pp. 20-26.

Bourgois, P. (1989), 'In Search of Horatio Alger: Culture and Ideology in the Crack Economy', *Contemporary Drug Problems*, Vol. 16(4), pp. 619-49.

Breen, P. (1995), 'Beliefs About the Treatment of Catholics and Protestants by the Security Forces', in Breen, P., Devine, P., and Robinson, G., *Social Attitudes in Northern Ireland: Fourth Report*, Appletree Press, Belfast, pp. 49-62.

Brewer, J. D., Lockhart, B. and Rodgers, P. (1998), 'Informal Social Control and Crime Management in Belfast', *British Journal of Sociology*, Vol. 49(4), pp. 570-85.

Brewer, J. D., Lockhart, B. and Rodgers, P. (1997), *Crime in Ireland 1945-95: 'Here be Dragons'*, Clarendon Press, Oxford.

Brogden, M. (1995), 'An Agenda for Post-Troubles Policing in Northern Ireland – The South African Precedent', *Liverpool Law Review*, Vol. XVII(1), pp. 3-27.

Burton, F. (1978), *The Politics of Legitimacy: Struggles in a Belfast Community*, Routledge and Kegan Paul, London.

Casey, J. P. (1970), 'Republican Courts in Ireland 1919-1922', *Irish Jurist*, Vol. 5, pp. 321-42.

Casey, J. P. (1974), 'The Genesis of the Dáil Courts', *Irish Jurist*, Vol. 9, pp. 326-38.

Cavanaugh, K. A. (1997), 'Interpretations of Political Violence in Ethnically Divided Societies', *Terrorism and Political Violence*, Vol. 9(3), pp. 33-54.

Channel 4 News (2000), 'Brutal Justice', 21 May 2000.

Chief Constable's Report 1997/98 (The), Royal Ulster Constabulary, Belfast.

Cohen, A. (1985), *The Symbolic Construction of Community*, Tavistock, London.

Collins, E. (1997), *Killing Rage*, Granta Books, London.

Conway, P. (1997), 'A Response to Paramilitary Policing in Northern Ireland', *Critical Criminology*, Vol. 8(1), pp. 109-21.

Coogan, T. P. (1980), *The I.R.A.* (6th Impression, revised and expanded), Fontana, London.

Crawford, A. (1998), *Crime Prevention and Community Safety: Politics, Policies, and Practices*, Longman, London.

Darby, J. (1986), *Intimidation and Control of Conflict in Northern Ireland*, Gill and Macmillan, Dublin.

Davitt, C. (1968), 'The Civil Jurisdiction of the Courts of Justice of the Irish Republic, 1920-1922', *Irish Jurist*, Vol. 3, pp. 112-30.

Drummond, W. (1998), 'Not Trying to Undermine Police', *Belfast Telegraph*, 3 November, p. 12.

Feenan, D. (1998), 'Punish or Restore', *Fortnight*, May, pp. 13-14.

Feldman, A. (1999), 'Retaliate and Punish: Political Violence as Form and Memory in Northern Ireland', *Éire-Ireland*, Vol. XXXII, pp. 195-235.

Gallagher, T. (1995), 'Policing in Northern Ireland: Attitudinal Evidence', in O'Day, A. (ed.), *Terrorism's Laboratory*, Dartmouth, Aldershot, pp. 47-58.

Hillyard, P. (1985), 'Popular Justice in Northern Ireland', *Research in Law, Deviance and Social Control*, Vol. 7, pp. 247-67.

Human Rights Watch (1991), *Human Rights in Northern Ireland*, Human Rights Watch, New York.

Human Rights Watch (1992), *Children in Northern Ireland: Abused by Security Forces and Paramilitaries*, Human Rights Watch, New York.

Human Rights Watch (1997), *To Serve Without Favor: Policing, Human Rights, and Accountability in Northern Ireland*, Human Rights Watch, New York.

Ingram, A. (1997), 'Time to Find a Better Way', *Belfast Telegraph*, 20 December 1997, p. 7.

Ingram, A. (1998a) (Minister for Security, Northern Ireland), *Crime and Community – A Local Partnership Approach*, Northern Ireland Office, Belfast. (A paper tabled for the multi-party talks at Stormont, 19 March 1998.)

Ingram, Adam (1998b), *Restorative Justice*, Northern Ireland Office, Belfast. (A paper tabled for the multi-party talks at Stormont, 19 March 1998.)

Kennedy, L. (1995), 'Nightmares Within Nightmares: Paramilitary Repression Within Working-Class Communities', in Kennedy, L. (ed.), *Crime and Punishment in West Belfast*, The Summer School, Belfast, pp. 67-80.

Kennedy, L. (2000), 'We've Come For Your Boys', *Fortnight*, No. 382, pp. 14-15.
Kennedy, L. (2001), *They Shoot People Don't They? An Analysis of the Age and Gender of Victims of Paramilitary 'Punishments' in Northern Ireland*, The Author, Belfast.
Knox, C. (2001), 'The "Deserving" Victims of Political Violence', *Criminal Justice*, Vol. 1(2), pp. 181-99.
Kotsonouris, M. (1994), *Retreat From Revolution: The Dáil Courts, 1920-22*, Irish Academic Press, Blackrock.
Lacey, N. and Zedner, L. (1995), 'Discourses of Community in Criminal Justice', *Journal of Law and Society*, Vol. 22(3), pp. 301-25.
Lee, S. (ed.) (1990), *Freedom From Fear: Churches Together in Northern Ireland*, Institute of Irish Studies, Belfast.
Macardle, D. (1951), *The Irish Republic*, 4th edn., Irish Press, Dublin (first published in 1937).
Matthews, R. (ed.)(1988), *Informal Justice?*, Sage, London.
McCorry, J. and Morrissey, M. (1989), 'Community, Crime and Punishment in West Belfast', *The Howard Journal*, Vol. 28(4), pp. 282-91.
McDonald, H. (1998), 'Loyalist Ex-Terrorists Launch "Alternative Justice" Scheme', *Observer*, 7 May.
McEvoy, K., McElrath, K. and Higgins, K. (1998), 'Does Ulster Still Say No? Drugs, Politics, and Propaganda in Northern Ireland', *Journal of Drug Issues*, Vol. 28(1), pp. 127-54.
McEvoy, K. (2000), 'Law, Struggle and Political Transformation in Northern Ireland', *Journal of Law and Society*, Vol. 27(4), pp. 542-71.
McEvoy, K. and Mika, H. (2002), 'Republican Hegemony or Community Ownership?: Community Restorative Justice in Northern Ireland', in Feenan, D. (ed.), *Informal Criminal Justice*, Ashgate, Aldershot, chapter 5.
Merry, S. E. (1993), 'Sorting Out Popular Justice', in Merry, S. E. and Milner, N. (eds), *The Possibility of Popular Justice: A Case Study of Community Mediation in the United States*, University of Michigan Press, Ann Arbor, pp. 31-66.
Moriarty, G. (1995), 'IRA "Punishment" Attacks Double but Loyalist Rate Down', *Irish Times*, 7 December, p. 6.
Morrissey, M. (1980), 'The Limits of Community Action', M.Phil thesis, Ulster Polytechnic.
Morrissey, M. and Pease, K. (1982), 'The Black Criminal Justice System in West Belfast', *The Howard Journal*, Vol. XXI, pp. 159-66.
Munck, R. (1984), 'Repression, Insurgency, and Popular Justice: The Irish Case', *Crime and Social Justice*, Vol. 21-22, pp. 81-94.
Munck, R. (1988), 'The Lads and the Hoods: Alternative Justice in an Irish Context', in Tomlinson, M., Varley, T. and McCullagh, C. (eds), *Whose Law and Order?: Aspects of Crime and Social Control in Irish Society*, Sociological Association of Ireland, Dublin, pp. 41-53.
Nelson, S. (1984), *Ulster's Uncertain Defenders: Protestant Political, Paramilitary and Community Groups and the Northern Ireland Conflict*, Appletree Press, Belfast.
O'Mahony, D., Geary, R., McEvoy, K. and Morison, J. (2000), *Crime, Community and Locale: The Northern Ireland Communities Crime Survey*, Ashgate, Aldershot.
O'Shea, R. (1994), 'Rough Justice: Paramilitary "Punishment" Assaults in Northern Ireland', LL.M. thesis, University of Essex.
R. v. *Caulfield*, Crown Court, Petrie J., Unreported, Transcript, 25 March 1999.
Report of the Chief Constable 1998/99, Royal Ulster Constabulary, Belfast.
Report of the Chief Constable 2000-2001, Royal Ulster Constabulary, Belfast.
RUC (Royal Ulster Constabulary) (1987), 'Paramilitary Thuggery', Royal Ulster Constabulary, Belfast.

Ryder, C. (2000), *The RUC 1922-2000: A Force Under Fire*, Arrow, London (first published in 1989).

Santos, B. de S. (1979), 'Popular Strategy, Dual Power and Socialist Strategy', in Fine, B., Kinsey R., Lea, J., Picciotto, S. and Young, J. (eds), *Capitalism and the Rule of Law: From Deviancy to Marxism*, Hutchinson, London, pp. 151-63.

Santos, B. de S. (1982), 'Law and Revolution in Portugal: The Experiences of Popular Justice after the 25th of April 1974', in Abel, R. (ed.), *The Politics of Informal Justice: Volume 1*, Academic Press, New York, pp. 251-80.

Shamir, R. (2000), *The Colonies of Law: Colonialism, Zionism and Law in Early Mandate Palestine*, Cambridge University Press, Cambridge.

Silke, A. (1999a), 'Rebel's Dilemma: The Changing Relationship Between the IRA, Sinn Féin and Paramilitary Vigilantism in Northern Ireland', *Terrorism and Political Violence*, Vol. 11(1), pp. 55-93.

Silke, A. (1999b), 'The Lords of Discipline: The Methods and Motives of Paramilitary Vigilantism in Northern Ireland', *Low Intensity Conflict and Law Enforcement*, Vol. 7(2), pp. 121-56.

Silke, A. (1999c), 'Ragged Justice: Loyalist Vigilantism in Northern Ireland', *Terrorism and Political Violence*, Vol. 11(3), pp. 1-31.

Silke, A. and Taylor, M. (2000), 'War Without End: Comparing IRA and Loyalist Vigilantism in Northern Ireland', *The Howard Journal*, Vol. 39(3), pp. 249-66.

Sluka, J. A. (1989), *Hearts and Minds Water and Fish: Support for the IRA and INLA in a Northern Irish Ghetto*, JAI Press Inc., Greenwich.

Taylor, P. (1999), *Loyalists*, Bloomsbury, London.

Tomlinson, M., Varley, T. and McCullagh, C. (1988), 'Introduction', in Tomlinson, M. Varley, T. and McCullagh, C. (eds), *Whose Law and Order: Aspects of Crime and Social Control in Irish Society*, Sociological Association of Ireland, Dublin, pp. 9-20.

Toolis, K. (1995), *Rebel Hearts: Journeys Within the IRA's Soul*, Basingstoke, London.

Travis, A. (1998), 'Strong Public Backing for On-the-Spot Drug Fines', *Guardian*, 4 June 1998, p. 1.

Watters, D. (1999), 'Greater Shankill Alternatives', 'Let the Family Speak' Conference, Newcastle, Northern Ireland, June 17-18.

Weber, M. (1978), *Economy and Society, 2 Vols.*, ed. Roth, G. and Wittich, C., University of California Press, Berkeley.

Willmott, P. (1987), 'Introduction', in Willmott, P. (ed.), *Policing and the Community*, Policy Studies Institute, London.

Winstone, T. (1997), 'Alternatives to Punishment Beatings and Shootings in a Loyalist Community in Belfast', *Critical Criminology*, Vol. 8(1), pp. 122-8.

Winstone, T., Watters, D. and Drummond, B. (1999), 'Shankill Alternatives', *Fortnight*, September, pp. 18-19.

5 Republican Hegemony or Community Ownership? Community Restorative Justice in Northern Ireland[1]

Kieran McEvoy and Harry Mika

Introduction

One of the visible symptoms of the limitations of state policing in Ireland since at least the nineteenth century has been the periodic existence of alternative systems of vigilantism or 'self policing' (Johnston, 1996; Bell, 1996; Kotsonouris, 1995). Such alternate justice systems have developed in many jurisdictions which have undergone political, social or ethnic conflict (Abel, 1982; McDonald and Zatz, 1992; Burman and Scharf, 1990). In Northern Ireland official figures suggest that since 1973, approximately 2,300 people have been the victims of paramilitary punishment shootings (usually in the knees, thighs, elbows, ankles or a combination) and since 1983, approximately 1,700 people have been the victim of paramilitary punishment beatings (involving attacks with baseball bats, hurling sticks studded with nails, iron bars and other heavy implements (RUC website, 2000). While there is a heated debate as to the reliability of such statistics and the ways in which they have been used in the political arena,[2] there is little dispute concerning the realities of the extreme violence visited upon the victims of punishment attacks with a number having died of injuries or been permanently disabled. While organized paramilitary violence has reduced dramatically in Northern Ireland, with all of the main paramilitary groupings currently observing 'military cessations', punishment attacks and banishments have continued, albeit waxing and waning in the light of political developments and events on the ground (Silke and Taylor, 2000; Knox and Monaghan, 2001).

This paper is divided into three parts. Part one focuses upon the ideology and practice of the Republican paramilitary protagonists, their relationship with the communities from which they draw their support and suggests how such factors relate to the occurrence of punishment violence. Part two explores a number of practical interventions in Republican areas designed to offer non-violent alternatives to punishment attacks, largely based upon the theory and practice of restorative justice. Part three offers some critical reflections on the potential of these projects to end punishment violence and the complex interaction between community praxis, the state and transformation into a post conflict society.

Understanding Republican Punishment Violence

The Provisional IRA (henceforth IRA) is the largest and best known paramilitary organization in Northern Ireland. While it has attacked the security forces, political and judicial figures, Loyalists, economic and civilian targets as part of an overall 'military' strategy (O'Brien, 1993) its members have also 'policed' Republican areas against anti-social crime through punishments and banishments. A distinct section within the IRA known as the 'civil administration' has been given this task (O'Doherty, 1998). This system requires a considerable logistical and infrastructural commitment with personnel designated to hear complaints, investigate, make recommendations and carry out the punishment attacks. It became somewhat routinized during the conflict with designated buildings where complaints were made, relationships established with professionals seeking to make interventions regarding those under threat (discussed below), victims being made aware of the threat and occasional highly publicized accounts of victims or their families arranging to arrive at agreed destinations to be punished.

In justification of these attacks, Republicans pointed to the Royal Ulster Constabulary's ('RUC' prior to its reform as the 'Police Service of Northern Ireland') lack of acceptance or legitimacy amongst their community; the tradition of alternative justice in Ireland as a challenge to the legitimacy of the state (Kotsonouris, 1994); the inability or unwillingness of the RUC to 'properly' police Republican areas, and police toleration of the activity of 'ordinary' criminals in return for becoming 'informers' on suspected IRA activists (Helsinki Watch, 1993, 1992; Munck 1984, 1988). Equally, there has often been considerable grass-roots pressure in local communities to 'do something' about anti-social activity.

Some commentators have strongly criticized the activities of the IRA in carrying out these policing activities as an exercise in power and control, and a form of 'nakedly obvious intimidation' with moralistic justifications which are gauche and transparent (O'Doherty, 1998, p. 145). Similarly, Kennedy (1995) locates Republican punishment beatings within a framework of 'internal repression' within working class nationalist communities. He argues that punishments help to 'manufacture community support' against the state, exercise control through terror, appeal to puritanical punitive urges to 'clean up' society and keep IRA volunteers busy while on cease-fire. Kennedy also contends that punishments may in part be due to the influence of 'warped personalities' amongst the ranks of the paramilitary membership (1995, pp. 77-9). Silke (1999, p. 70) makes a similar point, arguing that the reduced status (within Republicanism) of those involved in punishment attacks has led to a small number of people 'with personality disorders' having become involved in the punishment squads.

Others, while equally critical of the brutality of punishment violence, place greater emphasis upon the community pressures to respond to anti-social crime and the failings of state policing in Republican areas (Sluka, 1989; Connolly, 1997). Such accounts also point to the considerable levels of community support for such activities (Morrissey and Pease, 1982; Connolly, 1997), a factor also acknowledged by Silke (1998). They point to the existence of a crude 'tariff' system (in which matters such as the seriousness of the offence, previous record, age and gender of the alleged offender all impacted upon the punishment imposed), suggesting a more systemic and organized use of violence rather than one subject to the whim of 'warped personalities' (Conway, 1997). Similarly, a number have suggested that while there is some danger from 'informers' amongst the ranks of petty criminals who pose security problems for the IRA, policing activities largely constituted a drain on resources away from the military effort (Munck, 1988; McCorry and Morrissey, 1989). These latter writers share, to a greater or lesser degree, a more subtle appreciation of Republican ideology and practice as well as a more complex understanding of the interaction between paramilitaries and the communities in which they exist.

As we have argued elsewhere (e.g., McEvoy and Mika, 2001), we would place greatest emphasis upon four related themes in understanding punishment violence in Republican communities which must inform any attempts at finding non-violent alternatives to Republican punishment violence. Firstly, the resurgence of the IRA in the early 1970s is widely acknowledged as being influenced in large part by the perceived need for the organized defence of nationalist communities from Loyalist mobs, either supported by or ignored by a belligerent police force (Bowyer Bell, 1979; Coogan, 1987; Bishop and Mallie, 1987). Thus this notion of 'responsibility' for the defence of their community is a key tenet in modern Republican ideology (MacIntyre, 1995; O'Doherty, 1998). It extends beyond defence from Loyalist or state violence to include defence and protection from anti-social crime. Secondly, among Republican communities, there is a parallel culture of dependence upon the IRA to deal with anti-social crime. A range of surveys and ethnographic research has produced candid acknowledgements of such reliance (Brewer *et al*, 1997; O'Mahony *et al*, 2000). As one Republican activist told one of the authors: 'the conflict has created a cycle of dependency, where the community expects the movement [IRA] to deal with anti-social crime, the IRA feels responsible and must act but lacks the resources to deal with it other than through violence and the result is damaging the kids who are after all part of the community'. Thirdly, with regard to formal 'state policing', the RUC's lack of legitimacy in working class Republican and Nationalist communities is well documented (e.g., McGarry and O'Leary, 1999; Ellison, 2000; O'Mahony *et al*, 2000). The sectarian composition of the force, its preoccupation with 'fighting terrorism' and its history of human rights abuses seriously undermined the RUC's capacity to effectively police 'ordinary' crime in such communities. Any process designed to end punishment violence is clearly linked to a transformation of state policing, and an overall improvement in police-community relations in such neighbourhoods.

Finally, the relationship between punishment attacks and broader political developments has become increasingly significant since the 1994 cease-fires. In the pre-1994 context of major explosions, killings and so forth, punishment violence was of less obvious political significance. However after the 'military cessations', the political significance of punishment attacks increased significantly. The continuance of punishment attacks, albeit without the use of firearms for a period on the

Republican side, has become a litmus test for some by which to measure the paramilitaries' commitment to peace. Urging the end to punishment beatings and taking effective action to prevent such activities became one of the key 'Mitchell Principles', a pre-condition to entry to participation in the all-party peace talks (Mitchell, 1996). Similarly, the debates concerning the early release of politically motivated prisoners after the Good Friday Agreement were peppered with efforts by Unionists and Conservatives to link such releases to an end to punishment attacks. Victims of punishment attacks have, like other victims of the conflict, become political objects to be utilized by different protagonists to support their broader political and ideological agenda (Knox, 2001). While the 'wall to wall' media coverage of punishment attacks may be justifiably linked to a process of 'reinventing and re-demonizing the enemy' (Tomlinson, 1995), the political reality remains that an end to punishment beatings is intricately linked to the overall process of conflict resolution.

Those who have been engaged in attempts at praxis on this issue on the Republican side have been informed by these four themes, but have focused in practice on the first two. The central thrust has been to create a process whereby Republicans could be encouraged to (in their terms) 'disengage responsibly' and local communities could be properly trained and encouraged to take greater responsibility and ownership over the process of justice.   Such a community centred focus has required a parallel process by which the past failings of formal state policing could be acknowledged and rectified and the political efforts at conflict resolution could be seen to be working. While the Patten report has been published and legislation on a new policing service has been passed, the political prospects for the future are less clear at the time of writing.

Punishment Attacks, Restorative Justice and Praxis

Before discussing in detail the attempts at using restorative justice theory and practice to make interventions with regard to punishment violence, it is important to offer a brief introduction to its central tenets in so far as they relate to the Northern Ireland context.

While an admittedly broad concept, restorative justice is at its core an approach to dealing with the harmful effects of crime as a breakdown in relationships which require healing, rather than focusing exclusively upon rule breaking (Zehr, 1990). It is often shaped by a critique of the traditional retributive justice focus upon the punishment of offender (Marshall, 1999). In the specific Northern Ireland context, restorative justice proposes three core concepts that underpin the values of pilot initiatives in Republican and Loyalist areas.

First, crime is fundamentally a violation of people and interpersonal relationships. Victims and the community have been harmed and are in need of restoration. While the primary victims are those most directly affected by the offence, the family members of victims and offenders, witnesses and others in the community are also victims and their input should be maximized (McCold, 1996). Second, restorative justice maintains that crime and anti-social behaviour create obligations and liabilities. Offenders are obligated to make things right, as much as possible (Braithwaite, 1989). Victims must have every opportunity to participate in defining these obligations, and offenders must be provided the opportunities and encouragement to understand the nature of the harms they have caused and the avenues for taking responsibility for what has happened (Wright, 1996). Since local communities bear a responsibility for the welfare of all of its members, communities are encouraged to support victims and to integrate offenders into community life (Bernd-Dieter, 1998). Third, restorative justice seeks to heal and put right the wrongs. The needs of victims for information, validation, restitution, testimony, safety and support are the starting points of a restorative justice process (Zehr and Mika, 1998). Such a process should be designed to maximize the possibilities for voluntary exchange of information, participation, dialogue and mutual consent between victim and offender, including opportunities for expressions of remorse, forgiveness and reconciliation where appropriate (Yazzie and Zion, 1996).

Restorative Justice and Praxis in Republican Communities

As was noted earlier, punishment violence was not afforded the same level of political significance during the Northern Ireland conflict as in the post cease-fire era. That said, the brutality of punishment attacks by paramilitaries has always been something of a public relations disaster (at least at a national and international level) for Loyalist and Republican paramilitaries. A number of international human rights organizations have, under the rubric of international humanitarian law, been extremely critical of such activities (Amnesty International, 1994; Human Rights Watch, 1992). Within the jurisdiction, a number of single-issue pressure groups emerged in the 1990s who dedicated themselves to the task of publicizing the brutality of such attacks. Although the activities of some of these groups provoked controversy,[3] they were nonetheless a persistent irritant to the paramilitaries and their political parties (McEvoy, 2001).

Perhaps in partial recognition of the damage done to their respective political causes, since at least the early 1990s Republicans (and Loyalists) have permitted individuals and agencies to intervene on behalf of those under threat. Since 1990 a program called *Base 2* has clarified with paramilitaries whether individuals were under threat, relocated such people outside their community (in Northern Ireland, the Republic of Ireland or England) and sought to arrange for their reintegration (Base 2, 1990-2000). This programme has become one of the primary sources of objective data on punishment attacks dealing with over 2,800 cases by the end of 2000.

It was in such a context of continuing punishments and limited interventions by professionals that in 1996 one of the authors (McEvoy) and a number of colleagues were approached by activists from Republican areas to provide training on issues concerning informal justice. A programme was devised which focused upon restorative justice, human rights, crime prevention, mediation and non-violence. A residential followed at which a model of non-violent community based alternatives to punishment attacks was devised. In December 1997, following extensive consultation with Republicans, statutory agencies, community representatives, political parties and others, a discussion document (The 'Blue Book') was produced detailing the process and outlining the model based upon restorative justice principles (Auld *et al*, 1997). That document, originally written as a discussion document for Sinn Féin and the IRA but subsequently amended and published by the authors in their personal capacity, was subsequently endorsed by both wings of Republicanism.[4] Following publication of the report, funding for four pilot projects in Republican areas and a co-ordinator position for three years was successfully achieved in September 1998 under the auspices of the Northern Ireland Association for the Care and Rehabilitation of Offenders (NIACRO), a major voluntary organization with whom all of the report authors were involved.

In their submission to the Patten Commission on Policing, Sinn Féin stressed community restorative justice as one of their five key demands.[5] Instructively the Sinn Féin submission was explicit that restorative justice was not viewed as supplanting 'formal' policing and specifically recommended the inclusion of some statutory organizations (other than the RUC) in the management of such projects.[6] After the first of the projects became operational in January 1999, the IRA also endorsed the projects and called upon people in Republican communities to use the projects where they were established rather than appeal for punishment attacks.[7] Indeed, opposition from the RUC to the restorative justice projects only served to enhance their credibility to Republicans.[8]

The model proposed in the *Blue Book* was designed to meet a number of specifications including non-violence; meeting the needs and responsibilities of victim, offender and community; community involvement in the delivery of the programme; acting within the law; proportionality between sanction and infraction; due process and consistency; utilization of existing community programmes and an inclusive and transparent approach to the management and staffing of the project (Auld *et al*, 1997). However, it was also stressed that such projects would not have relations with an unreformed RUC.

Between the publication of the *Blue Book* and the projects becoming operational, a number of the envisaged features have not been incorporated. For example, it was originally envisaged that projects would have an investigatory wing, a community forum wherein 'community hearings' would take place, and the power to 'boycott' persistent offenders (wherein goods and services in a local community would be withdrawn from persistent offenders). In practice, none of these features have been implemented. Rather, the work of the projects is taken up with the normal restorative justice activities of preparation of victims and offenders, mediation, family group conferencing and the monitoring of agreements. In addition, the *Blue Book* suggested that the process should include a Community Charter outlining the rights and responsibilities of local citizens and these are shortly to appear as murals on gable walls where the projects operate.

The Projects

Four pilot projects were launched in Republican areas (three in Belfast and one in Derry) in 1999 and, as noted above, are currently being evaluated by one of the authors (Mika). These launches led almost immediately to high levels of interest in programme duplication in Nationalist areas of Northern Ireland and a number of areas in the Irish Republic.[9] This has not been particularly surprising given considerable local and even international media interest and the advocacy by Sinn Féin of the initiatives. Such demands have led to a significant drain on scarce resources and energy in the four pilot schemes. With the central co-ordinating office, 'Community Restorative Justice Ireland' (CRJ) has become the formal designation for all Nationalist programmes. By early 2000, training regimens had been completed for 15 Community Restorative Justice programmes throughout Northern Ireland.

Case activity for the four pilot schemes in Republican areas included about 200 referrals-cases, greater than 90 per cent of which were resolved and closed in 1999. The 1999 and 2000 evaluation snapshot of Community Restorative Justice is highly suggestive of probable programme impact (Mika, 2001). During these two years, each of the pilots maintained a programme consultant/co-ordinator, and an administrator, a training officer and standards monitor of Community Restorative Justice (in a central office) were appointed. Local projects, in addition, had some success in securing their own premises through local grants and contributions. Management committees had been appointed in each of the areas, and each site had a least one full class of community volunteers who had received formal restorative justice and mediation training. For the two programme years, Community Restorative Justice opened about 700 cases, more than 90 per cent of which had been closed and resolved. It is anticipated that by the close of the 2001 programme year, Community Restorative Justice will have been involved in about 1,200 cases in Republican communities served by these four projects alone. This specific programme output is in addition to formally engaging more than 75 community groups, and voluntary and statutory organizations, and participating in approximately 150 separate radio interviews, television appearances, and newspaper articles. Case profiles reveal the standard fare of many community mediation programmes world-wide, including noise and nuisance, family conflict, burglary and damage to property. A portion of the caseload also involved individuals under paramilitary punishment threat for serious and chronic offending.

Evaluations

While the final evaluation of the projects in both Republican and Loyalist areas are not due to be completed until 2002, some preliminary trends have become apparent in the first year of the projects' operation.[10] First, the initial months of any site's programme have been dominated by rudimentary developments, including initial public education, community consultation, and training. Second, as noted above, significant demands have been made upon the fledgling expertise and resources of the pilot schemes in expanding into other areas. Third, each of the restorative justice initiatives has engaged in extensive and broad community consultation prior to formally launching their service, resulting in very high levels of community interest. Fourth, and following from the levels of consultation with the community, referral of cases has been both immediate, and at such high levels as to often overwhelm the capacity of the new initiatives to respond. Fifth, given the number of referrals, the reputation of workers affiliated with the projects (including ex-prisoners) appear to have enhanced programme credibility in local areas. The final factor is the highly politicized environment in which these projects have been operating. Given their origins in dialogue with paramilitary organizations and the explicit involvement of former prisoners, programme activities are (perhaps understandably) closely scrutinized by the media, statutory organizations and others for malpractice. While the latter places considerable pressures on developing projects, on balance, most of the other factors noted here appear to bode favourably for the development of the projects at least in the short run.

Restorative Justice as a Means of Ending Punishment Violence

As academics and practitioners with ten and twenty five years respectively of experience of working on the Northern Ireland conflict (McEvoy) and mediation, dispute resolution and restorative justice in the USA and internationally (Mika), the authors are acutely aware of the need for critical reflexivity in attempts at praxis such as these. We have grouped the possible criticisms of these initiatives into three overlapping categories. These are: restorative justice as an expression of 'the totalitarian community'; restorative justice as a tool for the maintenance of paramilitary hegemony and the diminution of state power; and restorative justice as the absorption of revolutionary struggle and the legitimation of the British state.

Restorative Justice as an Expression of the 'Intolerant' Community

> We should stop thinking about communities as homogenous neighbourhoods and start recognising them as interest groups which are often in conflict. (Shearing, 1994, p. 5)

Shearing's salutary reminder concerning the dangers of romanticizing the notion of community when thinking about the role of ordinary citizens in 'policing' activities is quoted approvingly in the research on Restorative Justice commissioned by the Northern Ireland Criminal Justice Review. In that research, Dignan argues that 'such warnings are relevant for those who might be tempted to opportunistically invoke the concepts of restorative justice to lend a spurious legitimacy to attempts to perpetuate illiberal attitudes and practices that operate under the guise of informal "alternative justice" processes' (Dignan, 2000, p. 19). Few would dispute the need to problematize reductionist or rose-tinted notions of community when considering any community based justice system (Mika, 1987). The familiar danger of community justice whereby a process of net-widening may occur (in which the expansion of intolerant social control encourages unnecessary intervention with a larger group of individuals concerning often petty issues; for example, see Cohen, 1985) is equally applicable in this context. Indeed it is often the most punitive and illiberal elements of working class communities in Northern

Ireland who have been at the forefront of demanding ever more violent physical punishments from paramilitaries against alleged anti-social offenders.

Such dangers have not however been lost on those involved in the establishment of restorative justice projects in Northern Ireland, a fact that Dignan inexplicably fails to mention. As Auld *et al* (1997, p. 28) argued: 'our concept of "the community" is not an undifferentiated mass with identical interests. Rather it is made up of diverse groups of people with different incomes, interests, political affiliations, housing types and views on anti-social crime'. Similarly, the authors cautioned that '...the spectre of vigilantism, unchecked by notions of due process or the rights of individuals and minority groups, must be ensured against by any community justice system' (Auld *et al*, 1997, p. 28). More recently the *Community Restorative Justice Standards and Values* noted, '...restorative justice initiatives embrace the diversity of the community without regard to the ethnicity, religious belief, political opinion, disability, gender, age and sexual orientation' (Community Restorative Justice, 2000, p. 5).

While recognizing the dangers regarding intolerance and vigilantism (Johnston, 1996),[11] it is our view that they can be successfully managed. An organizational ethos on non-violence and protecting the human rights of victim and offender; a broad-based recruitment process; high standards of training; operating in an open, transparent and accountable fashion in line with published standards; and ongoing self monitoring and independent evaluation, represent systemic ways in which such dangers should be addressed. While the risk of 'net-widening' will become clearer after a longer term analysis of the case load, it is apparent from the early cases of the projects in Republican areas that a significant proportion (15-20 per cent) of them would previously have resulted in punishment violence. High levels of commitment, energy and enthusiasm in local communities has seen a throughput of over 1,000 cases across Northern Ireland in just over two years. Several hundred volunteers have completed training on restorative justice, non-violence, human rights and a range of other key themes relevant to restorative justice theory and practice. Both the projects in Republican and Loyalist areas have now developed and published sophisticated Standards documents and put in place mechanisms to ensure that they are complied with. As John Braithwaite (2001, p. 16) argued recently at a conference held in Belfast,

> Northern Ireland has a more mature debate on standards and principles of restorative justice than any society I know...I suspect this is because Northern Ireland has a more politicized contest between state and civil society models of restorative justice than can be found in other places. Such fraught contexts are where there is the greatest risk of justice system catastrophes. But they are also the contexts with the richest prospects for rising to the political challenges with transformative innovations through restorative justice. In my short time in Northern Ireland I have found the restorative justice programs in both the Loyalist and Republican communities inspiring.

We would argue that restorative justice, if properly managed, has the potential to encourage tolerance and respect for human rights in local communities. One of the reasons for punitive attitudes towards crime and anti-social behaviour is the social distance between communities, offenders and those tasked with the punishment of crime. For example, the lack of familiarity or empathy amongst the American electorate, particularly towards young African American males who make up a disproportionate number of prison inmates, may be linked directly to the upsurge in support for incarceration and ever more punitive sanctions for criminal behaviour (e.g., Welch, 1999; May, 1999). In the Northern Ireland context, the notion that 'dealing with' anti-social behaviour was primarily the responsibility of the paramilitaries in certain communities encouraged similarly punitive attitudes. However, if restorative justice projects can foster greater involvement in and ownership over crime management, a variation of what some commentators have referred to as a 'responsibilisation strategy' (e.g., Crawford, 1998, p. 247), then they may become a tool for greater community tolerance, cohesion and non-violence.

Restorative Justice and Paramilitary Hegemony

The second major concern voiced with regard to the restorative justice projects is that they represent an attempt by paramilitaries to maintain control and influence in local communities. These projects emerged from direct dialogue with paramilitary constituencies and have been explicit about the desire to include former prisoners amongst their staff and volunteers activists. The involvement of such individuals has been a constant source of criticism by the Northern Ireland Office and the RUC since the projects emerged. This view was summed up in the recent Criminal Justice Review Report:

> We heard a wide range of concerns expressed about community restorative justice schemes and their relationship to paramilitary punishment beatings, including: the motivation for the development of community restorative justice schemes. Many believed that community restorative justice schemes were being developed by paramilitaries because of the growing unacceptability of punishment attacks within the community, and the need to replace such attacks with other methods of controlling their communities; The risk that those involved in meting out sanctions arising from such scheme would resort to or threaten punishment beatings; The perceived or potential involvement of those with paramilitary links in such schemes, and the risk of the schemes being driven by people who did not represent the community as a whole, for reasons that had little or nothing to do with concerns about crime... (Criminal Justice Review, 2000, pp. 196-7) [12]

After three decades of a violent conflict it is hardly surprising that many in the state justice system and elsewhere are suspicious about projects which emerge from a direct dialogue with paramilitary constituencies. One needs to be acutely aware of the corrosive dangers of direct or implied paramilitary coercion on the credibility and effectiveness of these fledgling projects. Indeed we would argue, and have done so both privately and publicly to a range of the actors involved, that the continuance of any beatings and shootings by paramilitaries (albeit in reduced numbers) in areas where restorative justice projects are operational, places an unfair pressure on the restorative projects themselves. The perception in Republican areas that the IRA continues to punish a number of the most serious and persistent offenders (leaving restorative justice to deal with the rest) is likely to impact negatively upon the projects in the medium-long term. With those caveats acknowledged, it is important to look more closely at some of the assumptions regarding the concerns of paramilitary hegemony in local communities.

The first and most obvious point is the notion that paramilitaries may use restorative justice to 'control' or exert a 'stranglehold' over local communities (Knox and Monaghan, 2001). This suggests a relationship between paramilitaries and their communities which is essentially one of coercion by the former visited upon the latter. Such a view is narrow and inaccurate. There is a much more complex dialectic between paramilitaries and the communities in which they operate in Northern Ireland (Sluka, 1989, 1995; McAuley, 1994), one which we have characterized above as a cycle of 'responsibility and reliance' in the area of punishment violence. While particularly in Republican communities, Republican activists, Sinn Féin members and former prisoners are highly active throughout civil society, they are only part of a diverse, vibrant and heterogeneous community sector of womens' groups, church groups, tenants' associations and so forth. The notion that power is maintained by physical coercion or the supine acceptance of Republican directives by such groups is conspiratorial fantasy, seemingly prevalent amongst those with little or no direct contact with Republicans or the communities from which they come. If restorative justice projects can attract a diverse range of recruits from within local communities and are professionally managed, then the power of Republicans or Loyalists in such settings can only be exercised as one organic element as part of a broader contested space.

The second point concerns the origins of the projects in dialogue with paramilitary constituencies and the motivation of paramilitaries for becoming involved. It is undoubtedly true that the IRA wished to end (or at least reduce) punishment violence because of their perceived growing unacceptability. Certainly the political pressure on Sinn Féin regarding such attacks during the peace process may well have focused minds more acutely within the Republican Movement generally. That said, it is difficult to imagine how effective attempts at praxis concerning punishment violence might have been achieved without direct engagement with such constituencies. In a process of post conflict transformation, the aim has been to persuade and encourage those constituencies to support and feel ownership over the changes being wrought rather to seek to impose such changes upon them.

The third element of the concerns regarding paramilitary hegemony and restorative justice is the view that restorative justice projects may be used by paramilitaries (particularly Republicans) to exclude the institutions of state justice from such communities. As Mulcahy (2000, pp. 77-8) has pointed out, the RUC claimed a base of 'hidden support' in nationalist areas, suggesting that individuals were intimidated (by the IRA) from expressing their outright co-operation with the force. Such a view has permeated much of the official reaction to restorative justice projects. To a limited extent, it explains why the parallel Loyalist project (which sought unsuccessfully to develop relations with the RUC) have received comparatively little media criticism despite the UVF's limitations on the scope of their intervention.[13]

In fact, however, there has been no attempt on the Republican side to exclude the state system *per se,* and project leaders have been adamant that their aim is to supplant paramilitary punishments. As the report of the Criminal Justice Review acknowledges, relations have been developed with the Probation Service, the statutory Youth Services, Social Services, Educational Sector, and the Housing Executive. Similarly, practitioners and spokespersons have made it clear that they do not regard it as a problem if victims also contact the police (e.g., in the case of car theft or burglary for insurance purposes) or where the police are informed as a matter of course, through restorative justice referrals to specialist agencies (e.g., in cases of domestic violence or child abuse). Community Restorative Justice spokespersons made clear that their objection was to relations with an unreformed RUC, not necessarily to a new policing service.[14] It is our view that in the context of a reformed policing service, restorative justice projects can actually provide an excellent vehicle for the development of organic links between state policing and communities traditionally estranged from the police, albeit at a pace dictated by local communities. Partnerships cannot be imposed however, and it is simply an unachievable political demand to expect such a partnership in the absence of police reforms.

Restorative Justice as the Co-option of Revolutionary Struggle and the Legitimation of the State

> Community Restorative Justice is British double speak for collaboration with Crown Forces...NIACRO is dedicated to recruiting ex-prisoners into a new police force which will serve as an auxiliary wing of the RUC...It is clear that the establishment of a new British police force in the guise of community justice is the initiative of a British colonial agency operating from Stormont.[15]

For Republicans, the complex dialectic of notions of 'responsibility and reliance' between paramilitary organizations and their communities means that for those opposed to the peace process the apparent abandonment of 'policing' functions is viewed as symptomatic of a broader 'corruption of the struggle' and an abandonment of traditional objectives.[16]

While the charge of co-option by the formal justice system is a traditional one faced by the advocates of informal justice (e.g., Fitzpatrick, 1992; Nina, 1992), it is a charge of considerably augmented political significance in a context in which dissidents see the potential for political destabilization through the policing debate. In our view, this is not however an argument for the retention of paramilitary punishment violence as a means of protecting that political flank. Rather we would argue that it represents an opportunity to present restorative justice as a more progressive means of achieving political objectives (such as the protection of communities from anti-social crime) more in keeping with an era of transformation and conflict resolution.

Given crime's inherent tendency to bifurcate the 'rough' from the 'respectable', Adam Crawford has questioned the role of crime in the development of 'open, tolerant and inclusive communities' (Crawford, 1997, p. 274). Such concerns are highly germane to the current discussion. However, as Crawford goes on to argue, the key to ensuring that anxieties concerning crime do not result in defensive or parochial communities is to link community activity with *social justice*.[17] The realities of the brutality of punishment violence have been a moral imperative for the establishment of these projects. Their origins in dialogue with paramilitary groups, the realities of operating in a hostile political environment and the background and skills of the staff and volunteers have meant that these projects have continuously demonstrated their commitment to principles of social justice in their recruitment, training and practice.

Conclusion

The failure of state policing during the Northern Ireland conflict contributed significantly to the evolution of a violent and brutal system of paramilitary punishments. As well as the complex interaction of notions of paramilitary responsibility and community dependence, such violence was symptomatic of fractured relationships between the state criminal justice system and working class communities.

The restorative justice projects detailed above represent attempts at praxis designed ultimately to end paramilitary punishment violence in local communities. A range of features are required to ensure that restorative justice practice in such areas is operated legitimately.[18] However, such communities cannot do it alone. In the final analysis, that process can only succeed if the new policing service and a reformed criminal justice system prove capable of much more nuanced engagement with the needs of local communities, demonstrating local democratic accountability and a reconfigured set of state/community power relations (see McEvoy *et al*, 2001). We are convinced that these restorative justice initiatives are indicative of a commitment at a local community level to change a culture that had largely become immunized to the human consequences of using violence to resolve its problems of crime and anti-social behaviour. Whether state agencies prove themselves capable of a similar transformation remains to be seen.

Notes

1   A fuller version of this chapter, which examines attempts to supplant both Loyalist and Republican punishment violence, is published in *Policing & Society* (2001), Vol. 11(3-4), pp. 359-82. We are grateful for permission from the editor to reproduce some of those arguments here.

2   See, e.g., 'Statistics Show Drop in Punishment Attacks', *Ireland on Sunday*, 5 February 1999.

3   'FAIT Faces Breakup After Scandal: Future of Group is Bleak Says Member', *Irish News*, 29 July 1997; 'FAIT is Rocked by Former Director's Attack', *Belfast Telegraph*, 28 September 1998; 'Union Asks For NIO to Investigate FAIT', *Belfast Telegraph*, 21 October 1998; 'McKenna Quits FAIT to Start New Project', *Belfast Telegraph*, 1 May 1999. Families Against Intimidation and Terror folded in 1999.

4   'Sinn Féin is in total agreement with the use of non-violent mechanisms for making offenders more accountable for their crimes, giving victims an input and involving communities in the ownership of the justice process. In particular, the report is to be

welcomed for acknowledging the limitations of the formal justice system in the North as well as providing practical non-violent alternatives to beatings and shootings. While obviously considerable work would need to be done to arrive at a stage of actually implementing local systems of restorative justice on the ground, this document provides a helpful framework within which to discuss moving that process forward.' Gerry Adams, Sinn Féin President, quoted in the *Irish News*, 18 December 1997, 'Community Policing Without the Balaclavas'.

5   In the section of their submission entitled Community Restorative Justice, Sinn Féin referred to the *Blue Book* and argued; '...this is a process which Sinn Féin supports and which we are encouraging in areas where we have significant political support. It needs to be clearly stated at the outset that these proposals are set in the context of a new police service that can enjoy widespread support from, and is seen as an integral part of, the community as a whole. The RUC quite clearly do not fit this criteria.' Sinn Féin (1998, pp. 20-1).

6   'Local structures should not be seen as an alternative to formal policing. In our view restorative justice...is an approach which can build trust and empower individual communities affected. Effective liaison between police and community can also serve to deal more effectively with neighbourhood disputes and less serious offences in a way that also frees up police time and resources to deal with more serious crime...Local management committees will be established which must be broad based, involving political representatives of all local parties, church people, business people and local community organizations. We would also like to see statutory bodies represented locally – such as the Probation Board – sitting on management committees. This will assist in ensuring effective delivery of services as well as monitoring of local structures by statutory bodies and monitoring of statutory bodies by the local community' (Sinn Féin, 1998, p. 21).

7   'Republican terrorists haven't carried out any beatings or shootings in the city for four weeks after pledging its support to Community Restorative Justice programmes...Republicans in Belfast are telling the people to go to the Restorative Justice programme co-ordinators with their problems.' *Belfast Telegraph*, 10 April 1999, 'IRA Calls Halt to Beatings'.

8   As one IRA spokesperson told a local newspaper, 'We know the RUC is fiercely opposed to the Restorative Justice programmes...In fact, the opposition of the RUC to the programme is the finest recommendation it could receive...We want people to support the Restorative Justice approach by bringing their problems to the dedicated and highly trained workers operating in the programmes rather than to the IRA.' *Andersonstown News*, 20 March 1999, 'IRA Pledges Support for "Community Justice" Plan'.

9   For example, the pilot project in Brandywell, a very small Nationalist estate in Derry, gave rise to programmes in seven other housing estates in Derry by the end of 1999.

10   The evaluations are based upon the range of variables appropriate both to restorative justice values and principles (see, for example, Zehr and Mika, 1998).

11   Johnston (1996, p. 220) has defined vigilantism as consisting of six necessary features. These include: (a) planning and premeditation, (b) voluntary engagement by private citizens, (c) a form of autonomous citizenship which constitutes a 'social movement', (d) the use or threat of force, (e) it arises when an established order is under threat, and (f) it aims to control crime or other social infractions by offering assurances of security.

12   The Review report appears to use the phrase community restorative justice as a general description for the projects in both Loyalist and Republican areas rather than just those in the Republican communities which, as was discussed above, operate under the name of Community Restorative Justice Ireland.

13 The original premise upon which Greater Shankill Alternatives was created was explicit that they would not intervene in matters concerning internal disciplinary matters within Loyalist paramilitary groupings, disputes between paramilitary groupings concerning territory, drugs or other matters, or offences of a sexual nature (Winstone, 1997).

14 'We do want a partnership with a reformed police service in the future. We know that our kind of restorative justice scheme works best with a good relationship with the formal system. We intend to plan for that day. But it is not, unfortunately, here yet'. (Community Restorative Justice, 2000).

15 'Blue Book for New British Police', *Saoirse,* September 1998. Saoirse is the magazine of Republican Sinn Féin. Republican Sinn Féin, the political wing of the Continuity IRA (not currently on cease-fire), is opposed to the peace process.

16 An upsurge in punishment shootings has been linked in some quarters to tensions within the mainstream IRA concerning the lack of political progress and a sense that dissident Republicans were making political capital from the IRA's moratorium on punishment attacks. 'Violence Blamed on Tensions within the Provisionals', *Irish Times,* 16 March 2000.

17 'The challenge for local participatory initiatives is to mediate competing claims through processes and strategies which are open, inclusive, democratic, egalitarian – in the sense that they recognise and appropriately compensate for power differentials – and are grounded in principles of social, rather than local, justice'. (Crawford, 1997, p. 291).

18 Elsewhere we have written in some detail about the requirements of 'legitimating restorative justice practice' in local communities, grouped under seven themes. These include a mandate from local communities, moral authority, partnership, competency, practice, transparency and accountability (Mika & McEvoy, 2001).

References

Abel, R. (ed.) (1982), *The Politics of Informal Justice, Vols. 1 and 2*, Academic Press, New York.

Amnesty International (1994), *Political Killings in Northern Ireland*, Amnesty International, London.

Auld, J., Gormally, B., McEvoy K. and Ritchie, M. (1997), *Designing a System of Restorative Justice in Northern Ireland (The Blue Book)*, The Authors, Belfast.

Base 2 (1990- 2000), *Annual Reports*, NIACRO, Belfast.

Bell, C. (1996), 'Alternative Justice in Ireland', in Dawson, N., Greer, D. and Ingram, P. (eds), *One Hundred and Fifty Years of Irish Law*, SLS, Belfast, pp.144-67.

Bernd-Dieter, M. (1998), 'Restorative Justice: A New Paradigm in Criminal Law?', *European Journal of Crime, Criminal Law and Criminal Justice*, Vol. 6, pp. 125-39.

Bishop, P. and Mallie, E. (1987), *The Provisional IRA*, Corgi, London.

Bowyer Bell, J. (1979), *The Secret Army: The IRA*, Poolbeg, London.

Braithwaite, J. (1989), *Crime, Shame and Reintegration*, Cambridge University Press, Cambridge.

Braithwaite, J. (2001), 'Reconciling Models: Balancing Regulation, Standards and Principles of Restorative Justice Practice', in Mika, H. and McEvoy, K. (eds), *International Perspectives on Restorative Justice: A Conference Report*, Queen's University Belfast, Belfast, pp.16-25.

Brewer, J., Lockhart B. and Rodgers, P. (1998), 'Informal Social Control and Crime Management in Belfast', *British Journal of Sociology*, Vol. 49, pp. 570-85.

Burman, S. and Scharf, W. (1990), 'Creating People's Justice: Street Committees and People's Courts in South Africa', *Law and Society Review*, Vol. 24, pp. 693-735.

76 *Informal Criminal Justice*

Cohen, S. (1985), *Visions of Social Control*, Cambridge University Press, Cambridge.
Community Restorative Justice (2000), *Values and Standards of Practice*, Community Restorative Justice, Belfast.
Connolly, J. (1997), *Community Policing in the North of Ireland*, Centre for Research and Documentation, Belfast.
Conway, P. (1993), '"The Threat of Violence" and "Working with the Threatened"', *Criminal Justice Matters*, ISTD, London, pp. 2-10.
Conway, P. (1997), 'A Response to Paramilitary Policing in Northern Ireland', *Critical Criminology*, Vol. 8, pp. 109-22.
Coogan, T. P. (1987), *The IRA*, Fontana, London.
Crawford, A. (1997), *The Local Governance of Crime: Appeals to Community and Partnerships*, Clarendon Press, Oxford.
Crawford, A. (1998), *Crime Prevention and Community Safety*, Longman, Harlow.
Criminal Justice Review (2000), *Review of the Criminal Justice System in Northern Ireland*, Her Majesty's Stationery Office, Belfast.
Dignan, J. (2000), *Restorative Justice Options from Northern Ireland*, Her Majesty's Stationery Office, Belfast.
Ellison, G. (2000), 'Reflecting All Shades of Opinion: Public Attitudinal Surveys and the Construction of Police Legitimacy in Northern Ireland', *British Journal of Criminology*, Vol. 40, pp. 88-111.
Fitzpatrick, P. (1992), 'The Impossibility of Popular Justice', *Social and Legal Studies*, Vol. 1, pp. 199-215.
Helsinki Watch (1992), *Children in Northern Ireland: Abused by Security Forces and Paramilitaries*, Human Rights Watch, New York.
Helsinki Watch (1993), 'Northern Ireland: Human Rights Abuses by All Sides', Vol. 5(6), Human Rights Watch, New York.
Human Rights Watch (1992), *World Report 1992: An Annual Review of Developments and the Bush Administration Policy on Human Rights World-wide*, New York: Human Rights Watch.
Johnston, L. (1996), 'What is Vigilantism?', *British Journal of Criminology*, Vol. 36, pp. 220-36.
Kennedy, L. (1995), 'Nightmares within Nightmares: Paramilitary Repression in Working Class Communities', in Kennedy, L. (ed.), *Crime and Punishment in West Belfast*, The Summer School, Belfast, pp. 67-80.
Knox, C. (2001), 'The "Deserving" Victims of Political Violence: Punishment Attacks in Northern Ireland', *Criminal Justice*, Vol. 1(2), pp. 181-201.
Knox, C. and Monaghan, R. (2001), *Informal Criminal Justice Systems in Northern Ireland*, Report to the Economic and Social Research Council, London, The Authors.
Kotsonouris, M. (1995), *Retreat from Revolution: The Dáil Courts, 1920-24*, Irish Academic Press, Dublin.
MacIntyre, A. (1995), 'Modern Irish Republicanism: The Product of British State Strategies', *Irish Political Studies*, Vol. 10, pp. 97-122.
Marshall, T. (1999), *Restorative Justice*, Her Majesty's Stationery Office, London.
McAuley, J. (1994), *The Politics of Identity: A Loyalist Community in Belfast*, Avebury, Aldershot.
McCold, P. (1996), 'Restorative Justice and the Role of Community', in Galloway, B. and Hudson, J. (eds), *Restorative Justice*, Criminal Justice Press, New York, pp. 85-103.
McCorry, J. and Morrissey, M. (1989), 'Community, Crime and Punishment in West Belfast', *Howard Journal*, Vol. 28, pp. 289-92.
McDonald, J. and Zatz, M. (1992), 'Popular Justice in Revolutionary Nicaragua', *Social and Legal Studies*, Vol. 1, pp. 283-305.

McEvoy, K. (2001), 'Human Rights, Humanitarian Interventions and Paramilitary Activities in Northern Ireland, in Harvey, C. (ed.), *Human Rights, Equality and Democratic Renewal in Northern Ireland*, Hart, Oxford, pp. 215-48.

McEvoy K. and Mika, H. (2001), 'Punishment, Policing and Praxis: Restorative Justice and Non-Violent Alternatives To Paramilitary Punishments In Northern Ireland', *Policing & Society*, Vol. 11(3-4), pp. 359-82.

McEvoy, K., Gormally, B. and Mika, M. (2001), 'Conflict, Crime Control and the 'Re'-Construction of State\Community Relations in Northern Ireland', in Hughes, G., McLaughlin, E. and Muncie, J. (eds), *Crime Prevention and Community Safety: New Directions*, Sage, London, pp. 183-212.

McGarry, J. and O'Leary, B. (1999), *Policing Northern Ireland: Proposals for a New Start*, Blackstaff, Belfast.

May, J. (ed.) (1999), *Building Violence*, Sage, London.

Mika, H. (1987), 'Mediating Neighbourhood Conflict: Conceptual and Strategic Considerations', *Negotiation Journal*, (October), pp. 397-410.

Mika, H. & McEvoy, K. (2001), 'Restorative Justice In Conflict: Paramilitarism, Community And The Construction Of Legitimacy in Northern Ireland', *Contemporary Justice Review*, Vol. 4(3).

Mika, H. (2001), *Interim Evaluation Report of Four Pilot Community Restorative Justice Programmes*, NIACRO, Belfast.

Mitchell, G. (1996), *Report of the International Body*, Her Majesty's Stationery Office, Belfast.

Morrissey, M. and Pease, K. (1982), 'The Black Criminal Justice System in West Belfast', *Howard Journal*, Vol. 21, pp. 159-66.

Mulcahy, A. (2000), 'Policing History: The Official Discourse and Organisational Memory of the Royal Ulster Constabulary', *British Journal of Criminology*, Vol. 40, pp. 68-87.

Munck, R. (1984), 'Repression, Insurgency and Popular Justice: The Irish Case', *Crime and Social Justice*, Vols. 21-2, pp. 81-94.

Munck, R. (1988), 'The Lads and the Hoods: Alternative Justice in an Irish Context', in Tomlinson, M., Varley, T. and McCullagh, C. (eds), *Whose Law and Order? Aspects of Crime and Social Control in Irish Society*, Sociological Association of Ireland, Belfast, pp. 41-53.

Nina, D. (1992), *Popular Justice in a New South Africa*, Centre for Applied Legal Studies, Johannesburg, Occasional Paper 15.

O'Brien, B. (1993), *The Long War: The IRA and Sinn Féin 1985 to Today*, O'Brien Press, Dublin.

O'Doherty, M. (1998), *The Trouble with Guns: Republican Strategy and the Provisional IRA*, Blackstaff, Belfast.

O'Mahony, D., Geary, R., McEvoy, K. and Morison, J. (2000), *Crime, Community and Locale: The Northern Ireland Communities Crime Survey*, Ashgate, Aldershot.

Patten Report, The (1999), *A New Beginning: Policing in Northern Ireland*, Her Majesty's Stationery Office, Belfast.

RUC (2000), *Official Website of the Royal Ulster Constabulary, http://www.ruc.police.uk*, (accessed 2000).

Shearing, C. (1994), 'Participatory Policing: Modalities of Lay Participation', *Imbizo*, Vol. 2, pp. 5-10.

Silke, A. (1998), 'The Lords of Discipline: The Methods and Motives of Paramilitary Vigilantism in Northern Ireland', *Low Intensity Conflict and Law Enforcement*, Vol. 7, pp. 121-56.

Silke, A. (1999), 'Rebel's Dilemma: The Changing Relationship between the IRA, Sinn Fein and Paramilitary Vigilantism in Northern Ireland', *Terrorism and Political Violence*, Vol. 11, pp. 55-99.

78   *Informal Criminal Justice*

Silke, A. and Taylor, M. (2000), 'War Without End: Comparing IRA and Loyalist Vigilantism in Northern Ireland', *Howard Journal of Criminal Justice*, Vol. 39, pp. 249-66.

Sinn Féin (1998), *Sinn Féin Submission to the Independent Commission on Policing for Northern Ireland*, Sinn Féin, Belfast .

Sluka, J. (1989), *Hearts and Minds, Water and Fish: Support for the IRA and INLA in a Northern Ireland Ghetto*, JAI Press, London.

Sluka, J. (1995), 'Domination, Resistance and Political-Culture in Northern-Ireland Catholic-Nationalist Ghettos', *Critique Of Anthropology*, Vol. 1, pp. 71-102.

Taylor, P. (1997), *Provos: The IRA and Sinn Féin*, Bloomsbury, London.

Tomlinson, M. (1995), 'Can Britain Leave Ireland? The Political Economy of War and Peace', *Race and Class*, Vol. 37, pp. 1-22.

Welch, M. (1999), *Punishment in America: Social Control and the Ironies of Imprisonment*, Sage, Thousand Oaks, CA.

Winstone, T. (1997), 'Alternatives to Punishment Beatings and Shootings in a Loyalist Community in Belfast', *Critical Criminology*, Vol. 8, pp. 122-8.

Wright, M. (1996), *Justice for Victims and Offenders*, Waterside Press, London.

Yazzie, R. and Zion, J. W. (1996), 'Navajo Restorative Justice: The Law of Equality and Justice', in Galaway, B. and Hudson, J. (eds), *Restorative Justice: International Perspectives*, Kugler, Amsterdam, pp. 157-75.

Zehr, H. (1990), *Changing Lenses: A New Focus for Crime and Justice*, Herald Press, Scottsdale, PA.

Zehr, H. and Mika, H. (1998), 'Fundamental Concepts of Restorative Justice', *Contemporary Justice Review*, Vol. 1, pp. 5-17.

6 Informal Crime Management in a Northern British City: Crime Fear and Locality

Sandra Walklate

Introduction

In the second term of the current Labour government in Britain it is clear that the problem of crime and its management continues to feature as a key policy issue. In 1997 the Labour government made a clear commitment that crime prevention would become a statutory duty of local government. In the implementation of that duty local authority personnel were charged with conducting local crime audits, writing corporate community safety strategies, and setting local crime reduction targets. Indeed the Crime and Disorder Act 1998, the centrepiece of 'New Labour's' stance on crime and social disorder, expressly put to the fore crime reduction as its main target. As an Act it addressed a wide range of issues. The purpose of this chapter is to address two of those issues: the requirement made of local partnerships to tackle crime reduction and how to deal with young offenders. These two themes also comprised two of the three ministerial priorities for the criminal justice system for 1999-2000 and therefore constitute a useful means through which to examine the legitimacy, or otherwise, of the underlying presumptions embedded in the 1998 legislation. Put simply, those presumptions reflected a belief that it is possible to put in place some universally applicable policy recommendations that will work in a diverse range of socio-economic situations. The implications of these presumptions are explored in this chapter, not just as a purely academic exercise, but in the context of understanding the *lived experience* of crime in two, predominantly white socio-economically-similar high crime areas in northern Britain, a description of which follows below. In this sense this discussion, by implication, is concerned to consider this legislation from the perspective of the 'socially excluded'. These communities also comprise in some respects the socially and politically unacceptable face of contemporary British society. As a consequence, then, this chapter is also concerned to explore some of the policy problems associated with the concept of 'Bringing Britain Together' as highlighted in the government report of the same name also published in 1998 (Social Exclusion Unit, 1998).

The chapter falls into three parts. The first will offer a brief overview of the research in these two northern British communities and its main findings, on which the subsequent observations made in this chapter are based. The second will consider the relevance of these findings to the questions of dealing with young offenders and for the development of partnership initiatives as required by the Crime and Disorder Act 1998. The third will offer a critical analysis of the implications of these observations for the likely success or otherwise of the Crime and Disorder Act as a whole.

The Research Areas and Key Findings

The research areas on which this discussion is based were located in the City of Salford, part of the Greater Manchester conurbation. The city of Salford itself is a multiply deprived, predominantly white area battling with the full effects of the closure of the docks in 1972 and years of de-industrialization. It is an area in which the City Council has attempted to sow the seeds of economic regeneration including the creation of one of the first Enterprise Zones in 1981 and latterly with the development of its dockland into an office, leisure and residential development akin to London's Dockland scheme. Arguably the economic and structural changes affecting Salford as a whole have taken their toll on particular parts of the city referred to as 'Old Salford' (its inner-city areas) rather than 'New Salford' (the comparatively wealthy and suburban areas which became part of the City of Salford after 1974). Both these research areas, called Oldtown and Bankhill respectively, are in 'Old Salford'.

These areas comprise two, predominantly white, local authority wards with similar unemployment rates (Oldtown 22.9 per cent; Bankhill, 22.8 per cent), and similar youth unemployment rates (32.4 per cent and 37.8 per cent respectively) but with differing patterns of housing tenure (Oldtown; owner occupied 23.8 per cent, council 61.2 per cent, housing association 7.1 per cent: Bankhill; 34.6 per cent, 28 per cent, and 23 per cent respectively). The two wards are, however, physically quite different and have a very different history.

Oldtown was the residential ward, which historically housed a great number of the city's industrial workforce and dock labour. It is now predominantly a council owned estate, part of which, known locally as the Oldtown Triangle, is situated in the heart of the estate and which includes much of the area's lowest standard of housing. The ward has undergone a number of transformations in the last three decades, its back-to-back terraces being largely demolished in the 1960s and 1970s and replaced with system-built high and low-rise housing stock. From the early 1980's Salford Council, controversially, embarked on a policy which sold off many of its worst housing in this area to private developers who transformed these hard-to-let estates on the periphery of the ward into owner-occupied 'yuppie' flats. At the same time some residents of the Triangle area were improving their own housing through the setting up of Salford's (and indeed Manchester's) first housing co-operative.

The defunct and derelict dock area became, by 1990, the city's prestigious docklands development. Situated on the other side of a busy four-lane highway from the main body of the ward's residential area it is visible from all parts of the estate. It is at once separated from, and yet a part of the ward. In the 1990s the remaining council stock is being improved by Estates Action monies in five distinct phases so that, in mid 1995, the further one travels into the estate the more untouched the area is. Nevertheless housing for owner-occupation has been built; indeed it is a condition of the Estates Action funding that mixed residential tenure is promoted in such areas, and Oldtown is no exception.

Bankhill, on the other hand, is a more physically diverse area which, in turn, is more physically connected to surrounding areas so that there is some local confusion as to where the ward boundaries actually are. It is an area of very large early Victorian and Georgian merchants' houses as well as late Victorian and Edwardian terraces. In Engels' *The Condition of the Working Class in England* it is cited as an area of middle-class flight from the squalor of the city. Its reputation as a more middle-class area, a step up from the inner city on the way to the suburbs, persisted well into the latter half of the twentieth century.

It is, at present, however, very much a part of the 'inner-city'. Its larger dwellings are, on the whole, residential homes for the elderly or community care hostels. Many are divided into flats, rented out by private landlords. Small pockets of council housing have been built in the ward from the 1960s, including a small number of tower blocks. Many of the smaller terraced houses have been bought wholesale by housing associations and improved for rent. Owner occupation is the largest form of housing tenure in the area. Bankhill covers a smaller area than Oldtown but is more densely populated and a higher proportion of its properties are of a poor standard, lacking amenities such as central heating.

These brief pen portraits provide some initial clues as to how these areas might be viewed in relation to criminal justice policy. It is certainly the case that the historically greater visibility of Oldtown as a problematic area (see for example, Roberts, 1971) has left its mark on the area's relationships with official agencies (including the police). However, it is also the case that both areas witnessed and experienced civil disturbances in the early 1990s (potentially) earmarking them as part of Britain's 'dangerous places' (Campbell, 1993). The extent to which such a characterization is, or is not appropriate, is open to debate, of course.

What emerged from the data gathered during the course of this project was that these two research sites, whilst seemingly so similar on official indicators, and geographically less than two miles apart, were actually exhibiting very different responses to their situation. These differences have been fully discussed elsewhere but in summary they can be characterized in the following way. On the one hand Oldtown has been identified as an example of a 'defended community'; that is an ordered community (not disordered as the Chicago school would suggest), trusting (of those who are local) and whilst certainly disadvantaged well defended from interference from 'outsiders'. However, on the other hand Bankhill has been identified as an example of a 'frightened community'; socially disordered, where there is an absence of the trust of 'being local' found in Oldtown, and where there is no general collective community infrastructure. The residents of Bankhill will, however, offer generalized trust to the official agencies (see Evans and Walklate, 1996; Evans, 1997; Walklate, 1998). Such dynamics reflect the differing and differential relationship people living in these areas have in their relationship with crime and, as a consequence feed and fuel policy possibilities.

It has been argued elsewhere that the processes that underpin the surface manifestation of these community dynamics reflect different kinds of trust relationships. These relationships demonstrate the salience of the questions of; whom can you trust, how do you trust, how much can you trust, and when can you trust? (Nelken, 1994). The sense of well-being that individuals construct for themselves in the two high crime areas discussed above is mediated by their understanding of where they find themselves in relation to a 'square of trust' — see Figure 6.1 (Evans, Fraser, and Walklate, 1996; Walklate, 1998).

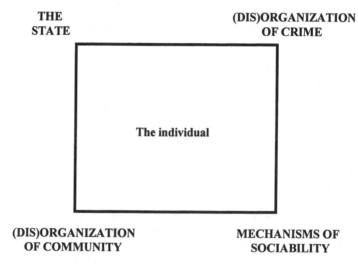

Figure 6.1: The Square of Trust

In these two research areas trust relationships were certainly differently constituted. In one, Oldtown, it meant not trusting state officials to sort things out in favour of expecting the more locally organized criminal gangs to do something. In the absence of the gang doing anything other issues might be managed as a result of the presence of kinship and family networks; knowing someone's father or brother. Both processes, arguably, contributed towards local social solidarity. In the other, Bankhill, it meant offering a generalized trust to state officials to sort things out but with little expectation that this might happen and moreover with little to put in the place of an official response. A detailed analysis of the way in which these trust relationships manifest themselves is discussed in greater detail in Evans and Walklate (1999a). For the purposes of this discussion the key concern is the questions that are raised by such an understanding for managing and developing response to crime in such areas by the strategies suggested by the Crime and Disorder Act 1998.

Responding to Crime and Disorder: Legislation and Social Reality

The Crime and Disorder Act 1998 is vast in its coverage and has already been subjected to some general critical scrutiny (see for example, Ashworth *et al*, 1998; Loveday, 1999; *Policy Studies* Special Issue, 1998). The purpose of this chapter is not to engage in such a general critique. As a piece of legislation it has raised all sorts of questions from how its implementation was to be funded (about which it says nothing) to the extent to which it addresses the perceived shortcomings within the workings of the criminal justice system (the matching or otherwise between the Crime and Disorder legislation and the proposed changes for the Crown Prosecution Service, for example). This chapter is primarily concerned to examine this legislation against social reality; not the social reality of managing the implementation process (the barriers to which at an organizational or inter-agency level we already know a great deal about); but the social reality of living one's routine, everyday life in a high crime area. In so doing it will take up two themes within the legislation: the notion of getting young people to 'make amends' and the concept of 'partnership'.

Making Amends or a Short, Sharp, Shock?

Over the twentieth century policy responses concerned to deal with young offenders have vacillated between treatment and punishment. The idea of 'making amends' arguably falls into the treatment model and proved to be increasingly popular during the 1990s. However, research suggests that making amends as a policy directive within the criminal justice system faces considerable practical difficulties (see, for example, Marshall and Merry, 1990). In addition, as a policy response, it appears to have failed to date to meet the objective for wider society of either re-integrating and/or re-educating the offender. The much-lauded Thames Valley project may stand as an exception to this. But in the light of the overall evidence from initiatives of this kind in this country to date, it would be easy to conclude that making amends is doomed to failure as a systemic response to offending behaviour. Such a conclusion, however, would be short-sighted.

The idea of 'making amends' can take many forms; not all of which are given expression to within the formal policy or legislative framework. As has been observed above, one of the dilemmas faced by initiatives informed by such a notion is how to render such a process meaningful to the participants. In other words, the idea in and of itself may be sound; what is required is a better understanding of how to make the idea work. Thus the question is raised concerning how, in what form, and under what circumstances does making amends work and for whom?

The literature on 'making amends' is full of rather nostalgic references to the concept of community as an ideal form of social control (Cohen, 1985). Yet, when the possibility of alternative forms of conflict resolution is raised, such community images seem rather less than nostalgic. One alternative is the idea of a self-policing community. It is an idea that constitutes a fundamental challenge to the assumptions frequently made about high crime areas in policy, political and academic debate. This has perhaps been made most explicit in the current embrace by the Labour party of

Etzioni's (1996) version of communitarianism. However, high crime communities are not necessarily disordered, disorganized, fearful places as either current policy initiatives may assume or the more historically informed notion of social disorganization led criminologists to believe. As has been suggested already in this chapter high crime areas can be experienced as highly ordered and safe places for the people who live there (see, for example, Walklate, 1998; Merry, 1981). During the course of our research the importance of understanding both the differences and the similarities between our research areas as potentially self-policing communities in this respect became apparent. Indeed in Oldtown, the defended community, part of the understanding of the dynamics underpinning this community was rooted in understanding the local processes of making amends. The following stories are illustrative of aspects of these processes.

The first is presented here in the words of a retired police superintendent who spent some considerable time during his career working in this area. In referring to a warehouse incident of 1992 he says:

> Carpetworld came about as a response to the police and the community in the area, trying to solve a particular problem of stolen vehicles being used against property in the area. But again to raise their own profile, to inspire intimidation and to create the myth. They were then doing public displays of handbrake turns. There was a considerable amount of danger to resident kids in the area. In fact, there was one team who were doing it a lot and knocked three thirteen year old girls down. They were not badly hurt, fortunately, but they could easily have been killed...
>
> The same people still live in that sort of area [---- Road], those three girls, initially the incident was reported to us – this is one of the areas which you mentioned at the beginning where an approach was made from Mr M and some of his friends to intercede and sort the business out. Eventually the people in the car had to pay £650 or make an offer, they didn't have to make an offer of £650 to the parents of the kids concerned. The other side of that offer is that if you don't take it you get done over for being a grass, so it's a bit like an offer you can't refuse.

The second is articulated in this quote from a middle aged female resident in this area;

> There's also a positive side sometimes. It doesn't always work one way, sometimes it works...I've heard of a case a few months ago where a lad had broken these pensioners' windows and he'd run off. Now a couple of people found out who he was, dragged him back to this house and asked if it was him. When they said it was, they made him apologize, gave him a thump and told him if he was anywhere near there again they would come back for him. Needless to say he's never been anywhere near. It has its own rules as well they sort things out their selves.

These stories allude to the importance in this local context of a 'no grassing' rule (Evans, Fraser and Walklate, 1996). They also allude to the belief in the powerful presence of a 'Mr Big'; 'I can't name any names, but what's his face up the road will sort it out'. They are comments that acknowledge the presence of a local organized criminal gang commonly referred to as the 'Salford Firm'. The presence of this gang in the locality is widely acknowledged both in official discourses about the area and in individual community members' articulations about their locality. The nature and extent of its presence and its influence can be disputed, but what is less in doubt are the aspirations of the gang and the local credibility associated with the gang's activities.

In reality this gang probably comprises twenty to thirty 'full-time' members, involved in criminal activity at varying levels of seriousness. Understanding the underlying aspirations associated with these activities provides a different insight into the phenomenon of 'no grassing'. This is alluded to and then clarified in the following quotes taken from an interview with the spokesperson for the 'Salford Firm'.

> ...Cos a lot of people accuse us, saying 'That ----, you know, encourages them to break the law', but I don't have to encourage them to break the law, people who make them break the law are those who are responsible for them breaking the law, you know the councillors, the politicians – *these* are the ones who are responsible, not me. I only advise them how *not* to get caught, you know, don't do this, don't go robbing off old ladies, mugging old ladies – it's not on – you know, don't go robbing and burgling ordinary people's houses of televisions, you know, if you want to go and rob, go to Canalside.

So:

> ...You've not got to be a grass, I mean, there's a code in that – when is it right to inform the police about a certain thing, and when is it not correct. You know, if someone rapes somebody or interferes with a kid, or mugs an old lady, as far as the correct-minded thing for people, you know what I mean, the concern – if somebody hands them in then they're not grassing, you know, but if somebody goes and says 'so and so has done a ram-raid' or 'so and so has done a post office', then it's grassing, it's not acceptable.

Moreover, when incidents occur which break this moral code:

> ...we try to find out who's done it and if they're really young people, then we'll given them a talking to, you know, to say 'it's out of order', you know what I mean, but if it's someone who's supposed to be, you know, responsible and knew what they was doing – knew that it was a woman on her own or a woman with three kids and no husband, you know what I mean, they get a smacking ... [this is] street politics, you know, 'It's not on – there's too many burglaries going on, we've got to put a stop to it', you know what I mean. We don't go and tell the police, you know, we've got to handle it ourselves, you know, there's got to be some kind of, you know, street justice, so when the lads find out who's going round breaking into people's houses, they get a smacking, you know what I mean, and it's called 'taxing', you know.

The importance of this expressed 'moral code' lies not so much in what it does and does not deliver but in the fact that for local people it has a saliency for them in their routine daily lives; 'I can't name any names but what's his face up the road will sort it out'. This belief is given an added 'truth content' in two main ways: a clearly identifiable arena of 'public shaming' in the locality; and the viability of local stories of 'sorting things out'.

In this locality there is an area in which nearly all the local amenities are located: a supermarket (now closed), a chemist, a betting shop, a job shop, a post office, a public house and a hardware store. This area provides the physical location and space for 'public shaming' ceremonies. In other words, if there is graffiti to be written, and if there is graffiti to be written about a particular person who it is believed has 'grassed', then their name will appear in this location. It is here that people are named for the rest of the community to see: and since this is the only place where there are any local amenities in this locality it serves its purpose as a public arena of shame very well.

The use of this arena in this way serves a number of functions in the local community. It certainly provides a very real forum in which members of the local community are made very much aware of not only who has been accused of 'grassing' but also of the consequences of being so accused. The desire to avoid such 'public shaming' is one basis on which local choices are made concerning who to inform about what. Moreover, the actual appearance of names in this arena serves a deeper function: it marks, potentially, those whose behaviour has been deemed outside of the locally accepted norms and values. As such it serves to remind all members of this community of those norms and values. In this sense, there may be a similar functional relationship between these processes of public shaming and the further maintenance of social solidarity and cohesion found within this local community (see, also, Erikson, 1966).

Of course, the naming of 'grasses' is not the only way that people can be made to pay for offending the community norms and values. As the quotes above have suggested other informal mechanisms also exist for bringing offending behaviour into line. Those mechanisms might be monetary or physical but they nevertheless appear to exist as meaningful in the local stories of making amends. Such stories, of course, do not only highlight the ways in which recalcitrant young offenders are brought back to the community line; they can also highlight the ways in which 'grasses' can be reminded of the penalties for the more serious forms of this behaviour. For example;

> There is a sort of code, I think I touched on this briefly, that you do not victimize women. For instance, we persuaded a woman to go as a witness on two really serious assaults against a gang member. One was really an attempted murder and it took ages to get to court, it was before we had the sophistication of witness-protection that we have got today, but we did our best but they kept intimidating this woman. They kept shouting at her and calling her names, making threats towards her, but when they eventually did something physical they didn't do it to her, they did it to her son. They caught him, he was in his late teens – nineteen – and they stuck a screwdriver up his bottom which caused all sorts of terrible internal injuries which is one of the traditional techniques of dealing with what they call a grass. (Retired police superintendent)

Embedded in the processes described here is a recognition and acceptance that crime and the criminals are part of the community (not outside it), are often known by name, and that people can be made to make amends in a whole range of different informal but none the less meaningful ways. In some respects the examples offered here are clearly suggestive of a hierarchy of local mechanisms of making amends which mirror the conventional criminal justice process. Such a hierarchy may start with a warning; (the use of graffiti for 'public shaming'), may then move to the requirement to pay compensation (as in the case of the car accident), may then take the form of an assault (if the offence has been to harass old people or engage on other behaviour which offends the local code of ethics), and finally may take the form of serious physical assault (if the 'no grassing' rule has been broken in a way which is threatening to the local structures of control). The presence of this hierarchy of 'making amends' is well understood locally, reflects a sense of local justice that bears some similarities (and obviously some significant differences) to that of more conventional conceptions of justice, but nevertheless seems to have an effect. They are certainly a sure and usually quick response to unacceptable behaviour – the short, sharp, shock version of making amends.

Of course, not all high-crime areas share the same heterogeneous view of the crime problem. In Bankhill, as has already been suggested above, the experience of the crime problem looked somewhat different. In this area people did not feel protected by what they knew to be going on in their locality but felt threatened by it. As one female resident observed:

> When I see blokes on bikes now, they might be innocent, but to me they're part of the gang and that's who they are and I do not like to see anyone on a bike. (Established female resident)

Or as one elderly resident reported:

> There was a boy with a wheelbarrow full of tools, he broke into the park keeper's shed and walked out of the park with the wheelbarrow.... I'm sixty-three, I was frightened to stop him; it was a boy of about twelve. I know he'll come back with his pals.

Or expressed more graphically; 'It's like terrorism really' (Male established resident).

In an area like this it is the absence of the belief that 'what's his face up the road will sort it out' which is problematic; in other words, it seems to be the absence of the highly organized criminal gangs and the associated gang culture which is a salient factor here in contributing to a lack of sense of well-being in this locality especially for older people (Walklate, 1998). For people in this area, they knew about the nature of criminality there, but they did not know specifically who the criminals were (other than 'all young people'), and moreover, they also knew that no one, including themselves, were likely to call such problematic young people to account. There was no working formal means, or no publicly articulated informal means for making amends. For people in this area the belief that 'This area is going downhill rapidly' acted as a metaphor for not only what they saw going on in their locality, but also what was not happening along with their own sense of helplessness to intervene in what was going on around them.

To summarize: the preceding discussion has highlighted the importance of understanding community dynamics in order to offer a fuller picture of what 'making amends' might look like. It has clearly demonstrated that, formal policy response notwithstanding, the presence and absence of informal processes may also make a significant contribution to what might be considered to be locally meaningful processes of reparation. Understanding processes such as these leads to a more fundamental appreciation of what mechanisms might need to be in place which enable not only the informal processes to work but what may be also necessary for more formal processes to work. This leads us to a consideration of the question of partnership.

The implementation of the Crime and Disorder Act is heavily dependent upon the successful co-operation of a range of different agencies working within the criminal justice system. As was stated earlier much is already known about the conditions for the success or otherwise of inter-agency co-operation (see, for example, Sampson *et al*, 1988; Gilling, 1997) and the potential undercurrents within the more recent use of the term partnership (see, for example, Crawford, 1997). Such difficulties notwithstanding, the Crime and Disorder Act makes partnership working a statutory requirement. As a consequence local authorities have been busily engaged in conducting their Crime Audits and preparing their local plans of implementation for tackling locally identified problems. Again the purpose of this discussion is not to revisit what is already know about partnerships but to situate such knowledge within the two high crime areas under discussion. We shall do this, to begin with, by using those very data sources recommended by the Morgan Report (1991) which were further endorsed within this legislation.

The locations that were under investigation are part of the Salford Division of the Greater Manchester Police. The recorded crime rate for Salford as a whole was, at the time of the study, significantly higher than the national average; for example, in 1992 the incidence of recorded crime in England and Wales was 10,500 offences per 100,000 population, in Salford it was 16,660. The two areas under investigation did not correspond with police boundaries, but the recorded burglary rate, for example, for the sub-division in which Bankhill was situated was 70.3 per 1,000 population in 1993, and was 88.4 per 1,000 population for the sub-division which included Oldtown. Moreover, police officers believe that there is a significant under-reporting of crime in each of these areas (see Evans and Walklate, 1999b). Indeed, our own criminal victimization survey conducted in August 1994 reports that 23.7 per cent of people in Oldtown and 36.9 per cent of people in Bankhill were victims of crime in the previous year. Analysis of Command and Control data covering the beats relevant to these two localities for the month of January 1995 suggests that on a daily average 21 incidents are reported in Oldtown (1 per 11 residents) and 24 in Bankhill (1 per 24 residents); though, of course, it must be remembered that not all of these incidents (calls for service) are necessarily crime related nor are they necessarily recorded as crimes. A more detailed analysis of that Command and Control data suggests that these two wards report a different pattern of incidents – see Table 6.1.

On their own, these data offer a superficial insight into the nature of *reported local* (crime) problems. What they highlight is the level and kind of demand made on local policing resources as initiated by members of the public. Consequently they reflect the kind and type of incidents which those same members of the public are comfortable with defining as appropriate for police action. Taking such factors into account, this distribution is particularly interesting in (at least) two respects. First in respect of the differential proportion of reported incidents in each area relating to vehicle and property crime. Second, in respect of the proportion of reported incidents relating to drugs/drink. Each of these concerns is differentially reflected in other sources of data gathered during the course of this project but in particular in the criminal victimization survey data gathered.

Table 6.1   Incidents by Ward (command and control data, January 1995)

TYPE OF INCIDENT	OLDTOWN	BANKHILL
Vehicle crime	33%	24%
Property crime	15%	26%
Personal crime	8%	14%
Nuisance/suspicion	12%	9%
Child at risk/abuse	<1%	2%
Road traffic accident	1%	2%
Drugs/drink related	<1%	<1%
Activated alarms	20%	9%
Non-crime related	9%	14%

(The total number of incidents for Oldtown was 649 and for Bankhill was 737)

Table 6.2   Issues Considered to be a Problem or a Big Problem in Their Area

PROBLEM/BIG PROBLEM	OLDTOWN		BANKHILL	
Vandalism	187	(63.6%)	228	(78.8%)
Crime	162	(55.0%)	224	(74.0%)
Young people hanging about	152	(51.7%)	190	(62.9%)
Unemployment	151	(51.7%)	166	(54.9%)
No play area	141	(47.9%)	160	(52.9%)
Graffiti	107	(36.3%)	126	(41.7%)

(Numbers listed reflect total number of mentions by respondents in each area in order of frequency mentioned. Respondents could mention more than one issue)

This kind of listing in Table 6.2 is indicative of the degree of consensus that exists between people living in these areas in relation to what they considered to be local problems. The ordering of these problems changes somewhat when respondents were asked in a further question what was a particular problem for *them* in *their* area (whose responses are not tabulated). In answers to this question for people in Bankhill crime still topped the list, with vandalism coming second. For people in Oldtown this concern with vandalism was superseded by having nowhere for their children to play, with crime coming second. So the ordering of local problems changes; but crime still features as an issue affecting people. This was reiterated by the evidence of the kinds of crime people worried about happening to them during the day and during the night in their area — see Table 6.3 (overleaf).

Table 6.3   Crimes Worried About During the Day and During the Night in Each Area

CRIME WORRY	DAY-TIME		NIGHT-TIME	
	OLDTOWN	BANKHILL	OLDTOWN	BANKHILL
Being burgled	131 (1st)	173 (1st)	130 (1st)	168 (1st)
Car being stolen	80 (2nd)	80 (3rd)	78 (2nd)	82 (5th)
Vandalism	65 (3rd)	92 (2nd)	57 (6th)	89 (4th)
Being robbed	40 (4th)	65 (4th)	50 (8th)	76 (6th)
Young people	39 (5th)	45 (5th)	57 (6th)	69 (7th)
Being attacked	30 (6th)	44 (6th)	51 (7th)	60 (8th)
Being out alone	29 (7th)	43 (7th)	74 (3rd)	108 (2nd)

(Numbers reflect relative frequency of mentions by respondents with relative ranking in brackets)

Whilst there is little of surprise here given the more general findings of the criminal victimization survey industry, these figures do endorse the extent to which people living in each of these localities shared common concerns about crime and the crime problem. Although, of course, the variable frequency with which some crimes were mentioned may reflect different levels of concern. For example, those respondents in Oldtown who reported having been a victim of crime in the previous year (69 in total) reported 20 burglaries, 2 robberies, 31 thefts, and 27 incidents of criminal damage. Those respondents in Bankhill who reported having been a victim of crime in the previous year (111 in total) reported 53 burglaries, 5 robberies, 35 thefts, and 38 incidents of criminal damage. These expressed concerns reinforce the reporting pattern indicated by the Command and Control Data.

Using data sources such as these, it could be taken that the crime problem in these two localities is of a fairly conventional nature, that is, burglary, car crime and criminal damage. Consequently practitioners may be persuaded that policy could also be conventionally informed; for example, the introduction and resourcing of Neighbourhood Watch Schemes as a means of tackling burglary. However reliance on such data sources alone would address only the surface manifestation of the crime problem in localities such as Oldtown and Bankhill. These data do not penetrate its deep structure. Other sources of information provide an insight into this. One place that clues to this deep structure can be found is in the discussions which took place in the local Police Community Consultative Forums in each of these areas.

Police Community Consultative Group meetings, held monthly, were attended regularly by around thirty people from Oldtown and towards sixty in the Bankhill area. Analysis of the minutes of these meetings from February 1994 to July 1996 reveals that there were four recurring themes to those meetings in both areas; how to deal with troublesome youth, the problem of intimidation, the impact of force restructuring, and the slow response to 999 calls. In addition, in Bankhill frequent concern was expressed about the possible closure of the local police station and the rapidity of turnover of local police personnel.

So whilst what went on in police community consultative meetings does not match exactly the concerns highlighted in other sources of data, there is enough similarity in the concerns expressed to suggest that such meetings were not just giving a voice to those who chose to attend, but were tapping more widely held community concerns. What is particularly interesting in respect of those more widely held community concerns is the expressed problem of intimidation. In-depth interview and focus group data gathered in both of these areas facilitated a deeper understanding of what this more qualitative talk about crime was articulating. This returns us to the question of trust with which this paper began.

Talk about Crime in Oldtown

Depending upon where you live in Oldtown the experience of crime can be very different. In the Canalside and The Way parts of the ward (where the incidence of home ownership is at its highest), people were concerned that their houses or sheds might be broken into or objects taken from their garden. In discussion groups in these areas we found that people were much more likely to talk about taking preventive measures against crime, for example, planting prickly shrubs near fences or buying alarms for houses and cars. Crime here was talked about as a nuisance rather than a major threat to peace of mind. However in other parts of the ward, commonly known as The Triangle, the central talk about crime focused on groups of young males who gathered in particular parts of the estate and were seen to be involved in a good deal of anti-social behaviour. It is here that we can begin to get a feel for the problem of intimidation.

The problem of intimidation has been discussed in the context of Oldtown in greater detail in Evans, Fraser, and Walklate (1996). Indeed, in 1994 the area was chosen as part of a Home Office sponsored survey dealing with the question of intimidation but the survey was left incomplete as the interviewers were 'asked' to leave the area after two days! Here the idea that 'you're alright round here if you're local' has considerable force; and such 'being local' has less to do with length of residence than sticking to a particular code of conduct as has been highlighted earlier. Indeed even those residents who called the police, reported feeling undermined by the length of time it took for the police to respond which further marginalized them and fostered a reliance on the view that local people would sort things out (see Evans and Walklate, 1996). Crime Audits cannot capture this sense of what the issues might look like in a particular locality. The picture looked a little different, however in Bankhill.

Talk about Crime in Bankhill

Walking around Bankhill the pedestrian can encounter areas, which differ in their appearance and their 'feel'. Some areas look well-cared for and largely clear of rubbish and vandalism; whereas others are heavily painted with graffiti and may have other signs of disorder such as large numbers of boarded up windows, rubbish strewn back alleys and houses with windows which are shuttered and/or barred. Such places might amount to 'hotspots' for crime; and indeed in discussion groups a number of people said that they found it easier to cope with burglary than the petty crime engendered by such locations. For example, if the grids and drain covers along their street were stolen people must wait for the appropriate agency to act; if empty houses were vandalized then it would be up to others to initiate repairs. But such signs of disorder also signalled a more general deterioration and loss of faith in their neighbourhood. The view was frequently expressed that, 'this area is going downhill rapidly'. This view, alongside the construction of young people as 'people to be feared' had an enormous impact in Bankhill.

As the survey data cited above for Bankhill indicated, a substantial percentage of people living in this ward worried about young people hanging around on the streets. Indeed in many parts of the ward groups of young people, primarily male but not solely, are very visible. And whilst a proportion of these young people will be involved in criminal activity, such activity was (at the time of this study) not as well organized as in Oldtown. As a consequence, local residents appear to see all young people as people to be feared, avoided, and mistrusted. As one middle aged woman stated:

> We've reached the stage where we suspect children, all children, and youths and girls. You suspect them all.

Such views have an enormous impact on old and young in this neighbourhood. They have not as yet, however, undermined the willingness of people living in this area to work with the official agencies to try to improve matters and to look to such agencies for guidance and solutions (for a fuller discussion of these issues see Evans and Walklate, 1999a).

To summarize: for Oldtown, people feel they know who the criminals are, and feel that they know who will solve local 'disputes'. They also know something about the highly organized nature of crime in their area. Based on this knowledge they know who to trust, whom not to trust, when and how (Evans, Fraser and Walklate, 1996). Police officers managing and working in this area also know some of these things. They also know that they are, for the most part, marginal to these processes unless the equilibrium between them, the community, and the criminals becomes unbalanced in some way. In these circumstances Oldtown becomes a policing problem for both the police and the residents alike. They both 'know' that targeting troublesome youth, in and of itself, would not begin to penetrate the organized nature of crime in this area.

For Bankhill, people also know who the criminals are: 'young people'. What they do not know is who is going to sort out their local 'disputes'. What they do know is that they would like the 'officials' to do something, whilst at the same time they lack the belief and level of sociability to know how or what to do for themselves. Crime in this area is prevalent, but relatively disorganized, and people know who they want to trust ('the officials') and who they distrust (young people). However, because of the relative disorganization of criminality and community relationships in this area, this knowledge remains fragile. Such fragility, alongside the belief that 'This area is going downhill rapidly' means that there is little for people to rely on in terms of community and/or social infrastructure. Targeting the troublesome behaviour of young people in this area, which a simple aggressive policing style like Zero Tolerance might do, *might* have an effect on the local fear of crime (Hope and Hough, 1988) but would not solve other problems for people in this area (for example, vandalism, neglect of properties, and absence of community relationships).

Putting all these observations together, this data is clearly suggestive of the need for a finely nuanced policy response in areas such as these based on an understanding of the specific difficulties faced by *both* the agencies working within an area *and* the potentially variable community dynamics of that area. To reiterate; the areas under discussion here were less than two miles apart, yet the question of what might work in each of them looks potentially very different. That question of what might work is rooted in the lived reality of the crime problem in these areas and how the people living there are responding to it and is not necessarily penetrated by reliance on more formal sources of data alone. So where does such a view lead in respect of the notion of community safety partnerships?

Whose Partners in Crime?

At the time this research was conducted in Bankhill there was a great willingness on the part of the community to work for change. Such willingness was expressed in both the desire to work with the 'authorities' and the trust and expectation invested in them to be able to make things happen. In return, people in Bankhill wanted their concerns, which may appear petty and trivial (criminal damage and vandalism), to be taken seriously by the 'authorities'. Consequently, in an area like this, the local authority and the police may be able to take a lead in local developments and will find support for such in the local community. Such support may be best harnessed by exploring interpretations of the notion of partnership above and beyond the more normatively prescribed multi-agency approach.

This kind of strategy implies the view that crime is a local problem to be *managed* locally, not necessarily prevented or reduced. So the result may not be crime prevention or even crime reduction, but management; that is, ensuring that people feel better about, and more in control of, what is going on in their area. By implication this vision of the relationship between partnership and crime embraces the importance of managing incivilities as highlighted by the much maligned 'broken windows' thesis (Wilson and Kelling, 1982), with perhaps a rather different focus on who is responsible for that process.

The construction of young people as 'people to be feared' in Bankhill might demand a different response again. On a longer-term basis this is, arguably, the most pressing problem in this area. At present Bankhill offers little to young people and they in return are hesitant to go out of 'their area' to use what facilities there are. This may well be the space in which partnerships between teachers, youth workers, private enterprise, parents and the young people themselves (and other relevant agencies) might work most effectively.

On the other hand, in Oldtown the crime problem is already being managed, not by a community safety partnership strategy, but through the (fragile) equilibrium between the police, the local community, and the organized nature of crime in that area. A very different conception of what might constitute a partnership! Yet, the processes underpinning these relationships, in allowing people to feel alright about living in their locality, seems to work for most of the people living there most of the time. Of course, relationships such as these make agency-led interventions a difficult prospect in areas like Oldtown. Moreover in different localities in this ward, very local problems have been managed by local residents working together, sometimes with official aid coming afterwards, sometimes with that aid not being forthcoming at all.

In other words, partnerships in areas like Oldtown might well be formed but they may not have any of the characteristics of conventional organizational (voluntary or otherwise) allegiances; such partnerships may be with strategically placed individual residents, for example. Again, understanding the problem to be managed may be primarily about that, management; the desired result may not be crime prevention or crime reduction but restoring local equilibrium and the opportunity to discover what such an equilibrium might look like.

The implications of this discussion suggest that it is necessary to move away from either universalistic and/or simplistic solutions to crime in localities like Oldtown and Bankhill. The alternatives may be more complex (though not necessarily more expensive); they may have different outcomes than those valued by the crime prevention industry; and they may challenge conventional views of what is, or is not, acceptable as a crime problem. In addition they raise the questions of not only whose policy and whose process is crime prevention but also the question of what is democratically acceptable at a local as well as a national level. Locally informed and locally formulated policy responses may need to take account of the diversity of views which exist and which are acceptable. Moreover the meaning of 'locally' may need to be re-interpreted and re-defined in terms of quite small units (maybe at the level of street in some localities) in order to formulate policies which make sense to local people and therefore stand a chance of working.

Conclusion: Citizen, State, Market and Policy

Oldtown and Bankhill are not unusual places. Each urban (and increasingly rural) area has their equivalent Oldtowns and Bankhills. These are predominantly white areas, where the traditional working class historically co-existed with the 'social scum' alongside those who were endeavouring to better themselves as market forces permitted. Oldtown and Bankhill may be at different points on a socio-economic trajectory (which this research was not designed to accommodate); but this trajectory is suggestive (almost) of an ecological, historically driven, process which Oldtown has found a way of managing and that Bankhill is in the process of so doing. Such a process is characterized by a number of features; one of which is understanding the changing mechanisms of social inclusion and exclusion, especially in a context in which the nature of work is changing.

Evans, Fraser, and Walklate (1996, p. 379) state:

> ... your *place* in relation to crime *places* you in a community of belonging and exclusion ... It is consequently important to recognize who is seen to be protecting you and how: for many people it is not the police or the council but local families and/or the Salford Firm.

Moreover, it is the absence of confidence in the formal agencies which creates the space for those other forces to come into play.

This quote refers to Oldtown; a locality from which the state had, for the most part, withdrawn. It was apparent that parts of Bankhill were also in the process of suffering a similar fate. There are other similar localities throughout the United Kingdom, as Campbell's (1993) analysis suggests; some of them peopled by ethnic minorities; just as many not. They are all areas, which have been left behind by the market forces of the last two decades. These are the locations that have suffered disproportionately as the gap between rich and poor has grown and as we have become increasingly a 30/30/40 society. In other words a society in which only the top 30 per cent are economically secure with the middle group financially stretched on short-term contracts and the bottom 40 per cent left behind (Hutton, 1995). To reiterate, a critical reflection on the findings produced by this research reveals much about the ways in which the mechanisms of social inclusion and exclusion have operated and been managed at a local level. The question remains as to how much responsibility we should assume, collectively, for the most vulnerable in our society, however we might choose to define that vulnerability.

It is clear that whilst the relationship between the citizen and the state has changed in emphasis in the UK since 1945 there are also strong historical continuities in that relationship. Historical continuities informed by notions of a distinction between the deserving and undeserving, the principle of less eligibility, and the notion of the dangerous classes. These dangerous classes, of course, provide the criminal justice system with much of its work so for that reason alone it is important to grasp a clear understanding of how and why that these processes happen in the way that they do.

In a different context Currie (1997) has discussed the marketization of violence. By that he is referring to the processes whereby the 'pursuit of private gain' is 'likely to breed high levels of violent crime'. In the context of the empirical findings discussed here, that same pursuit seems to have produced communities which, when left to their own devices, devise their own management strategies. They have found ways of making life all right for themselves: the marketization of trust. The consequences of these processes are there to be seen (*inter alia*) in the Social Exclusion Report referred to at the beginning of this chapter. That report highlights communities, notably including Salford, for whom not only crime, but health, education, housing etc., still constitute issues for serious concern. In the foreword to that document the Prime Minister states:

Our goal is simple: to bridge the gap between the poorest neighbourhoods and the rest of Britain. Bridging that gap will not be easy. It will require imagination, persistence, and commitment.

The research discussed here certainly supports the view that bridging this gap will not be easy. Those who are socially excluded, and have found ways of managing that exclusion, will not be easily persuaded that it is in their interests to manage differently.

The partnership approach in tackling all kinds of crime has been well embraced in policy thinking. For example, the Audit Commission (1996) recognized the importance of understanding and working with the interconnections between the family, school, local authorities and the criminal justice system in dealing with the problem of young people (young men) and crime. The potential value, or otherwise, of reparation has also been well established. As the research discussed here has demonstrated, however, what can be understood by the term partnership is wide and varied, and how such partnerships might work is also wide and varied. For example, in Oldtown, it is possible to argue that partnership and reparation already exists. Young people who step over the boundaries of what is considered to be acceptable criminality in this area are quickly made to see the error of their ways through various shaming mechanisms from being labelled a 'grass' or being 'taxed', to more physical forms of punishment. Such mechanisms may not be what the professionals have in mind when they talk of 'reintegrative shaming' (Braithwaite, 1989), but they are public and they do seem to work. How might the Crime and Disorder Act improve on this for the people of Oldtown? In Bankhill, on the other hand, the fluidity of social relationships suggests that there is much more room for manoeuvre and meaningful inter-agency work around these issues.

So, the question remains as to whether or not the proposed policy strategies to tackle young people and crime are imaginative, persistent and committed enough to face this social reality: 'to think the unthinkable'. If the lived experiences of those people living in high crime areas are taken into account, there is clearly another layer of questions to be considered concerning what works, for whom, how, why, where and when. However in order for such accounting to occur it is important that academics, politicians, policy makers and the locally powerful pay constant vigilant attention to the questions of whose policy and whose community. As Giddens (1998, p. 88) states:

> In order to work, partnerships between government agencies, the criminal justice system, local associations and community organizations have to be inclusive — all economic and ethnic groups must be involved....To be successful, such schemes demand a long-term commitment to social objectives.

As he goes on to point out, such an approach neither necessarily means that any link between unemployment, poverty and crime is denied; but it does mean that policies need to be co-ordinated with common goals and objectives. However, to reiterate, above all else, a genuine desire for policy to work for change needs to be cognisant of the importance of the local context in which that policy is set. This desire needs to work with rather than against the historical and socio-economic circumstances which structure that local context. Such a desire does demand imagination, commitment and persistence. It also requires that the desire for policy to work needs to be both authentic and genuine for the communities themselves.

Note

The research referred to in this paper was funded under the Economic and Social Research Council's Crime and Social Order Initiative grant number L210252036. The researchers involved in the project were Sandra Walklate (now Professor of Sociology at Manchester Metropolitan University), Karen Evans (now Lecturer in Sociology at Liverpool University) and Penny Fraser (now working for NACRO).

References

Ashworth, A., Morgan, R., Smith, A. T. H., von Hirsch, A., Wasik, M. (1998), 'Neighbouring on the Oppressive: the Government's "Anti-Social Behaviour Order" Proposals', *Criminal Justice*, Vol. 16(1), pp. 7-14.
Audit Commission (1996), *Misspent Youth*, The Audit Commission, London.
Braithwaite, J. (1989), *Crime, Shame and Reintegration*, Oxford University Press, Oxford.
Campbell, B. (1993), *Goliath*, Virago, London.
Cohen, S. (1985), *Visions of Social Control*, Polity, Cambridge.
Crawford, A. (1997), *The Local Governance of Crime*, Clarendon Press, Oxford.
Currie, E. (1997), 'Market, Crime and Community: Towards a Mid-range Theory of Post-industrial Violence', *Theoretical Criminology*, Vol. 1(2), pp. 147-72.
Erikson, E. (1966), *Wayward Puritans*, John Wiley, New York.
Evans, K. (1997), '"It's Alright Round Here if You're Local": Community in the Inner City', in P. Hoggett (ed.), *Contested Communities*, The Policy Press, Bristol.
Evans, K., Fraser, P., and Walklate, S. (1996), 'Whom do you Trust? The Politics of Grassing on an Inner City Housing Estate', *Sociological Review*, Vol. 44(3), pp. 361-80.
Evans, K. and Walklate, S. (1996), 'Community Safety, Personal Safety, and the Fear of Crime: End of Project Report', Economic and Social Research Council, London.
Evans, K. and Walklate, S. (1999a), *Zero Tolerance or Community Tolerance? Managing Crime in High Crime Areas*, Ashgate, Aldershot.
Evans, K. and Walklate, S. (1999b), 'Zero Tolerance or Community Tolerance: Police and Community Talk About Crime in High Crime Areas', *Crime Prevention and Community Safety: An International Journal*, Vol. 1(1), pp. 11-24.
Etzioni, A. (1996), *The New Golden Rule*, Profile Books, London.
Giddens, A. (1998), *The Third Way*, Polity, Oxford.
Gilling, D. (1997), *Crime Prevention: Theory, Policy and Politics*, UCL Press, London.
Hope, T. and Hough, M. (1988), 'Area Crime and Incivility; a Profile from the British Crime Survey', in Hope. T. and Shaw, S. (eds), *Communities and Crime Reduction*, Her Majesty's Stationery Office, London, pp. 30-47.
Hutton, W. (1995), *The State We're In*, Jonathan Cape; London.
Loveday, B. (1998), 'Tough on Crime or Tough on the Causes of Crime? An Evaluation of Labour's Crime and Disorder Legislation', *Crime Prevention and Community Safety: An International Journal*, Vol. 1(2), pp. 2-24.
Marshall, T. and Merry, S. (1990), *Crime and Accountability*, Her Majesty's Stationery Office, London.
Merry, S. (1981), *Urban Danger*, Temple University Press, Philadelphia.
Nelken, D. (ed.) (1994), *The Futures of Criminology*, Sage, London.
Policy Studies (Special Issue) 1998, Vol. 19(3/4).
Roberts, R. (1971), *The Classic Slum*, Penguin, Harmondsworth.

Sampson, A., Stubbs, P., Smith, D., Pearson, G. and Blagg, H. (1988), 'Crime, Localities and the Multi-agency Approach', *British Journal of Criminology*, Vol. 28(4), pp. 478-93.

Social Exclusion Unit (1998), *Bringing Britain Together: A National Strategy for Neighbourhood Renewal*, Stationery Office, London.

Walklate, S. (1998), 'Crime and Community: Fear or Trust?', *British Journal of Sociology*, Vol. 49(4), pp. 550-69.

Wilson, J. and Kelling, G. (1982), 'Broken Windows: The Police and Community Safety', *Atlantic Monthly*, March, pp. 29-38.

7 Vigilantism and Popular Justice after Apartheid

Rebekah Lee and Jeremy Seekings

South Africa has a long history of vigilantism and popular justice. In both rural and urban areas, African people have regularly sought to maintain order – however defined – through policing the streets or hills, operating court-like institutions for dispute settlement, and meting out sentences and punishments as they deemed appropriate. At times these initiatives enjoyed the tacit and even active support of the state; at other times they were denounced as 'vigilantism'. Many of these variants of vigilantism and popular justice were tied to the system of racial discrimination that, after 1948, was known as *apartheid*. The state invested little effort in policing African townships, or in settling disputes, unless there was a clear threat to overall political stability. In rural areas, the state delegated authority to chiefs as part of its policy of establishing different political systems for different racial groups. The transition to democracy in South Africa might therefore have been expected to have led to a sharp decline in these forms of extra-state social ordering and control. But there is little evidence of any such sharp decline. Participation in and support for vigilantism of one kind or another remains very widespread.

Vigilantism and Popular Justice Before 1994

The African subjects of colonial, Boer or (after 1910) South African rule long sought to maintain order at the local level on their own terms through policing, settling disputes and disciplining offenders. The authorities recognized the benefits of such informal justice, so long as it was controlled by people acceptable to the authorities themselves. There thus developed a judicial and policing system that involved a combination of direct and indirect rule. This was obviously the case in the reserves, where authority was formally devolved to chiefs. But in urban areas, also, vigilantism was sanctioned intermittently (Seekings, 2001).

During the Second World War the government extended its Civilian Protection Service into African townships so as to counter the growing problem of disorderly youth (*tsotsis*). After the war, Civic Guard units were established in many townships, generally under the leadership of 'respectable' middle-class men. These were banned in 1952, but residents continued to organize in response to *tsotsis* (Goodhew, 1993; Glaser, 1994). Migrant workers, based in single-sex hostels, also organized against the *tsotsis* who preyed on them, and organized committees to settle disputes among themselves (Mayer, 1971). At this time most people in the towns, including families, had been born in rural areas and retained strong links with them. Migrants and settled urban families alike sought to impose an order that was deeply informed by rural 'tradition' (Wilson and Mafeje, 1963).

As people put down deeper roots in the towns, their ties to rural kin and customs declined. The better-off township residents, living in separate family accommodation, found it harder to organize collectively to settle disputes or contain the *tsotsi* problem. Moreover, they could less easily employ the sanction of ostracism, which underpinned other punishments (such as fines). Nonetheless, in townships such as Soweto (outside Johannesburg), residents combined successfully in the 1970s to form *makgotla*, named after the Setswana term for elders' courts in rural areas (*makgotla* being the plural form, *lekgotla* the singular). At their best, the *makgotla* sought to pre-empt violent crime, to find restitutive rather than merely punitive solutions to theft, and to reconcile members of the 'community' who were reneging on their obligations and responsibilities. But the *makgotla* generally drew on a moral code that was distinctively and controversially conservative, upholding the strongly patriarchal authority articulated as 'tradition'. Growing numbers of younger urban residents did not share this moral code, and became especially hostile to the *makgotla* when some of their leaders chose to participate in illegitimate, racially-segregated institutions of local government (Hund and Kotu-Rammopo, 1983; Glaser, 1994; Seekings, 2001).

In the 1980s a new generation of 'people's courts' was formed (Seekings, 1989; Allison, 1990; Moses, 1990; Scharf and Ngcokoto, 1991; Pavlich, 1992). These courts were often explicitly aligned with the progressive civic organizations that formed the organizational backbone of popular resistance to apartheid, and they championed a model of justice that was said to be pre-figurative of a post-*apartheid* order. The courts came to be seen as an integral component of 'people's power' in areas that had been 'liberated' from the authority of the *apartheid* state. According to the police, over four hundred people's courts were formed in townships across South Africa. Whilst many of the younger participants in these courts looked forward to a post-*apartheid* future, others continued to look back to a romanticized pre-colonial past. In the case of one well-documented 'people's court' in Soweto, the leading member of the court was a former card-carrying member of a *makgotla* group, and both the court's leadership and ordinary residents described the court as a *lekgotla* (Seekings, 1991).

The state became more hostile to informal policing and dispute settlement in the last years of apartheid, primarily because many 'people's courts' were run by opponents of *apartheid* as part of a revolutionary political project. But after 1990 the space for popularly-driven policing and dispute settlement opened up once again. Organizations allied to the African National Congress began to consider, openly and formally, the roles and activities of 'people's courts' in a post-*apartheid* context. The first priority was to ensure that existing courts operated in a disciplined way – meaning that they avoided the worst excesses of brutal or arbitrary practice. Non-government organizations initiated training programmes for leaders in 'people's courts' (Nina, 1992; Seekings, 1992).

Vigilantism and Popular Justice After 1994

Since 1994 newspapers have regularly published reports of vigilante action by members of the public, often involving the brutal punishment of supposed offenders. Intermittently, a vigilante movement with apparently extensive organization emerges and grabs media attention. A prime example of this is People Against Gangsterism and Drugs (PAGAD), based in formerly coloured areas of Cape Town. PAGAD members and supporters marched against drug-dealers, killing some and burning out others (later using pipe-bombs to do so). Surveys conducted in Cape Town in 1996-97 found strong support for direct action against known criminals, and minority support for PAGAD (Africa *et al*, 1998). In the years since 1997, however, PAGAD has veered away from its original mission and is alleged to have been responsible for the bombing of restaurants and the assassination of a magistrate (see the chapter by Minnaar in this volume). Another high-profile group is *Mapogo a Mathamaga*. *Mapogo* seems to have been formed by local black businessmen in 1996, after a spate of murders of businessmen and robberies. It 'investigates' incidents reported by paid-up members, mostly comprising theft and assault. It claims 40,000 members in its rural stronghold in the central part of Northern Province, but has subsequently formed branches in the Gauteng metropolitan areas and opened an office in Pretoria (*Mail and Guardian*, 21 January 2000). The movement attracted attention because its members were charged with assault and attempted murder, arising out of the corporal punishment that forms an integral part of its activity. *Mapogo* leaders are forthright about their approach:

> If the suspect hides information and there is strong evidence against him, a bit of *sjamboking* [whipping with a rawhide or plastic *sjambok*] will be done to dig out the truth. When they don't come out with the truth, they get a walloping. We don't encourage members to overdo the beating. But let me tell you, the criminal arrested by *Mapogo* – the one who is *sjamboked* – will never repeat the deeds, he'll be born-again. (Quoted in *Mail and Guardian*, 14 February 1997)

This 'Mapogo medicine' supposedly helps cure suspects of their bad ways. In May 1999 a suspected thief was reportedly dangled over a crocodile-infested river until he confessed (see, also, *Sunday Independent*, 25 June 1999; *Mail and Guardian*, 21 January 2000, 15 June 2000; see, further, Minnaar's chapter in this book).

Struggles over crime occasionally erupt into extraordinary violence. In the Tsolo and Qumbu districts of the Eastern Cape, more than four hundred people died between 1993 and 1996 in cycles of violence revolving around stock-theft. *Umfelandawonye wa Bufuyi* was formed in 1994 to stop stock-theft. It had strong support among migrant workers from the area who worked in and around Johannesburg, and who both retained a strong sense of 'tradition' and sought to invest in livestock. According to a report by the Human Rights Committee (1997, p. 5):

> The community was concerned not only with the violence but [also] with the negative impact stock-theft was having on their culture. Cultural practices, such as slaughtering cattle

during funerals and sacrificing goats during the graduation ceremonies for traditional healers, needed to be protected.

In response, alleged thieves organized themselves, drawing support from migrant workers who said that they had been accused falsely of stock-theft, and forced to quit their jobs. Whilst stock-theft provided the initial impetus to violence, and helped to sustain it, it seems that the conflict later developed a momentum of its own.

Groups like PAGAD and *Mapogo* (and to a lesser extent episodes like the Tsolo/Qumbu war) receive a lot of attention, but they are merely the visible tip of an iceberg. Moreover, they differ in important respects from the much more routine forms of vigilantism and dispute settlement that are practiced on an everyday basis in many parts of the country. Most 'vigilante' groups are highly localized, with groups of residents organizing and acting in their immediate neighbourhood. In African townships, many are organized by local street committees. It is less clear how vigilantism is organized in rural areas, although it is evidently widespread. Most such policing and dispute settlement is run by older, more conservative residents, but younger men and even women have become active in urban areas. Many focus on reconciliation (and compensation), since the parties to disputes often have to live together long after the dispute has been settled. Many, however, impose heavy punishments (in part to deter other prospective offenders). Lacking formal status, vigilante groups have a limited range of options when it comes to sentencing offenders, and many (or perhaps most) resort to corporal punishment. Vigilante groups clearly attract a measure of public support, and the police often turn a blind eye to them, grateful for their unfettered assistance.

There is no conclusive evidence on the extent of localized vigilantism. Press reports typically focus on the most controversial cases – such as *Mapogo* – in which there is a legal challenge to or popular outcry against physical violence or especially killings. Some such reports, nonetheless, point to the wide extent of vigilantism and popular justice, and to the high level of public support for them. In Durban's KwaMashu township, civic associations ran covert units which sought to sweep out criminal gangs (*Mail and Guardian*, 27 October 1995). In Mdantsane, outside East London, crowds of as many as five hundred people participated in the killing of a suspected thief (*ibid*, 3 September 1999). In Pretoria's Mamelodi township, for example, there are said to be more than twenty-two 'kangaroo courts' dispensing fines and corporal punishment (*ibid*, 11 August 2000). In Dube, Soweto, old women played the leading role in a fatal assault on suspect thieves and rapists (*Sunday Independent*, 4 March 2001).

There is little academic research into these forms of direct action by the public. Surveys are bedevilled by ambiguities in the meaning of 'vigilantism', and there are few detailed case-studies. A survey of the Eastern Cape province in mid-1999 found that about 60 per cent of the respondents thought that there had been an increase in vigilantism across the country since 1994 (although only 13 per cent said that there had been an incident of vigilantism in their own area). Five per cent said they had participated personally in vigilante activity and a further 20 per cent said they would consider participation. Almost exactly one half of the sample said that they supported 'alternative or traditional forms of punishment', such as 'people's courts, expulsion from a village, fines paid to a tribal chief, restitution or compensation to crime victims' (Schonteich, 2000, pp. 49-51). The percentage saying that they knew of vigilantism in their area is surprisingly low, but the percentage saying that they had participated is surprisingly large. Five per cent of the adult population of the Eastern Cape province would be about 150,000 participants, and five percent of the adult population countrywide would be an extraordinary one million people! *Mapogo*'s claimed membership of 40,000 seems small in comparison.

Another countrywide survey, in 1998, asked respondents where they went to ensure that criminals were punished, besides or instead of the police (Statistics South Africa, 1998). About 8 per cent in total mentioned 'street committees', 'people's courts' or vigilante groups. Such structures were especially common in the Northern Province and Eastern Cape. Almost all (91 per cent) said that they had nowhere to turn to. A second question asked where they could go for protection, besides or instead of the police. Again, almost all (82 per cent) said there was nowhere. Small proportions mentioned neighbourhood watch groups (6 per cent), and street committees, private security firms or local chiefs/headmen (3 per cent each).

Street Committees and Dispute Settlement in Guguletu, Cape Town

In both urban and rural areas, the intermittently reported high-profile incidents or episodes of conflict serve to obscure more everyday forms of informal policing and dispute settlement. The most common forms of urban 'vigilantism' are not the spontaneous actions of 'mobs' nor are they practised by 'kangaroo courts' which have no procedures, but rather are the everyday activities of street committees operating on a structured basis with broad popular support and on a routine basis at the very local level. Such activities are rarely labelled as 'vigilantism', in large part because they do not get reported in the press. Only when street committees combine together to mount policing activities in the township as a whole are they likely to be reported on and labelled as 'vigilantism'. But all of these activities need to be analysed if the dynamics and patterns of popular justice and ordering are to be understood fully. In this chapter we focus on local forms of ordering through a case-study of one township, Guguletu.

Guguletu is one of Cape Town's older African townships, with a well-established community. The infrastructure is good by South African standards, with tarred roads, water, electricity and sewerage in every house, and regular rubbish collection. The basic unit of civic organization is the street committee, typically comprising ten or so members who would be 'elected' in a public meeting (when 'elected' really means 'nominated' in that there would not be competition for places). Street committees have existed in Guguletu for decades, at least (see Burman and Scharf, 1990). There appears to be a regular turnover in active street committee membership, with an average length of service of about three years. This suggests that a large proportion of residents are active at one time or another.

In a survey we conducted in 1998, 95 per cent of respondents said that there was a street committee in their street. Street committees usually meet once per week or per fortnight, with larger 'community' meetings held less often (in some cases once per month, in others less often than this). A surprising 27 per cent of respondents said they were 'members' of their street committee, but this was probably understood to mean something more inclusive than full members of the committee that met weekly. As many as 58 per cent of respondents said that they attended meetings of the street committee, presumably referring to the 'community' meetings. These proportions were much higher among older residents and especially household heads, who comprise the key constituency for street committees. Among people aged 35 or more years, more than one-third said that they were 'members' of their street committee and over two-thirds said that they attended street committee meetings.

Street committees perform a range of tasks in two main areas. The first is liaison between residents and local state officials over housing and local services. For example, street committees played a central role in the transfer of formerly municipal housing to residents, identifying the person in whose name the house should be registered. Secondly, street committees are active in dispute settlement and policing. Some disputes involve housing. For example, street committees will help to resolve disputes over who should occupy a house. In this the street committees will often work with state institutions. In NY103 (a street in Guguletu), according to a local street committee leader, 'an old man was chased out of his own house by his wife's older children from another marriage; the street committee investigated this and is now attending court hearings to help the man get his house back'. Often, however, the street committee will resolve the matter on its own. Other disputes – such as thefts, petty assaults, family squabbles and even unfulfilled business transactions (such as incomplete repairs to a house) – will often be dealt with by street committees. Stolen goods are sought and, if recovered, returned to their owners. Street committees try to make peace between family members, including parents and their children, and between neighbours.

Sometimes the dispute will require street committees to co-operate. The following example was given by a street committee leader:

> A NY78 young man beat a youngster who lives at NY101. The beaten child's mother reported this to the NY101 street committee, who later handed the matter over to the NY78 street committee. Apparently the NY78 boy found out that this youngster stole his hi-fi. The thief was badly beaten and admitted to hospital. The mother of the beaten boy also reported this to the police, but was rejected, the police explaining that the dispute should first be solved by the street committee. Finally, the case was resolved: the hi-fi was rediscovered (where it had been sold), and apologies were sent to the beaten boy's mother.

As this example indicates, police often work closely with street committees, especially when juveniles are concerned (see, further, Ngcokoto, 1997).

Disputes that cannot be resolved by the street committee are sometimes taken to the civic organization – that is, the branch of the South African National Civic Organization (SANCO) – in that part of Guguletu. Intractable cases are even taken to SANCO's 'Local' structure that co-ordinates the four branches in the different sections of Guguletu. According to the chairperson of the Local, the executive spends every Saturday arbitrating disputes that could not be settled at street committee or branch levels.

Some evidence of popular engagement with street committees in Guguletu is evident from the 1998 survey. Asked 'Where do you go for help if a young man in your family does not obey his parents?', 41 per cent of respondents said they went to the street committee. In the situation of a neighbour who plays music too loud, 69 per cent said they went to the street committee. 'If a boy in the street stole a radio from your house', 66 per cent went to the street committee. For sure, Guguletu is a relatively well-established 'community', and responses to similar questions elsewhere are probably lower in residential areas settled more recently without the same degree of social cohesion in the community. But these results indicate how in some places minor misdemeanours and acts of disorder are routinely taken to street committees and other local, extra-state structures. These kinds of activity are much the same as those undertaken in the 1980s (Burman and Scharf, 1990) and probably also in preceding decades.

Street committees in Guguletu are also considered to be performing well. More than two-thirds (69 per cent) of respondents agreed that their street committee was doing a good job, with a further 18 per cent answering 'partly' or saying that they did not know. Only 13 per cent said their street committee was not doing a good job.

Women and Vigilantism

Most popular institutions for policing and dispute settlement have, in the past, upheld understandings of 'tradition' premised on generational and gender hierarchies. Informal courts and vigilante groups have generally been headed by middle-aged or elderly men (although the coercive capacity is generally dependent on younger men). There are few examples of women playing prominent roles in the past (one exception being *makgotla* leader Sinah Madipere Senakoane). For sure, some courts (including many of the people's courts of the 1980s) emphasized elders' responsibilities within the household. Most have come down hard on extra-marital rape. But almost all have been been dominated by men and have upheld essentially patriarchal forms of authority and responsibility in the household. As Scharf and Ngcokoto (1990, p. 349) note in their analysis of a 'people's court' in Guguletu: 'Non-sexism does not seem to have enjoyed much prominence as part of the new morality judging by the way in which gender-related disputes were dealt with' (see also Burman and Scharf, 1990, pp. 711-12).

The marginalization of women in local dispute settlement in the past reflected their social and economic marginalization more generally. African women in urban areas faced distinct challenges through much of the *apartheid* period. During the first three decades of apartheid, the state restricted the presence of African women in urban areas even more tightly than it did the presence of African men. Seen as wives and daughters and not as economic actors in their own right, most African women had to depend on their husbands and guardians for precious rights of residence to the city. Rights to tenancy were also closely linked to a dependent relationship to a man. Divorced or widowed women with children were evicted from their homes with alarming regularity, even if the woman herself had qualified rights of residence (Burman, 1984; Fast, 1995; Lee, 1999; Posel, 1991). Faced with restricted residency rights in towns, many women sought to remain invisible to the state, working in informal employment and living in shacks. This in turn shaped women's participation in collective organization. Few

African women participated in either trade unions or civic organization in residential areas. Women certainly mobilized and acted over civic grievances – such as rent increases, shack demolition and evictions – but were rarely involved in sustained organization (Seekings, 1991). In some areas, women were encouraged to form separate (and subordinate) arms to existing civic associations, which were to discuss women's concerns only (see, also, Burman and Scharf, 1990, 712).

This male-dominated pattern of organization began to give way in urban areas in the 1980s. The rapid expansion of secondary schooling among African girls, the relaxation and then abandonment of restrictions on women's urban residency and the opening up of new white-collar employment opportunities led to a generation of organizationally-active women. This was first evident in organizations of secondary school students and of young people ('youth') in general (*ibid*). As violence escalated and civic groups and the youth began more radical tactics of resistance, African township women were pushed into the background once again. Many women appear to have retreated into the extensive and dense array of associational structures that dealt with everyday problems but were largely apolitical in nature and did not intersect with the state on any level. These included the *umanyano* (church mothers' group), the burial society and the *umgalelo* (rotating credit association). These associations served women materially, spiritually and socially, but were for the most part neglected by the state because they did not interfere with state mechanisms of control. Within these largely women-only organizations, many African women 'came of age' in terms of their civic consciousness, and developed strategies of participation and communication which shaped the character of their associational life.

By the 1990s, younger women were playing prominent roles in street committees in places like Guguletu. This represents a major shift between the *apartheid* and post-*apartheid* periods, although it is not the direct result of the political transition. Our analysis of several street committees in Guguletu and one in Khayelitsha shows that the executive committees themselves comprise roughly equal numbers of men and women. As Ngcokoto (1997) notes, this was not the case in the past; in Guguletu, men used to predominate, and it is only in recent years that women have become active members and in some streets comprise a majority on the committees' members. In our interviews, several women confirmed that there had been a shift in the gender composition of the committees:

> Before, there were supposed to be men who are involved in a street committee. A woman was not supposed to be in a street committee, if you ask me the reason why, I don't know. Maybe the woman would be one, to be a secretary and the whole committee would be men. So we are trying to do a gender balance now because there are complicated cases sometimes that need women's understanding. (Interview with Ms. Duma, 3 March 2001)

Women on street committees said that having equal numbers of men and women was important and even encouraged, since it ensured a 'balanced' viewpoint. Gender balance within the committee ensures gender sensitivity. Certain cases brought before the committee are classified as a 'women matter', and these require the direction and understanding of female committee members, in particular the older women: 'Like if there is a fight between a sister and a sister, that matter is a women matter…, we are mostly women who are supposed to talk about this matter… because most of the time women are understanding the misunderstanding between the girls' (*ibid*). Women and men within the committee are seen to have different areas of expertise, and are charged with the responsibility for effectively carrying through an issue that is deemed to be within their particular realm of 'understanding'. Women also say that their presence has an educational effect on the men.

While there seems to exist a general acknowledgment that gender parity is a necessary characteristic of committees as a whole, the same cannot be said for all leadership positions in the committees. In our 1998 survey of Guguletu street committees, 28 out of 29 committees had a man and only one had a woman as chairperson. Over half of the street committees had female secretaries, however. This gender difference coincided with a generational difference. The average age of surveyed chairmen was 58, the eldest being 76 years of age and the youngest 33. The average age of the secretaries was considerably lower (36 years of age), with two secretaries who were 20 years of age at the time of the survey. The eldest was 55 years old. The typical chairperson is thus an elderly man whilst the typical secretary is a young woman.

The predominance of men in the office of chairperson presumably reflects in large part a cultural legacy, with street committees being an urban extension of 'traditional' and patriarchal systems of community justice dominated by male elders. In addition, this male predominance was reinforced in town as a result of state policy. But the (almost) exclusively male character of the office of chairperson also reflects present dynamics within the community. The general perception among our interviewees in Guguletu (and Khayelitsha) is that the youth have become more rebellious and violent crime is on the rise. Given this, it is seen as important to have a chairperson in the street who has the authority to admonish young men. Even among women, many think that this is the province of men:

It [the chairpersonship] need a man, we know it need a man… You see it is dealing with family matters so to a chair you must be a man so that if you say this is not going to happen, take a stand, you must take a stand. It always give those chairperson be man… At times I will tell you what, at times we are dealing with these naughty boys and the word from a man is much stronger than the word from the lady and those boys will respect them… .(Interview with Mrs Gwenxe, 16 January 2001)

As this interviewee indicates, men perpetrate most of the crime within townships. If, as discussed above, there is an understanding that your gender dictates what matters you have authority over – men over 'male' issues and women over 'female' issues – it is perceived that male chairpersons must remain to oversee the majority of these cases.

It would be simplistic to assert, however, that women in street committees generally acquiesce to the authority of the chairperson, and to male members in general. When pressed to speak about their perceptions of gender differences within street committees, several women across various committees in both

Khayelitsha and Guguletu commented that women committee members are in fact more 'active' and effective than men in their participation. According to one:

> Yes it's women that speak more and it's women that got good advice... Men are very weak... They quickly get fed up and they just decide to keep quiet, understand. When they don't like something or they see this doesn't come right then they just decide to drop it and leave it like that you understand. Then we women because we are mummies you understand... We always like to see that it comes to end, you don't want to leave it hanging like that.... (Interview with Mrs Sohena, 26 January 2001)

And another woman street committee leader concurred:

> You know sometimes men, there are people who are very shy. We women we speak things as we want to say it, you know... Men they are not fast in thinking about something like women. You know women they always think things fast and do things quick. Men take their time and they don't rush things as it goes, as it comes. (Interview with Mrs Witbooi, 20 February 2001)

Thus, women perceive themselves as being more forthright in their opinions, and are able to see an issue through to its completion with efficiency. Men are seen as less committed, less inclined to voice their views. In addition, male street committee members are seen as more prone to township temptations such as drinking, which inevitably affects their judgement (Ngcokoto, 1997).

> Sometimes they've [male members] got no time for the meetings, you understand. They don't worry much, maybe one wants to go out and have a drink, one wants to go out and meet friends, you understand. But with women...when we are needed we are always available. (Interview with Mrs Sohena)

Perhaps women committee members' collective strength stems from the depth of their experience in community associations. Certainly, preliminary analysis of female committee members' organizational profiles thus far indicates that when women join street committees, they are already involved in a broad range of community-based groups. Two thirds of female secretaries interviewed in 1998 were involved in leadership positions in organizations apart from the street committee, ranging from church and sports through Reconstruction and Development Programme issues to SANCO. In addition, all ten women surveyed in 2001 were active members of a wide variety of organizations. Male committee members in contrast are apparently only involved in the affairs of the street committee and nothing more.

Women perceive their role and function in different ways to men, and see their responsibly presiding over 'women matters' as a key part of their duties. In one Khayelitsha street committee, women are entasked not only with guiding the process through deliberation. If a woman is found 'guilty' of a particular offence, it is the women of the committee who decide on the appropriate means and method of punishment. For example, a woman was found grossly neglecting her disabled child by leaving it alone at home for long periods of time without any supervision. When this case was brought before the committee, the women decided to address the case with physical force, and they themselves *sjambokked* her. Explaining the women's actions, one committee leader said: 'The whole must beat, even if it's a woman the whole women must give you a beating...we take over that case, all women must discipline that woman...' Each woman in the committee whipped the guilty woman once with the *sjambok*, in effect showing her that all women in the community were condemning her action, since each female committee member took part in the punishment. This punishment was seen as appropriate, especially given that that her misdeed struck to the heart of womanhood – neglecting motherly duties. Asked about the relative effectiveness of this technique, the interviewee stated: 'It worked because the women they are afraid to do such a funny thing to their kids because they know it's gonna cause the women to come to your place because we are not afraid to come to your house because we wanted to discipline you.' In this case, women committee members met as a separate body to decide on appropriate punishment, and carried that punishment out as a separate body, without the presence of fellow male committee members. Women could not *sjambok* men, or vice versa.

Street committees are complex bodies that contain complex dynamics. A gendered analysis allows us to consider how some of these complex dynamics are played out, especially when examining the evolution of mechanisms of popular justice in the post-apartheid period. Women have increasingly become involved in organizations such as street committees, which in turn has transformed both the mode and manner of dispute settlement. Given that key differences exist in how women and men participate and enforce decisions of the committee, and given the importance of street committees as mouthpieces of community grievances and arbiters of community morals, changing gender relations within committees are of great importance.

Policing and Punishment

Street committees may prove effective mechanisms for dispute settlement within households or between neighbours, and they can even liase over disputes involving residents in different streets, but they can do little in the face of armed criminal gangs. This constraint may even be accentuated by the growing role of women in street committees. Policing requires concerted action by local civic activists, covering many streets at one time. In this, civic leaders now work more closely with the police than they did before 1994. According to the regional chairperson of SANCO:

> We used to handle cases as a movement. If we had a dispute the community would handle that, not go to the police. People were saying we were having kangaroo courts. Those things have changed now that we have a government of our own. Now we encourage people to go to the police, if someone is stabbed. Before it was not like that. (Interview with R. Mrawu, 29 January 1997)

But civics have not stepped out of this arena altogether. In Guguletu, widespread dissatisfaction with the local police led civic leaders to participate in a series of organized, vigilante activities. Key individuals were involved in the Community Police Forum (CPF), which was established to provide a channel for communication between police and the community. Structures like the CPF – and SANCO – provide institutional opportunities for very local leaders to come together and co-ordinate community-based or community-driven initiatives for the policing of township streets. Such policing is beyond the scope of any single street committee.

At the beginning of 1997, civic leaders in the CPF, SANCO and elsewhere launched 'Operation Khululekani' in Guguletu. 'Khululekani' means, roughly translated, 'free the people from criminal activity'. The *Cape Times* reported:

> Street committees are turning away from taking the law into their own hands – and have formed neighbourhood watches that conduct special crime-prevention operations with police. ... Members of the group, which comprises street committees and a core band of volunteers, patrol the township streets, gathering information on suspected criminal activity. This is then given to the police. Where limited police resources prevent immediate action, the group will confront the criminals and confiscate stolen property and firearms. Suspects are then taken to the Guguletu police station. (*Cape Times*, 8 January 1997; see, also, *Cape Argus*, 28 June 1997)

Popular mobilization continued into 1998. In January 1998, about three hundred residents took action against two alleged rapists who had been granted bail by the magistrate in the formal criminal justice system; the alleged rapists' house was destroyed. Three days later a doctor was fatally stabbed in his surgery and R60 stolen. Street committee networks were mobilized, and three members of a juvenile gang were identified as the culprits; they were apprehended, assaulted and – having confessed – turned over to the police. As the chairman of the local CPF said at a public meeting: 'We will go from door to door and root out *skollies* [delinquent thugs] in our communities. It is time for us to arm ourselves and get rid of these criminals' (*Cape Times*, 24 August 1998).

Faced with continued neglect by the police, residents began to take their cases to a group of minibus taxi-drivers based at the Guguletu taxi-rank. The participation of local minibus taxi-drivers in Guguletu reflected a countrywide trend. Minibus taxi associations are well organized and heavily armed; the fact that they can call upon many others very quickly renders them a powerful force, well-suited to the task of apprehending and punishing suspected criminals. Moreover, taxi-drivers seem to hold the police in low regard, and are willing to flout legal constraints on their actions. In Guguletu, people would report alleged criminals at the taxi-rank, and taxi-drivers would then pick up the suspect and, often, assault them. The press quoted residents who were very supportive of this vigilante action. According to one:

> To those people who feel this is barbaric and against the law, I say: You people stay in safe houses protected by walls, electric fences and big dogs. You don't know how it is to be helpless in front of the children while being bullied by criminals in your house. I had to leave my house as I fear for myself and my children. Now I have put all my trust in the residents. I'm convinced that they will help me. To me, the police are useless, I have no trust in them. (*Cape Times*, 24 August 1998; see, also, Monaghan, 2000, p. 15)

The taxi-drivers themselves insisted they were not vigilantes because they only investigated cases that the police had failed to resolve, and because they only assaulted people who did not co-operate. The police themselves declined to intervene, and the CPF expressed guarded support:

> These youngsters are terrorising us and must be taught a lesson. I admit we are harsh, but we get results. We do not kill them. All we do is give them a public whipping, for everyone to see who they are and to show the children out there what could happen when they do the same (*ibid*).

The chairman of the CPF said that the taxi-drivers 'did abuse their power but it contributed also in eliminating this thuggery that was taking place in the townships' (quoted in Monaghan, 2000, p. 15).

But, whilst the focus was initially intimidatory – that is, to intimidate criminals and deter them from crime – the taxi-drivers soon began to act more indiscriminately. According to the CPF chairman, the activity was 'hijacked' and used for settling personal grudges (interview with D. Landingwe, 19 March 2001). As residents noted, suspects might be assaulted even if they were innocent. One person was reportedly killed when vigilantes raided a house, looking for stolen property. In 1999, the police arrested and charged eight men linked to the taxi association. In an ironic testimony to the inefficiency of the criminal justice system, the cases had not been settled as of March 2001! Meanwhile, crime was said to have increased once again (Monaghan, 2000, p. 15).

The Perceived Incapacity of the Criminal Justice System

The persistence – and perhaps even expansion – of vigilantism is clearly due in part to the perception that crime is worsening and the formal criminal justice system is incapable of dealing with it. The extent of participation in extra-state activity reflects the extent of this perception. The end of apartheid and the advent of democracy has not been accompanied by any perceived improvement in the efficacy of the criminal justice system. For sure, the leadership of the police and courts is now more representative of the South African population than in the past, when it was almost entirely white, and is formally committed to public 'service' rather than the maintenance of an oppressive regime. But this deracialization has not enhanced the system's efficacy, nor improved perceptions thereof. Indeed, in some respects the crime situation has clearly worsened. Of great importance here is the ever easier access to and use of firearms. Some writers have also pointed to the demobilization of former combatants in the armed wings of the African National Congress and Pan-Africanist Congress, arguing that this has fuelled crime. There are well-known cases in which such ex-combatants have turned to crime, but the scale of crime and insecurity in the country dwarfs any contribution made by the relatively small number of such ex-combatants.

Crime is shockingly commonplace. Unfortunately, the official statistics on reported crime are very inadequate as an indication of levels of crime. In 2000 the government placed a moratorium on the release of crime statistics (ostensibly on the grounds that the statistics from the police were unreliable, but most observers wondered whether it was not simply to disguise the worsening crime situation).

Moreover, surveys found that many crimes are not reported to the police (Statistics South Africa, 1998). Countrywide, one in five households say they have been the victims of housebreaking over the past five years; one in ten individuals say they have been the victims of assault over the same period. Crime rates are much higher in urban than rural areas (although stock-theft is surprisingly prevalent) (*ibid*). Crime repeatedly figures in public opinion polls as the second most important issue facing the country (behind job creation only). Polls also reveal widespread dissatisfaction with the government's performance, even among ANC voters. Polls in 1999 found that only 19 per cent of voters thought that the government had performed 'very well' or 'fairly well' with respect to crime; a massive 80 per cent of voters thought that the government had performed 'not very well' or 'not at all well' (with just 1 per cent saying that they did not know) (IDASA, 1999). Indeed, the public think that government control over crime actually declined after 1994. In that year 25 per cent of the public thought that the government was in full control; by 1997, the proportion had fallen to 10 per cent. In 1994 just over 40 per cent of the public thought that the government had little or no control over crime; by 1997 this proportion had risen to over 60 per cent. In 1994, 70 per cent of people felt safe; by 1997 only 47 per cent did so (Moolman, 1999; see, also, Schonteich, 2000).

Public opinion polls record low levels of public confidence in the capacity of the criminal justice system to curb crime. In a 1998 survey, only 38 per cent of respondents said they were satisfied with the police, 23 per cent said they were neither satisfied nor dissatisfied, and 40 per cent said they were dissatisfied. Furthermore, the predominant view among the public as a whole was that the performance of the police had worsened in the four years since the first general election (*ibid*; see, also, Seekings, 1998; and Gibson and Gouws, 1997). Public attitudes are understandable in light of the low rate of success of the police in investigating crime. It is reported that 'of every 100 crimes committed, about half are reported; there is sufficient evidence to open a docket in only 25 of these 50 cases, and suspects are arrested in only 12 or 13 cases'. Even with a conviction rate in court of about 75 per cent, less than one in ten crimes lead to a conviction (figures by Schonteich, quoted in Merten and Ntabazalia, 1999, p. 51; see, also, Moolman, 1999). An astonishing one in five awaiting-trial prisoners escape from police custody! Whilst the number of reported crimes has risen steadily, the number of convictions had actually declined (Moolman, 1999, pp. 16-19). Furthermore, the police themselves admit that they cannot police large parts of the country through a shortage of manpower (and equipment). In rural areas the police are generally invisible and inaccessible. One-third of the rural respondents in the 1998 survey said that they had never seen police in their areas, and another one-third said they saw police less than once per month. Two-thirds of rural respondents said that the nearest police station was more than 10 km away (Pelser *et al*, 2000).

Unsurprisingly, many South Africans believe that there are times when the 'rule of law' should be violated. Gibson and Gouws (1997) found that more than one-third of a representative countrywide sample agreed that 'Sometimes it might be better to ignore the law and solve problems immediately rather than wait for a legal solution'. A non-representative survey conducted in 1996-97 found similar attitudes. As many as 85 per cent of respondents agreed (or agreed strongly) that 'the rate of crime has reached a level which requires drastic counter-measures'. As many as 71 per cent agreed (or agreed strongly) with the statement that 'it is more important to ensure the protection of the community than to protect the rights of the individual accused person'. A similar proportion agreed that 'the justice system is too easy on criminals', and an even higher proportion agreed that 'there would be less crime if our laws were stricter' (Seekings, 1998). Gibson and Gouws (1997) conclude that 'support for the rule of law among South Africans is not particularly widespread. If law fails to produce the desired outcome, many believe it should be set aside, manipulated, or ignored.' The public favours severer sentences on the accused than the courts generally impose. There is widespread public support for the death penalty and for corporal punishment, both of which have been declared unconstitutional in the Constitutional Court (see, for example, Schonteich, 2000, p. 98).

Conclusion

The extent of citizen participation in and support for vigilantism reflects the extent of crime and disorder and the real (and perceived) incapacity of the formal criminal justice system to deal with it. The political transition to democracy in South Africa has neither reduced levels of crime nor raised sufficiently the efficacy of the criminal justice system. The belief that people should 'take the law into their own hands' in some situations is widespread, and actual action is commonplace.

Of course, whether or not the perceived incapacity of the criminal justice system and the presence of attitudes supportive of vigilantism convert into actual action depends on additional factors. Most important is the extent of cohesion within the community; that is, to use currently fashionable discourse), the stock of 'social capital' in the community. Where communities are relatively cohesive, like Guguletu, more sustained action is likely. Where there is less cohesion, vigilantism is likely to be more sporadic and more violent. In many poorer areas of Cape Town, including the long-established African township of Langa as well as most of the sprawling new townships and shack settlements that make up Khayelitsha, street committees and civic organizations appear to be weaker and vigilantism more brutal than in Guguletu.

It is tempting to try to distinguish between a non-violent and restitutive form of popular justice, rooted in and accountable to the 'community', and a violent and punitive form of popular justice executed by irresponsible and 'lawless' individuals. 'Community courts' (organized, responsible, restrained) are often contrasted with 'vigilantism' (spontaneous, reckless and brutal), and it is claimed that strengthening 'community courts' will lead to less 'vigilantism'. There is some truth in this. But the reality is not neat and tidy. Many communities will sanction the use of violence in a wide range of conditions, sometimes to an extent that seems excessive to observers. In a recent, well-reported case in Soweto, elderly women participated in the brutal and fatal assault on a suspected thief and rapist. One of the elderly women told the press: 'The whole thing had a festive mood to it. It was payback time. We agreed that this is the ultimate deterrent. It felt good to strike back' (*Sunday Independent*, 4 March 2001).

In a township like Guguletu most forms of vigilantism do not entail actual physical violence: disputes within families or between neighbours or even between people in different streets are settled through compensation or undertakings to change one's behaviour. But behind these settlements lies the threat of ostracism or of violence, and violence is widely used against rebellious juveniles. Vigilantism is *implicit* in even the most peaceful forms of community court. As the case cited above shows, violence is sometimes even used by women against women for neglecting responsibilities within the family. When citizens act against gangs they typically employ more overt violence, even if they subsequently hand over the accused to the police. In a situation where gangs themselves use violence routinely, counter-violence seems to be considered appropriate by many if not most citizens. In other words, there appears to be a tacit acceptance of violent forms of vigilantism if it is initiated by or has the consent of street committees or other legitimate local institutions. Evidence from the victims of local vigilantism would be valuable in understanding better the dynamics and legitimacy of violence at the local level. Of course, there are cases where vigilante groups begin to act arbitrarily, and lose popular support. These attract considerable attention. But it should not be thought that they are typical of the broader vigilante phenomenon.

The transition from apartheid to democracy has not led to an end to vigilantism. The underlying conditions underpinning popular vigilantism remain, and may indeed by deepening. The one change which we have noted is the changing composition of participants in institutions of popular justice in Guguletu. In the 1980s age hierarchies were challenged, with younger people taking on roles previously monopolized by older men. In the 1990s there has been a marked increase in the participation of younger women in street committees. The high-profile movements (such as PAGAD and *Mapogo*) are male-dominated, but on the ground gender hierarchies have been breaking down in at least some locations. We cannot say how widespread this has been, nor can we identify clearly the consequences; more research is clearly needed on the ground, and especially into the dynamics within street committees and 'communities' more broadly. But it does suggest that popular vigilantism continues to accommodate the processes of social change, as it has for decades, given the persistence of the underlying causes.

Note

Research in Guguletu comprised: a mini-survey of street committee leaders in 1998, co-ordinated by Jeremy Seekings; a survey in 1998 of a representative sample of two hundred households, co-ordinated by Kris Jones and Jeremy Seekings; and interviews between 1996 and 2001 with civic leaders and street committee leaders, by Jeremy Seekings and Rebekah Lee. Siviwe Mdoda helped with transcribing and translating interviews. We are grateful to Kris Jones, Siviwe Mdoda and the many undergraduate students who have provided valuable assistance.

References

Africa, C., Christie, J., Mattes, R., Roofs, M. and Taylor. H. (1998), 'Crime and Community Action: PAGAD and the Cape Flats, 1996-1997', POS Report no. 4, Public Opinion Service, Institute for Democracy in South Africa (IDASA), Cape Town.

Allison, J. (1990), 'In Search of Revolutionary Justice in South Africa', *International Journal of the Sociology of Law*, Vol. 18, pp. 409-28.

Burman, S. (1984), 'Divorce and the Disadvantaged: African Women in Urban South Africa', in Hirschon, R. (ed.), *Women and Property/Women as Property*, Croom Helm, London, pp. 17-139.

Burman, S. and Scharf, W. (1990), 'Creating People's Justice: Street Committees and People's Courts in a South African City', *Law and Society Review*, Vol. 24, pp. 693-744.

Fast, H. (1995), *Pondoks, Houses and Hostels: A History of Nyanga, 1946-1970*, Unpublished Ph.D. thesis, University of Cape Town.

Gibson, J. L. and Gouws, A. (1997), 'Support for the Rule of Law in the Emerging South African Democracy', *International Social Science Journal*, No. 152, pp. 173-91.

Glaser, C. (1994), *Youth Culture and Politics in Soweto, 1958-1976*, Ph.D. thesis, University of Cambridge.

Goodhew, D. (1993), 'The People's Police Force: Communal Policing Initiatives in the Western Areas of Johannesburg, circa 1930-1962', *Journal of Southern African Studies*, Vol. 19, pp. 447-70.

Human Rights Committee (1997), 'Dimensions of the Continuing Violence in Tsolo and Qumbu: Murder, Gunrunning, Stock-theft and Intimidation', Special Report 4, Human Rights Committee, Johannesburg.

Hund, J. and Kotu-Rammopo, M. (1983), 'Justice in a South African Township: The Sociology of *Makgotla*', *Comparative and International Law Journal of Southern Africa*, Vol. 16, pp. 179-208.

IDASA (1999), *The Public Agenda*, Fourth Report, IDASA, Pretoria.

Lee, R. (1999), *African Women, Urban Areas and the Development of the Apartheid State: The Case of Cape Town, 1945-1970*, Unpublished M.Phil thesis, University of Oxford.

Mayer, P. (1971), *Townsmen or Tribesmen: Conservatism and the Process of Urbanisation in a South African City*, Oxford University Press, Cape Town.

Merten, M., and Ntabazalia, E. (1999), 'Wielding the Whip', *Siyaya*, No. 5, pp. 49-51.

Monaghan, R. (2000), 'Vigilantism in South Africa', unpublished paper.

Moolman, N. (1999), 'Escaping Justice? Let Us Look at the Scoreboard', *South African Journal of Criminal Justice*, Vol. 12, pp. 13-40.

Moses, J. J. (1990), *People's Courts and People's Justice*, Unpublished Ll.M dissertation, University of Cape Town.

Ngcokoto, B. (1997), 'Street Committees in Guguletu Section 3, 1982-1995', Occasional Paper, Community Peace Foundation, Cape Town.

Nina, D. (1992), 'Popular Justice in a "New South Africa": From People's Courts to Community Courts in Alexandra', Occasional Paper No. 15, Centre for Applied Legal Studies, University of the Witwatersrand, Johannesburg.

Pavlich, G. (1992), 'People's Courts, Postmodern Difference, and Socialist Justice in South Africa', *Social Justice*, Vol. 19, pp. 29-45.

Pelser, E., Louw, A. and Ntuli, S. (2000), *Poor Safety: Crime and Policing in South Africa's Rural Areas*, Monograph No. 47, Institute for Security Studies, Pretoria.

Posel, D. (1991), *The Making of Apartheid, 1948-1961: Conflict and Compromise*, Oxford University Press, Oxford.

Scharf, W. and Ngcokoto, B. (1991), 'Images of Punishment in the People's Courts of Cape Town, 1985-1987', in Manganyi, N. C. and du Toit, A (eds), *Political Violence and the Struggle in South Africa*, Southern Books, Cape Town, pp. 341-71.

Schonteich, M. (2000), *Justice versus Retribution: Attitudes to Punishment in the Eastern Cape*, Monograph No. 45, Institute for Security Studies, Pretoria.

Seekings, J. (1989), 'People's Courts and Popular Politics', in South African Research Service (edn.), *South African Review 5*, Ravan Press, Johannesburg, pp. 119-35.

Seekings, J. (1991), 'Gender Ideology and Township Politics in the 1980s', *Agenda: A Journal About Women and Gender*, Vol. 10, pp. 77-88.

Seekings, J. (1992), 'The Revival of "People's Courts": Informal Justice in Transitional South Africa', in Moss, G. and Obery, I. (eds), *South African Review 6*, Ravan Press, Johannesburg, pp. 186-200.

Seekings, J. (2001), 'Social Ordering and Control in the African Townships of South Africa: An Historical Overview of Extra-state Initiatives from the 1940s to the 1990s', in Scharf, W. and Nina, D. (eds), *The Other Law: Non-State Ordering in South Africa*, Juta, Cape Town, pp. 71-97.

Seekings, J. with Murray, C. (1998), *Lay Assessors in South Africa's Magistrates' Courts*, Law, Race and Gender Research Unit, University of Cape Town, Cape Town.

Statistics South Africa (1998), *Victims of Crime*, Statistics South Africa, Pretoria.

Wilson, M. and Mafeje, A. (1963), *Langa: A Study of Social Groups in an African Township*, Oxford University Press, Cape Town.

8 The 'New' Vigilantism in Post-April 1994 South Africa: Searching for Explanations

Anthony Minnaar

Introduction

Vigilantism[1] in post-1994 South Africa remains a highly emotional and contentious issue not only politically but also on a community and policing level. In the post-1994 era there have been subtle changes from the pre-1994 forms of vigilantism. Vigilante activity in the period before 1990 has largely been explained in terms of political motivations (liberation and struggle ideology or the 'conservative' response of covert state supported actions by surrogates or proxy agent provocateurs). In the mid-1980s, individuals and groups often took the law into their own hands in what were perceived to be 'legitimate' attacks on agents and structures of the apartheid state. Alternatively, they were seen as pre-emptive, retaliatory or revenge responses to those attacks by other elements and groupings politically opposed to the politics of 'struggle' in the townships (Coleman, 1998; Du Toit and Gagiano, 1993).

Although vigilantism all but ceased to be a tool of repression and political contestation after the democratic elections in 1994 the current vigilantism remains complex in its structure, motivation and nature. In particular, this period saw the rise of more formal or organized vigilante groupings, chief among which were four groupings. First, People Against Gangsterism and Drugs (PAGAD) in the Western Cape province. Secondly, *Mapogo a Mathamaga*, which originated in the Northern Province. Thirdly, more traditional forms such as the *Mfelandawonye Wamapondomise Burial Society* and *Ilisolomzi* – both ostensibly formed or redirected in 1995 to curb stock-theft in districts like Tsolo and Qumbu in the former Transkei region of the Eastern Cape . And finally, the *Inkumpa*, which was ironically formed in the same area to 'protect' those victims of the vigilante actions of the former two organizations (Minnaar and Potgieter, 1998).

117

Searching for Explanations

Why do such acts of community or popular justice continue to be perpetrated when the overt political reasons would appear to have been removed by the implementation of a new democratic system in the post-1994 period?[2] Is the current vigilantism merely a response to perceived increases in, or a continuation of, high levels of crime? This latter question is posed since the current general perception of vigilantism associates this form of violence largely with fighting crime, protecting communities from criminals and punishing those alleged criminals caught. The perpetrators most often felt they were acting with sufficient justification or even legitimately as either semi-formal street committees, neighbourhood patrols or concerned citizen groupings in ridding their areas of suspected criminals.

Vigilante acts in South Africa are certainly not straightforward or simple but rather complex social reactions to varying and different situations. One of the complicating factors in examining and assessing vigilante activity in South Africa has been the wide-range of 'types' of incidents. Vigilantism in South Africa covers a range of activities. They encompass punishment of 'criminals' either by spontaneous mob gatherings, individuals taking the law into own hands or the organized activities of vigilante groupings or people's courts in communities, assassination of known druglords, and the burning of alleged witches (Minnaar, 1997). They include commercial farmers catching and beating alleged poachers or trespassers. And extend from shop owners/managers meting out their own 'justice' on shoplifters to the illegal eviction of squatters (Minnaar and Ngoveni, 2000).

Currently, the vigilantism occurring countrywide does little for the maintenance of law and order or of upholding any vision of community justice. In its crudest sense it is simply individuals in a community taking the law into their own hands and dispensing their own punishment on alleged criminals, who they see not being caught, convicted and sentenced. In essence the current vigilantism in South Africa is a brutal indictment of the whole criminal justice system and an expression of its failure and the inadequacies of the policing that is or is not occurring.

Rising crime levels would appear to be a worldwide phenomenon but while responses to high levels of crime vary widely, these responses have been of particular ferocity and violence in present-day South Africa. However, such vigilante activity in South Africa in the late 1990s and the first years of the new millennium is perfectly understandable in light of general public perceptions that crime remains at unacceptably high levels in most communities across the country. There are a number of other underlying reasons which further sustain and encourage this high level of vigilante activity in South Africa. One of the reasons for the continuation of vigilante activities are the operations of the so-called people's courts.

People's Courts

During the late 1980s and early 1990s – years when political violence was at a high level – and prior to the April 1994 elections, there occurred many incidents where township residents took the law into their own hands. Much of this community justice was labelled 'political' and took the form of people's courts (Nina and Stavrou, 1993) and 'necklace'[3] executions of political opponents. A large proportion were nothing more than kangaroo courts where certain people used community anger selfishly for revenge; to get rid of opponents or rivals, or to impose control over certain communities through intimidation.

While the system of people's courts was originally established with admirable principles of ridding communities of all criminals, they came, in time, to get out of control and became a 'law unto themselves'. But in those communities ravaged by lawlessness and having a minimal police presence they were seen as a legitimate effort in the struggle to maintain a semblance of law and order. However, many of the people's courts lent themselves to abuses of power within the whole context of the 'struggle against apartheid' and 'making the townships ungovernable' so that 'people's power' could be established. In this period it was estimated that about 400 so-called people's courts operated in various townships across South Africa. But the government's use of the Emergency Regulations powers had, by August 1988, all but put an end to their politicized and revolutionary struggle activities (Human Rights Committee of South Africa [HRC], 2001, p. 12). However, a number continued to perpetrate anti-crime vigilante acts in trying to self-police their neighbourhoods in a covert manner. In the period 1990-1991 many areas experienced a renewed upsurge in 'popular justice'. This 'new' informal justice was based on the strengthening of the old political street committees and many of the vigilante structures still operating today are based on this model (HRC, 2001, p. 14). However, the debate and concerns about their activities shifted from the 1980s link to the national liberation struggle to the question of their potential role as township courts in crime prevention and dispute resolution. (Seekings, 1992; Charney, 1991; Nina, 2000; Van der Merwe and Twigg, 1997).

Because of the stigma attached to people's courts a number of communities by 1992 had restyled their vigilante actions as Anti-Crime Committees that claimed to have the legitimate backing of civic and local groupings within specific communities (Minnaar, 1995a; 1995b). However, the fears of vigilantism overtaking these courts and the engagement of uncontrolled mobs in brutal, unlawful and unjust action seems to have been realized in the post-1994 period. In the post-1994 period it would also appear that people's courts have become more prevalent in the informal squatter settlements where very little official control by the authorities extends. These communities are often faced with either organizing their own policing and community guards or facing the very real threat of being swamped and controlled by criminal gangs and organized syndicates. The people's courts in these types of communities are also used to ensure the discipline of community members, the orderly occupation of plots and the implementation of and acquiescence to the local squatter committee decisions.

Because of the way people's courts operate and the aura of fear that they have built up around themselves many victims of their activities are too frightened to report the assaults to the police for fear of being necklaced themselves. Many victims refuse to testify against the perpetrators because they fear reprisals (Beaver, 1997). Furthermore, in some cases criminals have hijacked people's courts for the purpose of self-enrichment. However, many residents suffering from the depredations of people's courts maintain that if the police were more effective against crime then people's courts would not exist.

While the people's court system appears to have an orderly and structured component to it, much of the recent vigilantism in many of the informal settlements has taken the form of spontaneous mob justice. This is more than likely triggered off by saturation levels of crime in communities tired of the depredations of criminals, who seemingly go unpunished. The communities often act out of a sense of desperation and helplessness as victims of crime.

Some Underlying Sustaining Factors of Vigilante Activities

Vigilante activity is often sustained by a number of factors. The factors include a so-called 'conspiracy of silence' and a fear of being labelled an informer by reporting perpetrators of vigilante abuses. They include also community support or condonation, often born out of high levels of frustration (or open anger) at criminal depredations and from feelings that individual citizens need to 'protect themselves'. Sheer crowd apathy, which is often coupled to a fear of getting involved (amounting to avoidance or denial), is another factor.

Very often vigilante action by members of a community involves a conspiracy of silence by the whole community. There have been incidents of vigilante action whereby a group of residents kill a suspect but often they are never reported for the offence, nor do any witnesses come forward. The first inkling the police have of a crime having been committed is when they find a body lying in the streets either burnt or beaten to death. In some instances police merely receive an anonymous phone call telling them where they can find the necklaced body. Very few arrests are made in cases of necklacing unless the police are actually present but even then arrests sometimes do not occur. One reason for this being that the crowd perpetrating the necklacing is often too large and aggressive for the police to control the situation. Another reason is that the crowd sometimes physically prevent the police from arresting anyone.

Police say that it is extremely difficult to catch those involved in vigilante attacks. Police believe that prospective witnesses fear that they might themselves be arrested for participating in the mob beating if they talk. Witnesses may also realize that after seeing or being involved in a mob killing and experiencing the mindlessness and savagery of such an act, that the same wrath would be turned on them if they break silence. Besides the conspiracy of silence there is also a measure of apathy exhibited from bystanders. Such cases of 'do nothing' by spectators is sometimes fuelled by their own fears that they might themselves become victims if they intervene. Alternatively, in some communities there is in fact strong support for the vigilante activities on the grounds of 'protecting the whole community'. Regardless of the fact that punishment in people's courts can be extremely severe sections of communities still tend to support their operations. In a number of cases members of the public give as their reason for this support that 'they [people's courts] were more effective than regular courts' (Mostert, 1995).

Vigilantes have been able to claim the moral high ground. They claim, in the absence of any strong civic organizations in certain areas, as well as the widespread lack of a police presence or response to crime (especially at night), to be protecting the community, or administering justice for the benefit of the residents in their area. It is then no wonder that ordinary citizens give such support to vigilante activities.

There have also been cases in South Africa where individual private citizens, acting completely on their own, take the law into their own hands to punish/kill suspected criminals. After one such instance where an individual had killed members of a local criminal gang who had robbed his wife one local resident stated that the message in this case was clear to them: 'If we don't defend ourselves, no one else will' (Vernon and Bowyer, 1995). It is this anger that is often translated into mob action, and fuelled by high levels of frustrations at a variety of things.

Lack of Confidence in the Criminal Justice System and Ineffective Policing

In many townships around South Africa you will find that in the absence of any effective policing vigilantism and the operation of kangaroo courts will flourish. Many of the incidents that have occurred have been where criminals were caught in the act and either beaten up, stoned and burnt or killed outright by angry citizens. These actions are not only an expression of people's anger and frustration but also of their fear. They are symptomatic of a breakdown in the criminal justice system and effective policing. It has been the experience of ordinary people that if cases are reported to the police very often nothing happens (due more to police manpower shortages, case overload, and the police being overworked). Furthermore, if a suspect is apprehended the overloaded judicial system might well see the case being indefinitely postponed while a suspect might also be released on what can only be termed ludicrously lenient bail terms. In some serious cases such as murder a suspect has been released on R200 bail. People have lost faith and all confidence in the ability of the state to prosecute any criminal effectively especially when they see criminals out on the streets soon after being arrested. Misconceptions concerning bail have also led to communities taking the law into their own hands.

Many predominantly black communities perceive that the established legal system is for 'whites only', 'too expensive' for poor people, illegitimate and a tool used previously for state repression, which perception further prejudices them against making use of the official channels for reporting crimes (SA Law Commission, 1999, p. 3). There is also a general view in the townships that the legal process is too protracted and that the punishments handed down by the formal courts do not satisfy the needs of the complainants. Furthermore, in such cases where a criminal has been released on low bail there have been incidents where witnesses have been either intimidated, killed or simply disappear; resulting in such cases being dismissed for lack of evidence or witnesses being unwilling to come forward and testify in court. For angry communities it has become an easier and acceptable solution to take the law into their own hands.

There can be no swifter justice than mob justice and vigilantism. Such community justice is often administered almost immediately a criminal is caught in the act. After one incident in the Tembisa township, east of Midrand, where the two burglars caught had been stoned to death one resident had stated that 'It's our duty to protect ourselves from criminals' (Khupiso, 1994). Such attitudes are in all probability rife in most communities experiencing high levels of crime.

People's courts also flourish because victims of crime are often afraid of reporting the crime to the police since they fear they would be punished for by-passing the local people's court. Where specific communities have become weary of the criminal depredations of local gang members they do not even bother with the niceties of a formal people's court hearing but merely gather together and go and search for suspected gang members. When such suspects are caught they are summarily executed either by necklacing, stoning, beatings or shooting. Such community justice is based on almost immediate punishment without the benefit of a hearing or plea-bargaining. There is also certainly no option of what form of punishment will be meted out – death is more often than not the only result. Such vigilante action points to an inevitable conclusion that law and order can no longer be maintained in certain areas. Nor is it a pretty sight because of the inherent barbarism of its execution. However, for many township residents it is a reality with which they daily live. They claim that vigilante actions take place because they are not being protected from the continual depredations of criminals and also feel that the criminals are not being properly punished. It is then no wonder that in this atmosphere of anger and fear more organized groupings have stepped into the vacuum to provide communities with 'protection'. One of these rural-based, post-1994 organizations has been *Mapogo a Mathamaga*, PAGAD is an example of an urban-based group.

'It is Bitter Medicine, But it Cures'

Mapogo a Mathamaga, a vigilante group initially originating from the central and southern area (the former Lebowa homeland region) of the Northern Province, was established on 25 August 1996 in Sekhukhuneland Village near the provincial capital Pietersburg. It got its name from a Sotho proverb meaning 'the leopard can change its colours and become a tiger when provoked'. *Mapogo* is also known as the 'Business Shield'. Businessmen in the area set it up after the murder of six local businessmen and a spate of burglaries of business premises during the two-month period of July and August 1996. Businessmen in particular believed that criminals in the area were targeting them, while the police and the courts were unable or unwilling to offer them more protection or reduce the crime in the area. After a series of meetings a constitution was drawn up. A memorandum outlining their grievances and demands was sent to the provincial Member of the Executive Committee (MEC) for Safety and Security, Seth Nthai. The group soon grew from 1,000 paid up members to more than 2,000 operating in towns and townships in this region of the Northern Province. *Mapogo* were reported to have widespread community support. Stickers supporting the group adorn business premises in the region and people sport T-shirts bearing its logo – the head of a leopard facing a tiger. The group initially arrested suspects and handed them over to the police, but changed tactics after police released a number of the suspects. They started apprehending suspects after dark – taking them by surprise and beating confessions out of them before handing them over to the police. By February 1997 three suspects had died from injuries received under 'interrogation' and twelve members of *Mapogo* were charged with murder, while another thirty members were under investigation. This did not stop the vigilante activities of *Mapogo*, with members vowing to continue their anti-crime campaign. The members of *Mapogo* also refused to join forces with legitimate anti-crime structures like local Community Police Forums (CPFs) since they felt that the CPFs and police were too lenient when dealing with criminals. Most members give the same kind of reasons for joining: desperation about the crime rate and a belief that the police are either unwilling or unable to deal with the problem (Altenroxel, 1998).

However, one faction within *Mapogo* which was supported by the chairperson, Monhlo John Magolego, continued to use violent methods despite a formal agreement with the provincial Department for Safety and Security that they would co-operate with the police and work within the law. In addition, Magolego stopped attending the meetings of the joint task team. A complete breakdown in relations between *Mapogo* and the provincial Department for Safety and Security soon occurred. The breakdown was indicative of the ambivalent attitude of the authorities between recognizing and co-opting vigilante organizations like *Mapogo* by getting them to work within such anti-crime structures as the CPFs, and confronting them and putting a complete stop to their activities (Mulaudzi, 1998).

By May 1999 the group had expanded into the four northern provinces of South Africa (the Northern Province, Mpumalanga, Gauteng and Northern Cape), opening more than 90 branch offices and expanding further south into the Freestate province. The group also claimed a total membership of 35,000. Of these, *Mapogo* chairman, Magolego, claimed that 10,000 were white, paid-up members who had joined the group for protection. Magolego said that most of these whites were farmers who had seen the continuation of attacks on them in 1999 (Lubisi, 1999). *Mapogo*'s success was variously attributed not only to its violent methods but also to its ability to deliver instant 'justice'. The claimed reduction in crime also helped its growing popularity but it was also alleged that it was successful in its containment of crime largely by creating fear within communities itself.

Regardless of efforts by the authorities to stamp down on their activities *Mapogo* continued throughout 1999 and 2000 with their brutal vigilante activity. However, police complain that *Mapogo* members largely fail to provide substantiated evidence in court for each suspect handed over. Accordingly not a single conviction against such suspects handed over by *Mapogo* has been obtained in the Northern Province's courts (Lubisi, 1999; Mtshali, 2000). By mid-2000 hundreds of people had been subjected to *Mapogo*'s vigilante punishments and had suffered severe beatings. According to one report more than 20 people died from these beatings (Ngobeni, 2000a).

A number of internal problems within *Mapogo* led to a slowdown in its growth.[4] In 2000, the organization increasingly fragmented. During the year, in response to calls from a number of different quarters, the police in the Northern Province stepped up their efforts to prosecute *Mapogo* members for vigilante acts – with over 300 cases under investigation against 600 *Mapogo* suspects.

However, in August 2000 the authorities were eventually forced to dismiss the murder and assault charges from 1998 against Magolego and eleven other *Mapogo* members because of a lack of evidence. Apparently witnesses were too frightened and intimidated to testify in court against him and his accomplices. By October 2000 complainants in the Northern Province had withdrawn about 30 cases against *Mapogo* while another 20 were dropped because of a lack of evidence. Other cases had also been closed as unsolved. *Mapogo* members had only been tried in as few as 15 cases (Nkosi, 2000). Despite these setbacks the Northern Province Directorate for Public Prosecutions' Senior Prosecutor, Dr Silas Ramaite, announced in October 2000 that a special task team would be established to specifically look into all the unresolved cases pending against *Mapogo* (Nkosi, 2000). However, in the first three months of 2001 a special police unit was able to arrest nine members of *Mapogo* from the Malelane and Komatipoort areas in Mpumalanga for crimes ranging from murder, assault and feeding suspected criminals to crocodiles (Lubisi, 2001).

While the start of 2001 saw Magolego attempting a regrouping and tightening of his control over *Mapogo* structures it would appear that the organization as a whole, and in particular the professional security services company he started in June 2000, were experiencing a slowdown in momentum if not actual stagnation. There was also a growing realization that the long-term future of the organization lay within, rather than outside, the structures of the law. While *Mapogo* remains a force of considerable impact in the rural areas of the Northern Province the implementation of the wideranging Rural Farm Safety Plan and the reorganization of civil defence structures (FarmWatch and the former 'Commandos') would appear to be undercutting some of the motivations (lack of protection and crime) for its operations and the support given to it by members of the communities in which it operates. *Mapogo* can be compared, in certain ways, to the establishment and operations of the other major organized vigilante grouping in South Africa, namely the urban-based PAGAD.

People Against Gangsterism and Drugs (PAGAD)

Of the two illustrative cases of vigilante groupings in present-day South Africa used in this chapter PAGAD represents the most complex, as well as the most well organized in militaristic terms. It is also concentrates more on urban crime problems, in particular drug dealing and gangsterism. It was launched towards the end of 1995 in the Western Cape and drew support particularly from the conservative religious neighbourhoods of the Cape Flats of Cape Town. Its initial success in the Western Cape led to the manifestation of other offshoot anti-crime structures in South Africa such as People Against Gangs and Drugs (PAGAD) in KwaZulu-Natal; People Against Drugs and Violence in the Eastern Cape; and People Against Crime and Drugs (PACAD) in Gauteng.

Initially, its structures followed a loosely Muslim hierarchy. In September 1996 tension between the key founding groups that constituted PAGAD developed into factional polarization which separated the Qibla[5] Islamic extremists from the moderate and militant populists. Although PAGAD regards itself as a broad inter-religious movement, very early on it committed itself to the Shariah Islamic Code of Law as a broad ethical code (Tayob, 1996, pp. 34-5). Moreover, militancy within PAGAD provoked concern and criticism from more moderate Muslim scholars and clerics. In turn, they have become targets of a PAGAD bombing campaign, alongside PAGAD's attacks on alleged druglords on the Cape Flats. On 14 November 1996 at least 19 prominent academics and eight Muslim organizations made a combined public statement in which they stated, that while they had initially supported the emergence of PAGAD some months before, they were then deeply concerned at the level of militancy that was being displayed by the organization (in violently targeting alleged druglords and gang leaders) and that PAGAD's confrontational and intolerant approach was putting ordinary citizens at risk (Rossouw, 1996, pp. 4-5).

PAGAD's *modus operandi* in the Western Cape was to organize anti-crime campaigns comprising so-called 'ultimatum' marches to the houses of persons believed to be involved in criminal activities. In particular, they targeted drug dealing and other gang-related crime (extortion, prostitution, burglary and dealing in stolen goods) and delivered a 24-hour ultimatum. Demanding, typically, that all illegal activities by such persons stop forthwith, failing which the identified individuals would have to face the consequences of non-compliance with the demands (Nina, 1996). While the marches were at first deemed legitimate democratic protests they were soon supplemented by armed attacks and bombings of houses of known or alleged criminals, druglords and opponents – usually using home-made petrol, nail or pipe bombs.[6]

The increasing militancy of PAGAD members was fuelled by the refusal of the police (after clashes with PAGAD marchers) to talk to or deal with PAGAD and the police's stated intentions to deal with and treat them as 'just another gang' (*Mail & Guardian* Editorial, 1996). Although PAGAD never hesitated to use force against gangsters and drug dealers they viewed the police as fair game if the latter got in their way.[7] One of PAGAD's leaders, Ali 'Phantom' Parker, went so far as to declare a Jihad (holy war) on druglords and the police. The South Africa Police Service (SAPS) took this to mean that PAGAD was busy distancing itself from its original objective of combating crime. Consequently, the police began to treat PAGAD members as 'urban terrorists'.

Underlying PAGAD's militancy is their distrust of community police forums and the criminal justice system. PAGAD argues that its actions are a natural response of citizens feeling the brunt of the failure of the state to protect them (from the activities of criminals, and in the Western Cape particularly from the proliferation of gang-related activities such as drug dealing). The apparent failure by the state to deal effectively with high profile criminals in the Western Cape was a strong motivating factor for the continuation of the PAGAD activities of confrontation and force. There were also many complaints from PAGAD that the police themselves were in collusion with the criminals. PAGAD argued that was why they did not take action against criminals, let them out on easy bail terms, lost dockets or simply ignored them.

During 1997 there occurred a noticeable increase in the acts of violence by PAGAD members in the Western Cape in the form of explosives and shootings, while non-violent activity decreased proportionally. There was also the greater use of the so-called 'Pagad bomb'[8] in bomb attacks rather than the use of petrol or pipe bombs. Moreover, there was also the move from small bomb devices to much larger (stronger) explosive devices (Friedman, 1997). Due to these activities, PAGAD members have been charged with a variety of crimes, including; public violence, sedition, attempted murder, murder, malicious damage to property, and possession of illegal firearms.

PAGAD's violent activities continued into 1998 and at the beginning of August 1998 there was a pipe-bomb blast at the offices in Bellville of the Special SAPS Unit investigating PAGAD activities. June, July and August of that year had also witnessed numerous bombings of houses of alleged gangsters as well as opponents/critics of PAGAD. (In one bombing incident in July 1998 two members of PAGAD were killed and one was seriously injured when a pipe bomb exploded in their pickup van (bakkie) on their way to another bomb attack.) The police were able to raid a number of houses of PAGAD members and found evidence of bomb manufacturing.

The PAGAD campaign against identified druglords and gang members continued with renewed vigour throughout 1999 against both druglords and the police. 1999 had started with a bomb blast, a number of assassinations and an audacious raid on a police station in the Western Cape (all attributed to PAGAD). Even more shocking, on 14 January 1999 Capt. Bennie Lategan, a member of the Special Gang Investigation Team in the Western Cape who was also investigating a number of sensitive cases involving PAGAD, was assassinated in his car in a drive-by shooting at an intersection in Cape Town (SAPA, 1999). It was believed that one of the reasons he was killed was the fact that he was a vital witness in a number of PAGAD cases.

It would appear that while PAGAD started out, and prided itself, as being anti-drug and against gangsterism it soon became anti-government as well. In the early days it had garnered a fair amount of public support, specifically in the poorer neighbourhoods on the Cape Flats. The main reason for this support has been attributed to the lack of police action and the belief that the police services had no interest in solving or dealing with these crime problems since they only affected poorer communities. In addition, behind this perception of state agencies being either unable or unwilling to deal effectively with the Cape Flats criminal gangs there has also been the charge that many police and court officials are corrupt, that dockets are being 'sold' and that some public officials protect gangsters from prosecution. In support of this contention PAGAD members point to the fact that over the years very few gang leaders have been prosecuted for any crimes. If they are prosecuted and serve time in prison it is only for minor offences (HRC, 2001, p. 41).

While initially trying to project a broad-based support image, PAGAD has become largely associated with the Muslim sectors of the Cape Town community. Most of its meetings are still being held in local mosques, its leaders use Arabic words in describing their actions and its supporters chant slogans in Arabic, while some wear scarves covering their faces. Since their public launch in 1996 with mass demonstrations there has occurred a change in tactics to a more sophisticated terror campaign through a bombing campaign. Fear is also instilled especially in the law enforcement agencies through death threats and assassinations of officers. Apart from the attacks on police stations and individual policemen, members of the judiciary have also come under attack and threat. In September 2000 the magistrate for the Wynberg Court, Pieter Theron, was assassinated. It is believed he was killed because he was the presiding magistrate in a number of cases involving members of PAGAD charged with 'urban terrorism'. In addition, a judge of the High Court, Judge Nathan Erasmus, began receiving death threats after refusing bail to the National Co-ordinator for PAGAD, Abdus-Salaam Ebrahim, in December 2000. In March 2001 Judge Erasmus had also sentenced Mansoer Legget, a member of PAGAD, to 11 life terms on 11 counts of murder committed over a five-month period. After the murder of Magistrate Theron the police launched Operation Lancer as a national operation to investigate urban terror and PAGAD. Part of the functions of this operation were also to provide special 24-hour police protection to all investigators, prosecutors, magistrates and judges in the Western Cape who were working on PAGAD cases and had received threats.

However, one of the problems in the government's crackdown on PAGAD activities has been their inability to produce accurate intelligence for successful arrests and hard evidence with which to prosecute PAGAD members. While a number of G-Force (PAGAD's armed wing) members thought to be responsible for the vigilante violence have been arrested very few have been convicted.[9] In addition, a number of cases against PAGAD members have recently collapsed with the murder of several witnesses who were either in the Witness Protection Programme or had left their safe houses to return to their homes or to visit family.

While PAGAD continues to be blamed for many of the bomb attacks, questions have been asked about criminal elements exploiting the situation. Analysts have identified gang links and the possibility that protection rackets for targets like restaurants and nightclubs are being run as a result of the bombing campaign.

From the above descriptions of the activities and modus operandi of these two vigilante organizations it can be seen that both in fact represent 'new' forms of vigilantism. Their manner of organization, and their modus operandi are forms that originated in South Africa after the 1994 democratic elections. While both started off with their primary aim to combat criminals as 'anti-crime or protection' organizations both reverted to essentially extra-legal vigilante activities largely using violent methods. In time they have turned into vigilante-type organizations. Both saw their actions as having legitimacy, not only in their own eyes, but also having the sanction and approval of their respective communities or constituencies. However, both, in essence, became politicized – the former when they entered the arena of public protest and pressure politics at a local level – and the latter when its chairperson entered the national elections in early 1999 as a candidate for the United Democratic Movement (UDM) party. PAGAD were accused of pushing forward a conservative Muslim political agenda but were eventually labelled as 'urban terrorists' by the authorities. Conversely, while the provincial government in the Northern Province had first tried to co-operate and work together with *Mapogo*, its members later had criminal charges brought against them and the organization was labelled as no better than the criminals they were supposed to be fighting against.

'Muzzle Them or Regulate Them'

By the early 1990s people's courts had become totally discredited in the eyes of many following extensive media reports of their wide-scale abuses and gross punishments. In essence, they had become feared institutions violating human rights in the townships. This situation had lead to efforts to either replace them with other forms of community justice or to reassert community control and accountability over them. Prior to 1994 there were a number of efforts to do just that (Nina, 1993). Some of these initiatives were only partially successful since not all people's courts were prepared to follow strict guidelines.

In the late 1990s there were a number of efforts by the authorities to establish some form of official community courts for urban areas; in particular the informal settlements where little formal criminal justice structures existed. The idea was to have community courts similar to that in the rural, tribal authority communal areas, the *Khoro* or *Kgotla* system. A proponent of this approach was the then provincial premier of Gauteng, Mathole Motshekga (a lawyer by training). His idea was to have community courts in areas where there are few formal structures in order to bring 'justice to the people'. The community courts would have a lay magistrate drawn from the community (a community leader or respected resident). There would be a prosecutor, also drawn from the community. Neither would necessarily have any formal training although both would go on short orientation courses provided by the Department of Justice. Behind the community court proposals was the need to take away some of the load from formal courts which are currently being overloaded by petty cases. The community-based courts would essentially be able to deal with problems and disputes arising daily in a community. The advantage of such courts would be the immediacy of dealing directly with a case brought before it (one of the big problems in the criminal justice system being the long postponements of cases before they come to trial). The Department of Justice would oversee the operations and accredit lay magistrates and prosecutors. Unlike the people's courts, the Community Courts would adopt a constructive punishment role, whereby most sentencing would be of a community service nature or fines with the more serious cases obviously being passed on to the higher courts. The prime objective of the Community Court punishments was to be to educate and rehabilitate the offender. It was hoped that community control and accountability towards the Community Courts would undercut the kangaroo courts operating in the townships and also do away with the worst excesses and abuses of community justice. By being more accessible and addressing the problems of petty crime they would also address the community's concerns about rampant crime and the failure of the formal criminal justice system to deal with criminals (Mafata, 1998). A Community Courts Bill was drafted but is currently still under discussion before being presented in Parliament.

At the beginning of 1999 the Gauteng government tried to harness widespread public anger and outrage against perceived escalating crime by launching a public campaign to set up 1980s-era style street committees in an effort to constructively engage communities in the fight against crime. The then Gauteng Member of the Executive Committee (MEC) for Safety and Security, Paul Mashatile, was a strong proponent of setting up street and block committees. His view was that this would be the only way of getting the community involved by way of small units to really reach the people on the ground in order to achieve any sort of success in a provincial anti-crime campaign. The difference for Mashatile of the apartheid-era committees and the envisaged ones was that then it was an alternative to the state machinery, while it would now be complementary to the criminal justice system. He saw the future focus as the elimination of crime. The old M-Plan of the ANC consisted of command structures that in the past stretched from the local civic association that had representatives of block committees, who in turn consisted of representatives of street committees. The new street committees in the Gauteng model envisaged the community policing forum on top, followed by area sub-forums, block communities and eventually, street communities at the lowest level. The Gauteng Secretariat for Safety and Security planned to assist their establishment in each community so that they would not mushroom on their own in an uncontrolled manner. The structures would be monitored by the Secretariat on an ongoing basis. A further major safeguard built into the new model was that the police would be involved and informed of what the committees were up to. The first such street committee model was implemented in Ivory Park (the scene of the first vigilante killing in early January 1999). The Ivory Park CPF was divided into eight zones, each under a sub-forum, and in turn the local police station dedicated one policeman to liaise with every two sub-forums as a link between the police and community. Furthermore, to promote this new concept of community policing, to co-ordinate crime prevention and to deal with vigilantism the Gauteng government declared the month of March 1999 as 'Safety and Security' month during which Mashatile and the Gauteng Premier Motshekga toured the province promoting the street committee system (Masipa, 1999). At a series of 'Don't do Crime' rallies the new street committee/CPF model was strongly punted by Mashatile. However, in encouraging communities to 'fight crime' individuals were still inclined towards taking the law into their own hands.

The most important thing in this situation was for the authorities to formalize the whole system of 'informal vigilante' justice by channelling these anti-crime activities into a more formal structure; that is, the new CPF/street committees in liaison with the local police structures. This would then serve the purpose of legitimizing the already existing informal structures.

Conclusion: 'We Cannot Wish Popular Justice Away'

While it is important to understand the 'new' vigilantism in the South African context of a country in transition and change, vigilantism has a number of implications and consequences for any developing democracy. First, vigilantism is a form of usurping state power. No government can allow this to happen and still try to maintain the rule of law. However, vigilantism can only occur if vigilante organizations and ordinary citizens are given the space to act because of the perceived failure of the state to deal with the issues of criminal violence. Therefore the state needs to assert its authority, enforce its laws effectively and efficiently and put functioning systems of criminal justice and policing into those areas that need it the most, namely the poorer urban neighbourhoods, informal settlements and deep rural areas such as the former homelands.

Secondly, the state needs to be seen to act swiftly to counteract vigilante actions, and to prosecute and convict perpetrators. However, the flip side of the coin remains that the whole criminal justice system needs to be unclogged, speeded up, and corruption stamped out so that criminal cases can be dealt with quickly. The public needs to see justice happen to criminals caught and handed over to the authorities. In relation to the functioning of the criminal justice system, citizens need to be socialized into, and made aware of, the fact that everyone has the right to access a court of law to have his or her case heard in a fair and public hearing, irrespective of the crime. It is incumbent on the authorities therefore to provide better access to courts for the general public even if this is only the more informal Community Court system. All accusations must be tested in an independent and impartial setting. Vigilantism patently denies this right. The South African Constitution also protects the rights of arrested, detained and accused persons requiring that they be subjected to due legal process. Again the spontaneous and premeditated acts of 'community justice' happen so quickly that they circumvent this right.

Fundamental to trying to put an end to vigilantism is the right to life. Far too many of the incidents result in the arbitrary killing of alleged suspects. The state must be seen to better protect the rights of all of its citizens. Furthermore, many of the acts strip their victims of dignity by either making them undress, parading them naked through a community or subjecting them to degrading forms of assault or beating. The very public performance of these 'punishments' also leads to the public ostracization, shunning or even expulsion of victims from communities. Allied to the right to life and human dignity is the obvious right of the security of the person and democratic freedoms as guaranteed by our new Constitution and Bill of Rights. Overall, vigilantism represents a serious violation of all these human rights and no state wishing to claim to be fully democratic can allow vigilantism to be perpetrated and to thrive in a vacuum or the absence of state control. It represents a far too serious threat to the continued growth and strengthening of democratic principles at grassroots level.

The Human Rights Committee recommended *inter alia* more effective community policing, harnessing both the Community Police Forums and the new Community Safety Forums (CSFs)[10] approach, and the introduction of community courts, in order to curb vigilantism in those communities that have benefited little from the justice system. In particular the HRC stated that community courts would shift the emphasis from retributive justice to a more restorative one (Human Rights Committee, 2001, pp. 86-7).

This view is backed up by another research report by the Centre for the Study of Violence and Reconciliation (CSVR) (Harris, 2000) that recommended that the public and the community police should be trained to fight crime within the boundaries of the law. Furthermore, the CSVR recommended that the efforts and activities of anti-crime groups in communities should be harnessed in line with the provisions of the law. Moreover, the report stated that their vigilante actions should be deflected into positive crime prevention programmes regulated by local police and Community Police Forum supervision. This approach needs, according to Harris (2000, p. 58), to be implemented within a framework that addresses:

> the real and practical failings of the CJS [Criminal Justice System]; prioritising the tackling of vigilantism as a form of crime, and educating the public and authorities about the workings of the CJS (to address misperceptions about due process)....since contemporary vigilantism cannot be separated from the formal criminal justice system.

Overall, Harris (2000, pp. 61-3) postulates that any vigilantism prevention programme will need to be strengthened by a broader strategy of a public human rights education campaign so that a human rights culture can be further inculcated at a grassroots level. One of the aims of such a strategy would be to delegitimize violence as the primary solution to problems (especially of crime) in communities by offering 'individuals alternative, non-violent options for vigilante incidents that are explained as emotion-driven; i.e. motivated by revenge, anger, jealousy, prejudice and fear' (Harris, 2000, p. 62).

However, it is a fact that vigilantism has become embedded in many communities desperately trying to combat crime. It cannot be doubted that vigilantism in its various forms remains rife – as witnessed by vigilante incidents from across the country during the first three months of 2001 – and poses a continuing problem. It would appear that vigilante activities will continue in the foreseeable future, particularly so long as the perceptions surrounding the lack of police service delivery, poor success rate at apprehending criminals, and the continuing backlog in effectively prosecuting and convicting them remains so strong in all communities. This is tied to the lack of trust in the police, feelings that are exacerbated about perceptions concerning police corruption and their perceived involvement in criminal activities or their 'protection' of gangsters. It will be a long and hard uphill struggle to overcome the present culture of vigilantism in South Africa and to channel these unlawful activities into more formal legitimate systems and structures of crime prevention. As Nina (2000, p. 27) states:

> It is likely that South Africa's long tradition of popular forms of justice will continue. What is unclear, is whether this tradition will continue to adopt, on certain occasions, a vigilante mode. A clear, swift and intelligence response is needed from the state to handle this problem...The possibility exists that, should the state fail to take the necessary measures against vigilantism, this form of popular justice will remain a constant feature of South Africa.

Notes

1   I have chosen to adopt throughout this chapter the term vigilantism since it is my belief that it best covers in the broadest possible meaning the acts described. In the South African context many different terms have been used to describe these acts. Most are dependant on the perspective from which they are being analysed and range from 'popular' or 'informal justice' to 'mob', 'extra-judicial', 'street' or simply 'rough' justice. Additionally, other terminology associated with vigilantism refers to such structures as people's or community courts, 'kangaroo' courts, street or block

committees, neighbourhood watches or – in more legalistic terms – alternative dispute resolution (ADR) courts. Many are interchangeable but are also indicative that there is no one definitive perspective on the phenomenon of vigilantism currently being experienced in South Africa.
2   Nina (2000) has argued that the contemporary vigilantism in South Africa is merely a continuation by other means of the pre-1994 popular forms of justice.
3   The necklace method of execution, which involves placing a petrol-filled tyre around the neck of the victim and then setting this alight, is a particularly South African activity. See Minnaar (1999) for a more detailed description, and Minnaar (1997) for an explanation of its links to alleged witchcraft practices and its spiritual and cultural significance.
4   Magolego had briefly entered national politics as a candidate for the United Democratic Movement (UDM) in the 1999 elections, while a breakaway faction, unhappy at Magolego's dictatorial management style, established a rival organization called *Sekhukhuni se bonwa ke Sebataladi* (Ngobeni, 2000b).
5   From the Qibla Mass Movement – an anti-apartheid movement inspired by the Islamic revolution in Iran which was basically a pro-Shi'ite fundamentalist force.
6   Unfortunately the targets have not always been criminals and have included opponents of PAGAD, as occurred in the bombing of the house of Ebrahim Moosa, a senior lecturer in Religious Studies at the University of Cape Town and Director of the Centre for Contemporary Islam on 13 July 1998. In 1996 he had been part of the group of prominent clergy that had condemned the violence being used by PAGAD.
7   Five policemen were shot and wounded in a skirmish at the Bellville Magistrate's Court in Cape Town on 17 December 1996.
8   This is a home-made grenade with nails.
9   By April 2001 less than 20 PAGAD members (of which only two were from PAGAD's G-Force) had been successfully convicted and sentenced.
10   Pilot CSFs have currently been set up in a number of areas in the Western Cape. CSFs are a multi-agency approach incorporating representatives from a number of different bodies, *inter alia* the SAPS, local CPF, Justice Department, Correctional Services, Welfare, Education and the local authority or municipality in the area. Each CSF puts together a Community Safety Plan that analyses and prioritizes the safety needs of the community itself (Human Rights Committee, 2001, p. 94).

References

Altenroxel, L. (1998), 'Vigilante "Medicine" cuts Crime', *Pretoria News*, 29 July.
Beaver, T. (1997), 'Victims who Survive are Too Scared to Speak Against the Kangaroo Courts', *Sunday Tribune*, 6 April.
Botha, A. (1998), '*People Against Gangsterism and Drugs (PAGAD)*', Unpublished MA seminar paper, Department of Political Studies, Rand Afrikaans University (RAU), Johannesburg.
Charney, C. (1991), 'Vigilantes, Clientelism and the South African State', *Transformation*, No. 16, pp. 1-28.
Coleman, M. (1998), *A Crime Against Humanity: Analysing the Repression of the Apartheid State*, Human Rights Committee, Braamfontein.
Du Toit, P. and Gagiano, J. (1993), 'Strongmen on the Cape Flats', *Africa Insight*, Vol. 23(2), pp. 101-11.
Editorial (1996), 'The Depth Behind Pagad', *Mail & Guardian*, 20-23 December.

Friedman, R. (1997), 'Govt Blamed for Lack of Action as War Escalates', *Cape Times*, 24 January.

Harris, B. (2001), *'As for Violent Crime, That's our Daily Bread': Vigilante action during South Africa's Period of Transition*, Unpublished report, Centre for the Study of Violence and Reconciliation (CSVR) Violence and Transition Series, Braamfontein.

Human Rights Committee of South Africa (HRC), (2001), *Popular Justice*, HRC Quarterly Review, Braamfontein.

Khupiso, V. (1994), 'Street Justice: Quick, Deadly', *Sunday Times*, 24 April.

Lubisi, D. (1999), 'Vigilantes Include White Farmers and Township Businessmen', *City Press*, 2 May.

Lubisi, D. (2001), 'Mapogo Vigilantes up for Grisly Murders', *Sowetan Sunday World*, 4 March.

Mafata, M. (1998), 'Community Courts Soon to Get the Nod', *Saturday Star*, 30 May.

Masipa, M. (1999), 'Street Committees Returning to Cut Crime', *The Star*, 17 February.

Minnaar, A. (1995a), 'Desperate Justice', *Crime & Conflict*, 2, Indicator SA, Vol. 12(3), Winter, pp. 9-12.

Minnaar, A. (1995b), 'Should People's Courts still be Operating?', Paper presented to the South African Association for Conflict Intervention (SAACI) Conference, *Conflict Resolution and Good Governance*, Rand Afrikaans University, Johannesburg. 30 November-2 December 1995.

Minnaar, A. (1997), 'Witchpurging in the Northern Province of South Africa: a Victim Profile and an Assessment of Initiatives to deal with Witchcraft', Paper presented to the 9th International Symposium on Victimology, *Caring for Victims*, Vrije Universiteit, Amsterdam, The Netherlands, 25-29 August 1997.

Minnaar, A. (1999), 'The New Vigilantism in Post-April 1994 South Africa: Crime prevention or an Expression of Lawlessness?', Paper read at the Criminological Society of South Africa (CRIMSA) International Conference, *Crime Prevention in the New Millennium*, Arendsnes, Cintsa East, East London, South Africa. 25-28 May 1999.

Minnaar, A. and Ngoveni, P. (2000), 'The Eviction of Squatters in South Africa: Post-1994 – Victims and the Role of the Police', Paper presented to the Xth International Symposium on Victimology, *Beyond Boundaries: Research and Action for the Third Millennium*, Montreal, Canada, 6-11 August 2000.

Minnaar, A. and Potgieter, A. (1998), 'Violence in Tsolo and Qumbu (Transkei) (1993-1997)', Institute for Human Rights and Criminal Justice Studies (HRCJS) Occasional Paper No. 3, May 1998/Conflict Series 2/98.

Mostert, W. (1995), 'People's Court Found Guilty', *Pretoria News*, 19 May.

Mtshali, T. (2000), 'Sjambok Brutes to Wield the Whip in eGoli', *Sowetan Sunday World*, 7 May.

Mulaudzi, H. (1998), 'Vigilante Group Members in Hiding after "Week of Terror"', *City Press*, 24 May.

Ngobeni, E. (2000a), 'Vigilante Group Faces Split', *Mail & Guardian*, 5 May.

Ngobeni, E. (2000b), 'Mapogo Goes Mainstream', *Mail & Guardian*, 15 June.

Nina, D. (1993), 'Popular Justice is not Kangaroo Courts', *Weekly Mail*, 6-13 December.

Nina, D. (1996), 'Popular Justice or Vigilantism?', *Crime & Conflict*, Vol. 7, pp. 1-4.

Nina, D. (2000), '*Dirty Harry* is Back: Vigilantism in South Africa – The (Re)emergence of the "Good" and "Bad" Community', *African Security Review*, Vol. 9(1), pp. 18-28.

Nina, D. and Stavrou, S. (1993), 'Research on Perceptions of Justice: Interaction Between State Justice and Popular Justice', Centre for Social and Development Studies (CSDS) Working Paper No. 9, University of Natal, Durban.

Nkosi, P. (2000), 'Claws out for Mapogo', *Sowetan Sunday World*, 5 October.

Rossouw, R. (1996), 'Holy Warriors behind Pagad', *Mail & Guardian*, 16-22 August.

SAPA, (1999), 'Pagad Planning to Attack Police: SAPS', *The Citizen*, 23 January.

Seekings, J. (1992), 'The Revival of "People's Courts": Informal Justice in Transitional South Africa', in Moss, G. and Obery, I. (eds), *South African Review 6: From 'Red Friday' to Codesa*, Ravan Press, Johannesburg, pp. 119-35.

South African Law Commission, (1999), *Community Dispute Resolution Structures*, Discussion Paper No. 87, Pretoria, South African Law Commission.

Tayob, A.I. (1996), 'Islamism & PAGAD: Finding the Connection', in Galant, R. and Gamieldien, F., *Drugs, Gangs, People's Power: Exploring the PAGAD Phenomenon*, Masjid, Cape Town, pp. 30-9.

Van der Merwe, H. and Twigg, A. (1997), 'Mechanisms for Conflict Resolution in South Africa: Institutionalising Conciliatory Community Justice Structures', in Minnaar, A. and Hough, M. (eds), *Conflict, Violence and Conflict Resolution: Where is South Africa Heading?*, Human Sciences Research Council (HSRC), Pretoria.

Vernon, K. and Bowyer, J. (1995), 'Five Thugs and a Shotgun Vigilante', *Sunday Times*, 17 September.

Von Schnitzler, A., Ditlhage, G., Kgalema, L., Maepa, T. and Mofokeng, T. (2001), *Mapogo a Mathamaga – A Case Study*, Violence and Transition Series Report No. 1, Unpublished, Centre for the Study of Violence and Reconciliation (CSVR), Braamfontein.

9 From Informal Justice to Formal Injustice: The Decriminalization of Political Murder in Weimar and Nazi Germany

Arthur D. Brenner

Introduction

Following the murders of Nazi Storm Troop (SA) leader Ernst Röhm, former Nazi party organizer Gregor Strasser, former Chancellor Kurt von Schleicher, and dozens of others in the so-called 'Blood Purge' of June 30-July 1, 1934, the Nazi leadership quickly moved to legitimize its actions. Despite the lack of resistance by the victims, the regime asserted that it had been acting in self-defence to pre-empt what it asserted was a coup plot against Hitler's rule. Immediately after the conclusion of the purge, the cabinet approved the following law: 'The measures taken on 30 June and 1 and 2 July to suppress the acts of high treason are legal, being necessary for the self-defence of the State.'[1] Less than two weeks later, Chancellor Adolf Hitler, speaking about the affair before the Reichstag, declared himself 'Supreme Judge of the German People'. Legal theorists sympathetic to the Nazi cause approved this rationalization. Among them was Carl Schmitt, who wrote in the German Law Journal that the purge was a 'true execution of justice. It was not carried out under the administration of justice, but was itself the highest justice.' Schmitt further spoke of 'the jurisprudence of the Führer'.[2]

The *ex post facto* ratification of the murders of Röhm *et al* was the crowning step in the legalization of Nazi rule by terror. It was also the culmination of a long process by which the assertion of 'defence of the state' came to include the right of private citizens, acting with or without state authority, to commit extrajudicial executions in cases where the victim was deemed by the perpetrators to have committed or likely to commit treason. That is to say, the legitimization of the Third Reich's supra-legal authority rested on precedents established by and in response to the practices of informal justice in the Weimar Republic (1919-1933).

The most numerous and notable of these extrajudicial executions had taken place amid the civil violence that beset Germany in the years 1918 to 1923, but their importance to the subject of this essay goes far beyond their immediate impact. The rhetoric surrounding them, the criminal trials and political conflicts that attended all efforts at resolution, are a major part of what connected the violence of this early period with Nazi concepts of justice. In tracing these developments, I intend to show how discourses of violence and justice influenced the public, the criminal justice system, and the German political environment and were influenced by them in turn. Moreover, I will show how the moral bases of informal justice in the Weimar Republic became the intellectual underpinnings for formal justice in the Nazi era.

Background

The period immediately following the end of World War I was a violent time in Germany. Between its establishment in November 1918 and the end of 1923, the Weimar Republic was beset by conditions tantamount to civil war. While most political centrists only reluctantly embraced the republican system, neither extreme right nor extreme left accepted the legitimacy of the new regime. On the contrary, those on the political extremes 'were opposed in principle to the system of parliamentary democracy and did their best to destroy it'.[3] Both left and right tried and failed several times to overthrow the government and establish a dictatorship, and nearly every attempt set off a violent reaction by the other side. In between these more dramatic spasms of terror, quotidian violence – mostly the handiwork of the extreme right – grew in magnitude. Thousands of people were killed or wounded in street fighting, isolated attacks, lynchings, assassinations, and executions. Strong governmental action might have quelled the violence, but this was unlikely at a time when no party held an outright majority and a kind of parliamentary gridlock – which saw ten different governing coalitions between early 1919 and the end of 1923 – paralleled the instability in the streets.

Accompanying the violence was a cacophony of invective that drew deeply from the friend-or-foe conceptions that had become embedded in the Germany psyche during the long, bitter war. These, in turn, were exacerbated by the looming prospect of a Bolshevik revolution in Germany. In this climate, the right wing of the political spectrum had little patience for concepts like loyal opposition, honest mistakes, or good intentions gone awry. The army leadership blamed the loss of the war on defeatist and profiteering civilians who had 'stabbed [the army] in the back'.[4] The Catholic political leader Matthias Erzberger, one of the civilians who had signed the armistice at Compiègne and reluctantly advocated acceptance of the widely reviled terms of the Versailles Treaty, was subjected to an endless campaign of invective and denunciations that destroyed his political standing and climaxed in his assassination by nationalist assailants in the summer of 1921. Less than a year later, members of a right-wing conspiracy assassinated the German Foreign Minister, Walther Rathenau. He had served his nation with distinction by conceiving and directing the German war materials management agency from 1915 to 1918, but German chauvinists hated him because he was Jewish and because of his pursuit of a policy of fulfilling the reparations obligations imposed as a result of the Peace Treaty of Versailles. The democratic constitution, which had been adopted in August 1919, allowed his haters openly to call for Rathenau's murder in the months before he was ambushed while being driven to work in Berlin. 'Shoot down Walter Rathenau,' sang his opponents, 'the god-damned Jewish sow.'

One product of this situation was the flooding of the judicial system with cases that were fundamentally political in nature, and in this politically charged atmosphere, judicial authorities from police investigators to public prosecutors to judges often permitted their own political sympathies to play a role in their work. This, in turn, fed a left-wing critique of the criminal justice system that pre-dated the Weimar period.

Left-wing protests about the fairness of German justice rested both on the continuity of judges, prosecutors, and other administrative personnel from the German Empire to the Weimar era and on perceived injustices in political cases after 1918. In the Empire, socialists complained of a pervasive class justice that treated proletarians more harshly than others before the law. Bismarck and his successors kept the judiciary in conservative hands, so when the Republic allowed imperial civil servants to remain in their posts after the revolution, the new regime was saddled with judges and prosecutors who were antipathetic to democratic, parliamentary government *per se* and who accepted neither the legitimacy of a regime created by socialist revolution nor the laws it produced.[5] In the words of the head of the German association of judges, the Weimar regime was governed by 'partisan, class and bastard law'.[6]

From the earliest stages of the republic, anecdotal evidence convinced socialists and republicans that the old judges and prosecutors carried slanted justice with them into the new era. The few, mild sentences passed for the murders of the communist leaders Karl Liebknecht and Rosa Luxemburg in 1919 first aroused the indignation of the left (even though military rather than civilian justice was responsible for the botched investigation and verdicts),[7] and as whitewashes of right-wing criminality became a pattern, the anger of left-wing intellectuals, party members and leaders rose. Justice was miscarried in a variety of ways. Professional jurists and lay judges (who were chosen almost exclusively from the 'better', and therefore conservative, classes) acted 'with some consistency as the benevolent protectors of the so-called patriotic forces of society'.[8] Rightist criminals who claimed to have acted from patriotic motives were granted leniency; in murder cases their avowals that the victims were 'shot while trying to flee', 'killed in an accident', or 'condemned by military law' almost invariably resulted in acquittal – if they were tried at all. Prosecutors and police delayed investigations, lost files, and suppressed evidence in order to ensure that crimes against leftists or the republic itself went unpunished.[9] Meanwhile, proletarian defendants, whose motives the criminal justice system deemed either selfish or internationalist, but in no way patriotic, were more often prosecuted and sentenced to the full extent of the law. Commenting on these trends in 1922, the German human rights activist E. J. Gumbel, the most penetrating analyst of political violence and politicized justice of the day, lamented that the failure of the German criminal justice system to try, convict or penalize hundreds of cases of political murder was 'proof of the complete breakdown of justice, or better, for the positive approval that political murder enjoys in Germany today'.[10]

There was little public outcry against the normalization of the concept of 'patriotic murder', except voices like Gumbel's, which originated from socialist, pacifist, and human rights organizations. There was too little support in the Reichstag and the state parliaments for thorough and critical investigations, and not enough pressure from the public to make elected officials address the problems. Gustav Radbruch, a legal scholar who served three brief terms as Reich Minister of Justice in the early 1920s, pushed for inquests into the alleged politicization of justice in the cases of political murder documented by Gumbel. However, Radbruch was not only frustrated by the instability of the parliamentary coalitions, which repeatedly took him out of the ministry and therefore a position to pursue the issue, but was also stymied by dilatory and ultimately unrevealing replies to his queries by the justice ministries of the German states in whose jurisdictions most such cases had taken place.[11]

German Paramilitarism and the Roots of Informal Justice

Most of the 'patriotic murders' committed in Germany in the period under discussion were carried out by members of Germany's numerous paramilitary organizations. These units formed just after the end of the war at the behest of the central government, state authorities, private businesses and landowners. The shock of sudden defeat after the arduous and bitter war, combined with the collapse of the old regime, led to the disintegration of the German armed forces in November 1918. Yet that same armistice authorized the German military to continue fighting in the Baltic region, whereby, in effect, German forces acted as the military instrument of the victorious powers in their attempt to contain the Soviet Union. However, the new German government was itself poorly positioned to provide these soldiers, because its own army, the Reichswehr, was in an embryonic state. Moreover, the government, along with moderate and conservative opinion, were deeply afraid that a defeated and dismembered Germany, home to the world's largest and most politically powerful working class, would, like Russia, succumb to a communist revolution. In order to fight the border war and to protect itself against political threats at home, the government subcontracted the provision of state security to a wide variety of voluntary public, private, and mixed public-private paramilitary organizations, most notably the Free Corps. These were mobile, heavily armed units composed mainly of demobilized younger officers, NCOs, and enlisted men who were unable or unwilling to return to civilian life, and they were the bulwark of state defence of Germany's eastern borders and of its suppression of left-wing insurrection. In emergencies they were aided by auxiliary volunteer forces (*Zeitfreiwilligenverbände*), which were reserve troops formed and trained by government forces in Berlin. Throughout Germany, too, the Free Corps and auxiliary units were complemented by civil guards (*Einwohnerwehren*), locally recruited, armed organizations created with government consent by conservative interests to protect private property and maintain municipal order against the spectre of proletarian depredations. In ruthlessly fighting off the Soviets in the Baltic region and suppressing the left in 1919, these paramilitary forces 'evolved into independent power factors' bound only tenuously by the command of the provisional Reichswehr.[12]

The seriousness this problem posed to the regime was compounded by the fact that the paramilitary bands were violently opposed to the parliamentary republic as a form of government, and to the particular foreign policy conducted by the Berlin government. The leaders and members of the paramilitary organizations longed for the neater, superficially more harmonious, and recent authoritarian past. Not only were they instinctively distrustful of democracy, but they were particularly angered by the fact that this democracy had been established on the rubble of the Hohenzollern dynasty. They blamed socialists, pacifists, and Jews for having betrayed the wartime army while it was still effective in the field and for imposing an unwelcome, 'un-German' political system on the nation.

This militantly anti-republican and nationalistic spirit was given further impetus when the Weimar government accepted the terms of the Versailles Peace Treaty in the spring of 1919. Few Germans found any redeeming features in the document: it removed substantial territories from German control, blamed the entire war on Germany and compelled it to pay enormous reparations, excluded Germany from the new League of Nations, and plundered Germany's colonial empire. The treaty also limited Germany to an army of 100,000 men, with no armour and no aircraft and bearing only defensive weapons, while simultaneously decreeing the dissolution of the general staff, the war academy, and cadet schools. The treaty's military provisions struck the paramilitaries like a thunderbolt: of the roughly half million men still at arms in mid-1919, fewer than 20 per cent could expect to be incorporated in the truncated army. This was a devastating prospect for thousands of men for whom a career as an officer was the highest ambition. For the mostly young soldiers who formed the cadres, a return to civilian life seemed out of the question. In the latter stages of the Great War, when the German military was desperate for able-bodied men, they were drafted directly from school and sent to the front at age 16 or 17 and knew nothing about work, only the camaraderie of the corps and the excitement of battle. Moreover, the men at arms were furious with the abject response of the government to the treaty terms, which they regarded contemptuously as a dictated peace. Behind the soldiers stood an array of conservative and nationalistic interests that were spooked by the spectre of Bolshevism. Thus the paramilitary forces scorned the very state that engaged and sanctioned their services, and they were supported morally and materially by a vast right-wing movement that was determined to keep the so-called 'national' forces armed and ready. Collectively, this movement intended to rearm Germany, to suppress communism within Germany and at its borders, and forcefully to revise the Versailles Peace Treaty.

During the first half of 1919, these forces carried out the first two elements of this mission successfully and brutally. Disarmament was delayed while several hundred thousand paramilitary troops stemmed the westward surge by the Red Army and stamped out the domestic rebellions throughout Germany. Given carte blanche by Defence Minister Gustav Noske, the irregulars used overwhelming force to subdue armed opposition and frequently carried out murderous reprisals. Between the consent of the Weimar government and the leeway given by the criminal justice system, the right-wing forces concluded that they could act with impunity if they could plausibly claim that they were acting to defend the national interest.

This comfortable arrangement continued as long as the Entente powers averted their gaze from the proliferation of armed units throughout Germany, and that lasted only as long as doing so suited the aims of the victors. The success of German forces in the Baltic region and in securing the republic against the domestic threat from the left seemed to portend the end of their existence, as the Entente began in June 1919 to demand that the German government meet the force limits established by the Versailles treaty. Most of the soldiers and their officers grumbled but complied with orders and returned to civilian life, but a minority went underground into a flourishing panoply of secret armed units. A few of the larger Free Corps resisted dissolution, first by non-compliance and finally, in March 1920, by attempting a coup (the Kapp Putsch) in order to install a dictatorial government that would resist foreign pressure, abrogate the treaty, and restore the German army to greatness. A general strike by workers in Berlin and elsewhere forced the collapse of the coup but, paradoxically, also ensured that the paramilitary organizations would live on in some form. The successful general strike re-awakened communist hopes for revolution and touched off an insurrection in the industrial Ruhr region. To meet the threat, the government called on the head of the revived but truncated Reichswehr – who just days before had declined to order his rump forces to squash the right-wing coup – to lead Germany's armed forces to put down the left-wing rebellion, and he in turn engaged the temporary assistance of some of the same Free Corps units that had been the backbone of the Kapp Putsch.[13] The lesson was clear: in certain circumstances, the state wanted and needed the paramilitary forces to continue to exist. The difficulty was that this could no longer take place with the degree of openness that had marked state-paramilitary relations since the beginning of 1919, because of the likelihood that the Entente powers, particularly the French, would take a harder line on implementing other provisions of the treaty and possibly even invade Germany in order to enforce it. The solution to this dilemma was equally transparent: the paramilitary forces would have to continue to exist, but in forms that were sufficiently altered to make their functions – to act as military reserve forces and to stash illegal weapons – and their relations to the state, opaque.

Although they ostensibly disarmed and disbanded to comply with government orders, the remaining paramilitary organizations recast themselves as labour associations, security firms, sporting societies, or other fictitious entities whose real purpose was to keep units together, ready for the next battle for the borders or for control of the German state. In this semi-clandestine existence they sustained military command structures and arms caches and conducted exercises while the central and regional governments looked the other way. Many officials – particularly in the Reichswehr – sympathized with the organizations' goals, felt their existence offered a greater measure of security, or were simply afraid to enforce orders for these groups to disband, thereby enabling the secret military organizations to continue their shadowy existence throughout the early 1920s.

The Practice of Informal Justice

It was in this climate that informal justice became the norm within Germany's illegal paramilitary formations. Their members were not imbued with the professionalism that had characterized the pre-war armies of Prussia and the other states of the old German Empire. A substantial proportion of the ranks were composed of young men who had been socialized by the crudity and brutality of the German side in the last two years of World War I. Often they were poorly paid, which created motives for petty thievery, black marketeering, and the like. Deprived of the action they craved during periods of relative calm, they drank and quarrelled among themselves.[14] Since the illegal organizations were not part of the army, and since they could not risk blowing their cover by taking disciplinary issues to military courts or the criminal justice system, they imposed discipline internally, and it was based on brutality, not on a military code of conduct and punishment. Some units had their own *Rollkommando*, which one government official in 1926 described as follows: 'The "Rollkommandos" were groups of specially trusted members of formations, who were set up partly as penal commandos against members of their own formation, and partly as fighting commandos for special tasks against oppositionally-thinking elements.'[15] For internal purposes, they typically punished even minor offences, such as complaints about conditions or command, petty theft, and dereliction of duty, with severe beatings.

This particular form of informal justice was merely part of a larger phenomenon, however. In various parts of Germany there existed autonomous paramilitary organizations of dubious legality whose existence was nevertheless tacitly condoned by the state. Furthermore, there persisted a climate of violence that was reinforced by the leniency granted by the criminal justice system to rightwing political criminality. And finally, they remained largely hidden because foreign threats, in the form of an Allied military control commission, made publicity about these enterprises a danger to state security and the national interest, as this was defined by many participants, supporters, and observers. The paramilitary organizations lived in constant fear that someone would betray their existence, their secrets, or their illegal activities – in particular, their secreting of mountains of weapons in violation of Germany's international agreements. If any of this was made public, the Entente powers and their military inspectors could find out and compel the dissolution of a paramilitary band and seize illegal weapons, since the German government could not openly tolerate the existence of an illegal organization. Therefore, from their earliest days the paramilitary bands included in their regulations an oath of loyalty to the organization that concluded with the sentence 'Traitors will fall to the *Feme!*' (*Verräter verfallen der Feme*). This was a euphemism for murder.[16]

The term *Feme* or *Femgerichte* (sometimes rendered in English as Vehmic courts) originally referred to a kind of informal, frontier justice practised in medieval Germany. These vigilante courts, which were especially numerous in Westphalia, 'tried and executed common criminals in areas where an ordered judicial system was lacking'.[17] Princes extracted fees as the price for legitimizing *Feme* verdicts passed in their territories. The modern version used by the Weimar paramilitary organizations was actually closer in form to military field justice, except that the military units involved were illegal and therefore their proceedings lacked legitimacy. A group or organization usually initiated this kind of murder (commonly referred to as *Fememord*) when it determined that a renegade or suspect member, or sometimes a civilian non-member, had to be eliminated because of the danger this person posed to the illegal enterprises the secret society had undertaken.

Like the shadowy paramilitary organizations themselves, the murders took place in a murky netherworld between legitimate 'justice' and renegade police action. The perpetrators themselves had no public occasion to speak about the escapades until long after these had taken place, and when they did, the leading figure among them insisted that they had not been acting as 'judges'.[18] Both critics and defenders, though, sometimes spoke of them as *Femerichter* ('Feme judges') or their activities as '*Feme* courts',[19] and one of the leading defence attorneys for the perpetrators termed their actions 'self-justice'.[20] This same advocate consistently referred to their actions as 'killings of traitors', which implied that they were acting to execute justice, a sense reinforced by the fact that in no case was such a murder carried out against someone caught in an act of putative 'treason'. That is, there was no case in which detention of the suspected informer, rather than his execution, would have provided greater security to the state. Moreover, the paramilitary organizations responsible for these acts did not hand over the accused for prosecution by the regular criminal justice system. They acted not only as police, but also as judges and executioners of justice.

There were, essentially, four main episodes of organized *Fememord* in the Weimar period.[21] The first arose in Bavaria in 1920-21, when members of the Bavarian Civil Guard, a private militia established with the consent of the Bavarian government, were deeply engaged in a variety of arms smuggling proscribed by the Versailles Treaty. They played a sort of cat-and-mouse game with Allied military inspectors and weapons caches, and the region, beset by economic hardship, was a haven for gun runners and informants eager to sell their knowledge of such activity to the highest bidder, German (to keep silent) or foreign (to betray such caches). To protect the arms it was busily acquiring and secreting, the Business Affairs Division of the Einwohnerwehr initiated the murder of four individuals (and the possible attempted murder of another) suspected of providing information about weapons depots to British or Belgian arms-control agents. Among the dead was the only woman killed by a *Feme*, Marie Sandmayr, who was kidnapped and murdered in the night of October 5-6, 1920. Her body was found the following morning in a park in Munich, tagged with a note reading, 'You slut, you have betrayed your fatherland, the Black Hand murdered you'.[22] The complicity of the Munich police and the Bavarian government ensured that no one was ever brought to justice for these crimes.

Similar episodes occurred at about the same time in the eastern German state of Mecklenburg, where wealthy landowners provided a haven for various paramilitary associations which, in turn, protected the border against Polish insurgents and who helped ensure the docility of the labour force that served the estates. Three *Feme* murders took place in this area. A further, and more complex, set of cases, arose in 1920-21 in Upper Silesia in the period leading up to the plebiscite mandated by the Versailles Treaty to determine whether the territory would be retained by Germany or be ceded to Poland. It is known that 'patriotic' paramilitary organizations, which sought to defend German interests in an area that was off-limits to regular German armed forces, carried out a small number of *Feme* verdicts. Less clear is the veracity of claims by one German paramilitary leader who served in the area that his men murdered some 200 putative 'traitors', either Germans who they deemed sympathetic to the Polish cause, or Poles who they thought were undermining German interests in the region. A German-Polish agreement reached in 1921, after the plebiscite divided the territory, amnestied all crimes committed by partisans of either side during the struggle, thereby ensuring that the misdeeds of the German clandestine organizations would remain secret.[23]

The best documented incidence of informal justice in Weimar Germany were the eight *Feme* murders and several additional assaults committed in 1923 by a death squad working within Germany's so-called Black Reichswehr. Their importance for this study lies in the fact that the de facto decriminalization of political murder in Germany was a product of political decisions made specifically to clear these murders.[24]

The *Feme* Murders of the Black Reichswehr

The *Schwarze Reichswehr* (SR, or Black Reichswehr) was an informal designation for the collection of labour troops (*Arbeitskommandos*, or AKs) initially formed by the regular army in 1921. Their function was to collect, sort, and decommission or destroy weapons that exceeded the Versailles Treaty limits. AKs were usually commanded by former Reichswehr officers, and the ranks were composed mostly of veterans of other paramilitary enterprises of the post-war period, such as the Free Corps. They were housed in army barracks at active Reichswehr bases and wore regular army uniforms; they also received training in the use of weapons, participated in military exercises, and in some cases performed guard duty at various locales near Berlin and in eastern Germany. Most tellingly, they were issued regular Reichswehr identification that included a system of ranks that corresponded exactly to that of the regular troops.[25] They also stockpiled the useful weapons they collected and turned over to Allied military officials mostly material that was worthless anyway. Their formation served the Reichswehr's interest in co-opting Germany's dangerous paramilitary forces – especially the former Free Corps – and turning them into disciplined auxiliaries of the armed forces. In short, the AKs were a shadow force being trained to supplement the army in case of an emergency.

That emergency arose with the French occupation of the Ruhr in January 1923, and the passive resistance, hyperinflation, and political turmoil that followed. The far right, long frustrated with the Weimar regime's compliance with the Versailles Treaty, demanded that passive resistance be turned into bold action to redeem the honour and independence of Germany. The ultra-conservative and ultra-nationalist camps also asserted that the weakened state was vulnerable to other presumed enemies, namely the Poles and the proletariat. The Reichswehr shared this sense of danger, but the Treaty's limits on the army's manpower and weaponry prevented it from openly increasing its forces, so it allowed the SR to grow rapidly to a force that was later estimated to number between 50-80,000 men, most stationed in Germany's eastern territories (Prussia, Pomerania, and Mecklenburg-Schwerin).[26] The Reichswehr also wanted to be sure that these forces could be properly armed, if the need arose, so the scope of the arms stashing that the AKs undertook also grew dramatically.

This rapid enlargement of the SR compounded the disciplinary problems inherent in this entirely illicit enterprise. In addition to the usual problems of drunkenness, insubordination, and dereliction of duty, which were handled by *Rollkommandos* formed at each garrison or base, the SR faced special risks of betrayal. As far as the SR was concerned, the stockpiling and concealment of arms were vital to the national interest, which would be seriously endangered if knowledge of these activities was made public or otherwise transmitted to Allied arms inspectors. Since the AKs were officially civilians, they could not be subject to the military penal code; and because secrecy was so urgent, treason (as the SR defined it) could not be reported to the formal criminal justice system, lest the illicit military activity be revealed to presumed enemies.[27] The SR had to carry out its own, informal justice.

Paul Schulz, who was responsible for managing the SR acquisition, transport, and secreting of illegal weapons, therefore applied to such cases the disciplinary method that had become the norm among Germany's right-wing paramilitary forces after the war: *Feme* murder. There was a pattern to these death squad murders. The victim aroused suspicion or anger by remarks complaining of poor treatment or low pay, or by stealing and selling SR weapons on the black market. When word of such a 'traitor' made its way to Schulz, he would send out his minions: three to five of his most trusted subordinates would simultaneously converge at or near the base to which the prospective victim was assigned, take the man at night to an isolated location, shoot him, and dispose of the body by burial or by dropping it, leaden with weights, into a nearby body of water. The disappearance was usually explained as the result of the victim's desertion or his fatal encounter with communists during a failed arms transaction that had turned violent, but was in fact the product of an informal justice implemented in the interstices between military and civilian courts.[28]

For two years after the crimes, government and criminal justice officials declined to investigate and prosecute the Schulz death squad. The army was not eager to see its secret activities dragged into the open, and the central government, which was locked in delicate negotiations with France to gain modifications to the Versailles treaty, wanted nothing revealed that could upset the talks on reparations and security issues. The Prussian state government, which had jurisdiction for most of the SR cases, went along with the national government on this issue.

This conspiracy of silence was pierced by the aggressive assaults of pacifist journalists, who throughout the mid-1920s published dozens of reports about the continued existence of the SR. The revelations were a huge embarrassment for the German government and army, which repeatedly denied that the German armed forces exceeded the 100,000-man limit mandated by the treaty. The disclosures threatened to upset the Franco-German negotiations by damaging or destroying the credibility of the German side. At the same time, human rights activists – often the same writers and journals that published the revelations about the SR – were engaged in a campaign against the class justice they believed was being practised in Germany.[29] By 1925 these dual campaigns, and the facts they uncovered, converged to create pressure on the criminal justice system to prosecute the *Feme* murders.

The product of this confluence of factors was a series of sensational trials and, partly coterminously, investigations of the *Feme* murders by subcommittees of the Reichstag and the Prussian state parliament.[30] The daily press reported extensively on the proceedings, and the cases were analysed in pacifist and left-wing periodicals that also uncovered new information about the *Feme* murders.[31] The hearings and revelations provoked an uproar, and so did several related developments. Among these were the exclusion of the public from some trials because the courts – often at the urging of the Reichswehr – were concerned that state secrets might be made public. Germans were also bewildered by the testimony and counter-testimony of various high-ranking army officers (retired or active), who were called upon to explain the circumstances surrounding the murders or to elaborate on the atmosphere of paranoia that had prevailed in military circles when the SR death squad was active.

In these proceedings, the perpetrators, their attorneys, and friendly witnesses argued that Schulz and his operatives not only had regarded themselves as regular soldiers, but had believed that in committing murder they were acting on implicit government orders to take care of the business of building up clandestine units and stockpiling illegal weapons using all necessary means in a time of dire national emergency. According to many sources, including Hans von Seeckt, who had been chief of the army at the time of the events in question, the men of the SR also believed that since the government had tolerated *Feme* murder by the Free Corps in Upper Silesia in 1921, it surely wanted the same defence of its interests in the crisis of 1923.[32] As to the question of whether government or army officials ever ordered a murder, Schulz himself was inexact: among higher-ranking officers, he stated, 'responsibility was always denied if anything came of a treasonous act. Everything was loaded onto the poor chaps below. We stood under colossal pressure. That which you call *Feme* murder was known and left uninvestigated by officials for two years' time.'[33] As Schulz acknowledged, his unit had devolved far enough from official sources of power and command that his actions could reasonably be viewed as the autonomous efforts of an overzealous former officer.

The German state was all too happy to promote this interpretation of the events in question. Government and Reichswehr officials continually denied that illegal units had been allowed to exist with the knowledge of the state. Their whipping boy was SR head Major Bruno Buchrucker, Schulz's immediate boss, who in September 1923 was arrested to forestall a coup (the Küstrin Putsch) he was planning to mount using AKs and regular units. Buchrucker's arrest, together with the fact that in 1923 several AKs had been dissolved once their existence had been made public,[34] permitted the army to claim that any *illegal* forces were promptly shut down when they were found out. As far as the Reichswehr was concerned, this 'proved' that Schulz, in executing informal justice, had been acting on his own initiative.

In courts of law, these arguments held sway. The state attorneys were reluctant to challenge the testimony of respected, high-ranking Reichswehr officers and the official denials they presented, and they often avoided pursuing lines of questioning that would have led to examinations of the links between the Schulz death squad and the Reichswehr. Judges, too, whose collective ethos was notoriously anti-republican and deferential to the military, frequently agreed to avoid sensitive questioning. Moreover, the courts, while often acknowledging that the accused had been acting from patriotic motives, rejected defence assertions that the extralegal actions of the SR death squad were justified by the state of emergency that had existed at the time of the events in question. By early 1928, Schulz and several dozen co-defendants in a handful of cases had been unable to prove that they had been acting on orders from higher authorities and were convicted of ordering, planning, and executing a handful of *Feme* verdicts. Several more trials had yet to begin.

The Amnesty Campaign

At this juncture, political developments began to overtake the ongoing legal ones. Shortly after the Schulz conviction, the Reichstag passed an amnesty law which freed many individuals who had been convicted of committing violent political crimes in the tumultuous early 1920s. The whole discussion of amnesties in the interest of drawing a line against the past, which had the strong endorsement of the Communist Party as well as parties of the right – all of whom wanted to see *their* political prisoners liberated – motivated the formation of a publicity campaign for the liberation of the convicted *Feme* murderers. It was supported largely by the Nationalist and Nazi Parties and the Stahlhelm, a nationalistic veterans' organization. The front man for this movement was Friedrich Grimm, one of the lead defence attorneys for the Schulz death squad members.

Grimm's central argument was the same one that he and other attorneys had used without success in court: the state of emergency that had existed in 1923 justified the SR death squad in its execution of informal justice against putative traitors. These men, insisted proponents of amnesty, were not criminals but the victims of a tumultuous revolutionary era. In a long report he wrote in January 1930 at the behest of the 'Committee for the Promotion of the Amnesty Efforts',

Grimm referred repeatedly to the 'problem of the extraordinary' circumstances facing the Black Reichswehr in 1923. To support his contention that judgment of these unusual conditions demanded the application of a 'higher justice' rather than written law, he cited the words of a Berlin court in a 1929 hearing about Paul Schulz: 'The real difficulty lies in the fact that the court is compelled to assess events of the past with the standard of legal requirements that is appropriate for normal times.'[35] In other cases of politically motivated murder dating from the period 1919-24, such as the Kapp Putsch of 1920, judicial authorities had used their discretion to effectuate de facto amnesties, and in some *Feme* trials the courts had explicitly proclaimed that the defendants had been acting in good faith and from patriotic and altruistic (as opposed to selfish/economic) motives. So, for example, in a 1927 *Feme* trial, the court declared that the murder had been committed 'because [the defendants] had believed, in the confused times of the Ruhr occupation and the inflation, that they were carrying through a good thing out of patriotic interests with the – at least tacit – understanding of the Reichswehr'.[36] If the courts could not draw the logical conclusion and acquit these men, the pro-amnesty camp asserted, then it was the duty of the sovereign power of the state to recognize why Schulz and his cohorts had committed these acts and to exculpate them.

Further impetus for the amnesty campaign came as a result of the negotiations in 1929 to implement the Young Plan, which included an agreement for the early evacuation of the Rhineland. Leading up to and during the negotiations, the Reichswehr and Foreign Office argued within the government that national authorities should do everything in their power to persuade Prussia—the jurisdiction for most of the remaining *Feme* cases – to suspend its prosecutions, lest the German negotiations with France be upset by a revelation that the Reichswehr had, in fact, lied about its past.[37] This was no idle worry: attorneys for some of the remaining defendants made it clear that their clients would implicate the Reichswehr in their illegal activities, and some government officials therefore considered it 'urgently' necessary to pass the amnesty.[38] Grimm and other attorneys thus utilized their legal options to increase political pressure on the government to let their clients off the hook. These arguments won growing political support among some otherwise hesitant deputies in the Reichstag, which in mid-1928 had rejected a bill that would have resulted in freedom for the *Feme* murderers.

The conclusion of the Franco-Belgian-German negotiations further motivated the advocates of amnesty for Schulz and others. The agreement included a provision that all three governments would amnesty all politically motivated crimes that were connected with the occupation and that had taken place in occupied territory, except crimes that had resulted in death. Accordingly, German prosecutors were barred from prosecuting for treason anyone who had collaborated with occupation authorities or separatist efforts. The contrast with the treatment of the *Feme* murderers galled their supporters: from their perspective, traitors would walk free, while real German patriots would continue to languish in prison or face further prosecution.

For most of the period from 1928-30, resistance by the Social Democratic and Centre parties prevented the passage of an amnesty bill into law. The latter was morally opposed to the exculpation of homicide, although its growing conservative wing sympathized with the patriotic arguments made by Schulz's supporters. The Social Democrats, who in 1925-26 had helped initiate Reichstag and Prussian state parliamentary investigations of the death squad murders, wanted to see a full exposition of the background to the *Feme* murders and therefore would not agree to an amnesty, even if it was crafted to include some leftist political prisoners whose release the socialists also sought. Social Democratic opposition was critical: not only was it the largest party in the Reichstag but it also controlled the Prussian government and therefore supervised prosecutors in the jurisdictions in which most of the remaining death squad cases stood to be tried. Indeed, one measure of how deeply this frustrated the supporters of Schulz and his cohorts was the splenetic rhetoric the right used in discourse about these matters. The right saw the continuation of *Feme* trials as part of a leftist campaign against the right, regarded these trials as a political abuse of the law, and accused the Social Democratic government of Prussia of prosecuting the heroes of the Black Reichswehr out of revenge for a corruption trial that had embarrassed the Social Democratic Party. The pro-amnesty forces also attacked publications about the *Feme* murders by journalists and pacifists as 'cruelty propaganda' (*Greuelpropaganda*), and asserted that 'the *Feme* agitation of the left was the greatest of all political lies and an unconscionable incitement of the German people'.[39]

The shifting political climate of 1929-30 helped weaken opposition to an amnesty. In the first half of 1930, a period marked by the first steps toward the abandonment of parliamentary rule, by Reichstag passage of the Young Plan, and by the French evacuation of the Rhineland, leading members of the Centre, Democratic and People's parties began for the first time openly to support an amnesty bill, which heretofore had been the province of more rightist parties.[40] In the words of Friedrich Grimm, the day of the 'liberation' of the Rhineland could not be celebrated with 'unmixed joy' unless 'the last remainder of the occupation', that is, the convictions of and pending charges against the *Feme* murderers, was put completely in the past.[41] In June that year the proposed amnesty law passed the Reichstag by a vote of 291 to 135, with the Social Democrats opposed. The party regarded this as a matter of prestige for the Prussian government, which was just then conducting its trial of one accused *Feme* murderer who had asserted that he could show that there had been direct contacts in 1923 between the legal Reichswehr and the SR. The Social Democrats believed that the opportunity was finally at hand to shed light on these murky affairs. In the German Federal Council (*Reichsrat*), where each state government controlled a number of votes roughly proportional to its population,[42] the Social Democratic view prevailed. The party argued that an amnesty for these politically motivated murderers would only worsen the mounting political crisis and exacerbate a rising tide of political violence. Moreover, this argument actually established an effective roadblock to the amnesty campaign, for it persuaded the Centre, Democratic and Bavarian People's parties to abstain in the Reichstag, leaving the bill six votes short of the two-thirds majority needed to override the Reichsrat's negative vote. A few days later, Chancellor Brüning dissolved the Reichstag, leaving the German right in a state of shock and disappointment that, despite a clear majority in favour of it, no amnesty bill could be passed into law.

Following the Reichstag elections of September 1930, in which the Nazis scored significant gains, the outcome of the amnesty campaign could no longer be in doubt. Within days of the inauguration of the new Reichstag, the plenary passed without debate a new bill that was identical to the one that had failed in July. The Federal Council also approved the law and it went into effect on October 24, 1930. The chief beneficiaries of the law were 23 men who had been convicted of their involvement in the informal justice carried out by the Schulz death squad, along with several dozen others who were serving time for capital crimes committed in 1920-21. Two others, including Germany's most prominent communist prisoner, were also released.

In practical terms, the outcome of the amnesty was unspectacular. Many of the men freed had already had their sentences reduced under earlier amnesties. Some, like Schulz, were out of prison, awaiting the adjudication of their appeals, and those whose cases were still pending would have benefited anyway from the long time that had passed since the commission of their crimes, which had made the successful prosecution of their cases unlikely, at best. Its political impact, though, was more significant, for this implicit acceptance of informal justice only encouraged extremist parties, which already regarded violence as an acceptable tool of political life.

Conclusion

The more important consequence of the amnesty law of 1930, though, was the profound impact it had on the decay of legal norms in Germany. It provided a political solution to a dispute that had been festering through much of the Weimar era and had become acute during the second half of the 1920s, the period when the *Feme* trials were taking place. Walter Luetgebrüne, a leading defence attorney on behalf of right-wing clients in the period, commented, in a 1929 essay in the Nazi organ *Völkischer Beobachter*, that 'when the jury court in Berlin [in a *Feme* trial] holds that the concept of emergency would not apply, that self-defence can be committed only on behalf of individuals but not of such valuable goods as the system of defence of the country, then this is rather peculiar. When the Black Reichswehr − a secretly built defence system . . . built up secretly by the state − was threatened by treason, then this attack on the state is an attack on the state as a person in law.'[43] Yet at about the same time, a court in Schwerin, ruling in another *Feme* trial, recognized 'defence of the state' as exculpatory. This 'monstrous' notion, lamented the Frankfurt law professor Hugo Sinzheimer, 'legalises political murder'.[44] While the judicial system had not yet reached a conclusion on the matter, virtually the entire German political spectrum accepted the rightist argument that an instance of 'national emergency' or 'defence of the state' justified extralegal behaviour by private citizens, as well as agents of the state, who had acted on their own initiative.

This was a harbinger of what was to come during the Third Reich, when the law was thoroughly subordinated to political, racial, and ideological interests. The bench, the bar, the state attorney's offices, and the university law faculties were purged of Jews and those whose opinions and conduct did not accord with the principles determined by the Nazi party. Legal scholars, fully two-thirds of whom by 1939 had been appointed after Hitler's accession to power, outdid one another in their attempts to provide theoretical justifications for their attempts to place the state on an equal, if not higher, plane of authority than the law itself. One Nazi decree stripped the judiciary of its independence when it stated that any public official was subject to dismissal if he failed 'to act at all times and without reservation in the interests of the national state'.[45] Moreover, a core principle of constitutional law, *nulla poena sine lex* ('no penalty without law'), was completely violated in all its forms. For example, a plethora of new statutes included provisions for retroactive punishment for acts that had not been violations at the time they had taken place,[46] and the Gestapo's practice of taking suspects and others into 'protective detention' without approval by any court of law transgressed the concept that only the judiciary had the right to impose punishments.[47] Finally, during the 1930s the Third Reich established and expanded the jurisdiction of the 'People's Court', an institution that had all the trappings of the regular legal system but judged political cases by political criteria.[48] Under the Nazis, 'defence of the state' became the supreme value guiding the law.

In one way or another, nearly all of these measures rested on the one law that had the most direct connection to the notion, posited by the defenders of the *Feme* murderers and sanctioned by the amnesty bill of 1933, that a state of emergency justified the supersession of existing law. The Decree of the Reich President for the Protection of the People and State was issued on 28 February 1933 in response to the fire that destroyed the Reichstag building. The act granted the central government virtually unlimited power over the individual by suspending most personal and civil liberties, and compelled the compliance of the German state governments, not all of which had yet come under Nazi control, in applying the new rules. Although the preamble of the decree asserted that its purpose was 'as a defensive measure against Communist acts of violence endangering the state',[49] it remained on the books long after the destruction of the communists. Indeed, the law only ceased to exist when the Allied military government cancelled it in May 1945. Thus the National Socialists made permanent the 'state of emergency' that justified extralegal actions for the sake of the 'defence of the state'. This, in turn, provided the backdrop not only for the Röhm purge of 1934, but for the entire system of persecution and terror visited on Jews, Gypsies, homosexuals, and a long list of others whom the Nazis defined as 'enemies of the people' between 1933-1945.

Notes

1   *Reichsgesetzblatt* 1 (1934), p. 529; this translation from Noakes, J. and Pridham, G. (eds) (1990), *Nazism 1919-1945*, Shocken Books, New York, Vol. I, p. 182.

2   Schmitt, C., 'Der Führer schützt das Recht', *Deutsche Juristen-Zeitung* Band 39, Heft 15, 1 August 1934, p. 947. See also the discussion in Stolleis, M. (1998), *The Law under the Swastika. Studies on Legal History in Nazi Germany*, trans. Thomas Dunlap, University of Chicago Press, Chicago, pp. 94, 97.

3   Kolb, E., *The Weimar Republic*, trans. Falla, P. S. (1988), Unwin Hyman, London, p. 34.

4   Paul von Hindenburg, testimony given on November 18, 1919, in Stenographischer Bericht über die öffentlichen Verhandlungen des 15. Untersuchungsausschusses der verfassungsgebenden Nationalversammlung, Berlin, 1920, Vol. 2, p. 701, quoted in Kaes, A., Jay, M. and Dimendberg, E. (eds) (1994), *The Weimar Republic Sourcebook*, University of California Press, Berkeley, p. 16.

5   The best example from Imperial Germany is Kuttner, E. (1913), *Klassenjustiz*, P. Singer, Berlin. For historical analysis, see Wehler, H-U. (1991), *The German Empire 1871-1918*, trans. Traynor, K., Berg, New York, pp. 127-9; Stern, H. N., 'Political Crime and Justice in the Weimar Republic', Ph.D. diss., Johns Hopkins University, 1966, pp. 11-12; Petersen, K. (1988), *Literatur und Justiz in der Weimarer Republik*, Metzler, Stuttgart, pp. 37-45; Kuhn, R. (1983), *Die Vertrauenskrise der Justiz (1926-1928). Der Kampf um die "Republikanisierung" der Rechtspflege in der Weimarer Republik*, Bundesanzeiger, Cologne, pp. 15-18; Hannover, H. and Hannover-Drück, E. (1987), *Politische Justiz 1918-1933*, Second edn., Lamuv, Bornheim-Merten, pp. 21-5; Kirchheimer, O. (1961), *Political Justice. The Use of Legal Procedure for Political Ends*, Princeton University Press, Princeton, pp. 211-14; Müller, I. (1991), *Hitler's Justice. The Courts of the Third Reich*, trans. Lucas Schneider, D., Harvard University Press, Cambridge, pp. 10*ff.*; Schulz, B. (1982), *Der Republikanische Richterbund (1921-1933)*, Peter Lang, Frankfurt, p. 17; Koch, H. W. (1989), *In the Name of the Volk. Political Justice in Hitler's Germany*, St. Martin's Press, New York, pp. 7-14.

6   Johannes L., Chairman of the *Deutscher Richterbund*, quoted in Kuhn, pp. 16, 36 (note 116). One further indication of the conservative orientation of the *Stand* was that while Leeb's organization had some 12,000 members, no more than 600 belonged to a Republican Association of Judges (*Republikanische Richterbund*), which was founded in 1921 as an antipode to the *Deutscher Richterbund*.

7   Quack, S. (1986), *Geistig frei und niemandes Knecht. Paul Levi-Rosa Luxemburg. Politische Arbeit und persönliche Beziehung*, Revised edn., Ullstein, Frankfurt, pp. 25*ff.*

8   Kirchheimer, p. 213. On the lay judges see Gumbel, E. J. (1984), *Verschwörer. Zur Geschichte und Soziologie der deutschen nationalistischen Geheimbünde 1918-1924*, reprint, Fischer, Frankfurt, pp. 62-3; Hannover and Hannover-Drück, pp. 28-30; and Stern, p. 18.

9   Deak, I. (1968), *Weimar Germany's Left-Wing Intellectuals: A History of the Weltbühne and its Circle*, University of California Press, Berkeley and Los Angeles, p. 123.

10 Gumbel, E. J. (ed.), *Denkschrift des Reichsjustizministers zu 'Vier Jahre politischer Mord'*, Malik-Verlag, Berlin, 1924, pp. 178-82.

11 Gumbel, *Denkschrift*.

12 Diehl, J. M. (1977), *Paramilitary Politics in the Weimar Republic*, Indiana University Press, Bloomington, pp. 24-30 (direct quotation from p. 28); Waite, R. G. L. (1970), *Vanguard of Nazism. The Free Corps Movement in Postwar Germany 1918-1923*, Reprint, Harvard University Press, Cambridge; Schulze, H. (1969), *Freikorps und Republik, 1918-1920*, H. Boldt, Boppard; and Gordon, H. J. (1957), *The Reichswehr and the German Republic, 1919-1926*, Princeton University Press, Princeton. All organizations, including these paramilitary forces, were required by German law to register with government authorities.

13   Craig, G. A. (1980), *Germany, 1866-1945*, paperback edn., Oxford University Press, New York, pp. 426-32.

14   For a literary example, see Ottwalt, E. (1931), *Denn Sie wissen was Sie tun*, Berlin.

15   Kuenzer, Reichskommissar für die Überwachung der öffentlichen Ordnung (Commissioner for the Observation of Public Order), report to the Reichsminister des Innern, 20 February 1926, in Bundesarchiv Deutschland, Abteilung Koblenz (BAK), Akten der Reichskanzlei, R43I/2732, p. 101 (microfilm reel 557, frame 83).

16   Kuenzer report, 20 February 1926, in BAK, R43I/2732, pp. 98-115, esp. p. 100 (reel 557, frames 79-97).

17   Stern, H. (1963), 'The *Organisation Consul*', *Journal of Modern History*, Vol. 35(1), p. 24.

18   Schulz to Walter Buch, 30 November 1928, BAK, NS26/1374, cited in Nagel, I. (1991), *Fememorde und Fememordprozesse in der Weimarer Republik*, Böhlau, Cologne, p. 336.

19   For an example of a critic, see Gumbel, E.J., 'Edmund Heines, der "Femerichter"', *Acht Uhr Abendblatt*, 3 November 1930; for supporters, Felgen, F. (ed.) (1930), *Femgericht*, J. F. Lehmann, Munich. On this subject more generally, Nagel, pp. 332-3.

20   'Self-justice' in Grimm, Friedrich, 'Denkschrift über die Notwendigkeit einer Befriedigungsamnestie. Verfaßt im Auftrage des Ausschusses zur Förderung der Amnestiebestrebungen aus Anlaß der Rheinlandräumung von Rechtsanwalt Professor Dr. Grimm, Essen/Münster', printed manuscript, 20 January 1930, Bundesarchiv, Abteilungen Militärarchiv (Freiburg) (BAF), Nachlaß Hans von Seeckt, N247/128, p. 14.

21   The following section is drawn from Brenner, A. D., '*Feme* Murder: Paramilitary "Self-Justice" in Weimar Germany', in Campbell, B. B. and Brenner, A. D. (eds) (2000), *Death Squads in Global Perspective: Murder with Deniability*, St. Martin's Press, New York, pp. 57-83; and Nagel.

22   Gumbel, E. J. (1929), with collaboration from Jacob, B. and Falk, A., '*Verräter verfallen der Feme*'. *Opfer/Mörder/Richter 1919-1929*, Malik-Verlag, Berlin, pp. 102-6; Nagel, pp. 53-4; Reichstag, III. Wahlperiode 1924/28, 27. Ausschuß, (Untersuchungsausschuß) Feme-Organisationen und Feme-Morde (hereafter, RFA); reports and testimony on the Sandmayr case in sessions 17, 18, 21, and 23, passim. Because this investigating committee never issued a report, its transcripts were not made part of the bound Reichstag proceedings; instead they are housed archivally in Bundesarchiv Deutschland, Abteilungen Berlin-Lichterfelde (BAB), Reichstag, R101/1645-1648.

23   On the Mecklenburg cases, see Nagel, pp. 57-9 and 158-66; on Upper Silesia, see Gumbel, *Verräter*, pp. 155-97, and Brenner, pp. 66-8.

24   Grimm, 'Denkschrift', p. 90. The figure provided here should be taken as a minimum: these are the cases that went through the criminal justice system. There may have been additional murders that were never found or processed through the criminal justice system. Gumbel, *Verräter*, pp. 279-81, identifies an additional three failed *Feme* murders attempted by Schulz's squad, while pp. Nagel, 66-9, counts two failed *Fememorde*.

25   Kuenzer, report of 20 February 1926, pp. 102-5 (reel 557, frames 84-7); Reichswehrminister [Otto] Geßler, report to RFA, 2 March 1926, RFA Proceedings, Nr. 5, in BAB, R101/1645, p. 53.

26   Craig, G. A. (1964), *The Politics of the Prussian Army, 1640-1945*, paperback edn., Oxford University Press, New York, p. 402.

27   Buchrucker, [Bruno Ernst], 'Schwarze Reichswehr. Gessler und sine "Arbeiter,"' typescript, undated (ca. 1928/29), BAK, Nachlaß Walter Luetgebrüne, N1150/152, pp. 6-7.

28 See Nagel, 63-79, and Gumbel, *Verräter*, 265-330. For the exposition of a single case, see, e.g., the indictment in the death of Walter Wilms: Oberstaatsanwalt bei dem Landgericht III, Berlin, 'Strafsache gegen Stantien u. Gen. (Mord an Wilms)', 28 January 1927, BAK, N1150/65.

29 The most influential works on this were Gumbel, E. J. (1922), *Vier Jahre politischer Morde*, Berlin, Verlag der neuen Gesellschaft; and Gumbel, *Denkschrift*. Also, Kuhn, R. (1983), *Die Vertrauenskrise der Justiz (1926-1928). Der Kampf um die 'Republikanisierung' der Rechtspflege in der Weimarer Republik*, Bundesanzeiger, Cologne.

30 RFA proceedings in BAB, R101/1645-1648; Prussian Landtag investigation proceedings in Preußischer Landtag, *Sitzungsberichte*, Wahlperiode 1924/28, Drucksache Nr. 8924-8. See, also, Nagel, pp. 285-324.

31 For a sample, see the newspaper clippings files in Geheimes Staatsarchiv Preußischer Kulturbesitz, Rep. 84a/14408-14413; also Nagel, pp. 102-18.

32 [Seeckt, Hans von], 'Einige Hinweise für ein militärisches Gutachten zu dem Rechtsgutachten des Herrn Professor Dr. Grimm', typescript, undated (ca. 1928), BA-F, N247/126, pp. 6-7.

33 Extract from Schulz's testimony as a witness in a libel suit against two journalists who accused the army of having sanctioned the Schulz death squad murders, from *Berliner Tageblatt*, 17 December 1927, cited in Nagel, p. 241.

34 [Seeckt], 'Einige Hinweise', p. 6.

35 Grimm, 'Denkschrift', pp. 5, 6.

36 Oberstaatsanwalt bei dem Landgericht III, Berlin, 'Strafsache gegen Stantien u. Gen. (Mord an Wilms).

37 This trail is too long and complex to be recounted in detail. Some examples: transcript of the cabinet discussion of 30 January 1926, BAK, R43I/2732, p. 88 (reel 557, frames 69-70); Staatssekretär in der Reichskanzlei, note ('Vermerk') of 18 May 1927, BAK, R43I/2733, p. 39 (reel 557, frame 481); Martius, Auswärtiges Amt, letter to Friedrich Grimm, 7 September 1928, BAK, R43I/2733, p. 103 (reel 557, frame 548); Staatssekretär in der Reichskanzlei, note of [n.d.] June 1929, BAK, R43I/2733, p. 208 (reel 557, frame 653); and Staatssekretär in der Reichskanzlei, note of 2 October 1930, BAK, R43I/2733, p. 246 (reel 557, frame 691).

38 Tischbein, Berlin representative of Mecklenburg-Schwerin, to Senior Councilor Planck, Reichs Chancellery, 13 May 1930, in BAK, R43I/1243, pp. 629-35 (reel 271, frames 1093-6).

39 Quoted in Christoph, J. (1988), *Die politischen Reichsamnestien 1918-1933*, Lang, Frankfurt, p. 285.

40 The history of this amnesty campaign is chronicled in Christoph, pp. 219-321. See also Petersen, K. (1988), *Literatur und Justiz in der Weimarer Republik*, Metzler, Stuttgart, pp. 71-2 and 153-9; and Nagel, pp. 325-48.

41 Grimm to Reichskanzlei, Bundesarchiv Koblenz, R43I/1243, p. 281.

42 The exception was Prussia, which was given a smaller proportion than its due in order to preclude Prussian domination of German affairs, as had been the case in the German Empire (1871-1918). A good explanation of this body's origin and construction is found in Holborn, H. (1982), *A History of Modern Germany, 1840-1945*, Princeton University Press, Princeton, pp. 549-51.

43 Luetgebrüne, W., 'Femeprozess und Recht', *Völkischer Beobachter*, 9 October 1928, cited in Koch, p. 13.

44 Sinzheimer, H., 'Die Legalisierung des politischen Mordes', *Die Justiz*, V. Band, Heft 2, November 1929, p. 68.

45 Law for the Restoration of the Professional Civil Service, 7 April 1933, Article IV, reproduced in Noakes and Pridham, Vol. I, p. 224.

46   Müller, p. 74.
47   On the Gestapo's practices, see Johnson, E. A. (1999), *Nazi Terror: The Gestapo, Jews, and Ordinary Germans*, Basic Books, New York.
48   This is the central subject of Koch, *In the Name of the Volk*.
49   Reproduced in Pridham and Noakes, Vol. I, p. 142.

References

Brenner, A. D. (2000), '*Feme* Murder: Paramilitary "Self-Justice" in Weimar Germany', in Campbell, B. B. and Brenner, A. D. (eds), *Death Squads in Global Perspective: Murder with Deniability*, St. Martin's Press, New York, pp. 57-83.
Buchrucker, [Bruno Ernst] (1928/29), 'Schwarze Reichswehr. Gessler und sine "Arbeiter"', typescript, undated, Bundesarchiv Deutschland, Abteilungen Koblenz, Nachlaß Walter Luetgebrüne, N1150/152.
Christoph, J. (1988), *Die politischen Reichsamnestien 1918-1933*, Lang, Frankfurt.
Craig, G. A. (1980), *Germany, 1866-1945*, paperback edn., Oxford University Press, New York.
Craig, G. A. (1964), *The Politics of the Prussian Army, 1640-1945*, paperback edn., Oxford University Press, New York.
Deak, I. (1968), *Weimar Germany's Left-Wing Intellectuals: A History of the Weltbühne and its Circle*, University of California Press, Berkeley and Los Angeles.
Diehl, J. M. (1977), *Paramilitary Politics in the Weimar Republic*, Indiana University Press, Bloomington.
Felgen, F. (ed.) (1930), *Femgericht*, J. F. Lehmann, Munich.
Geheimes Staatsarchiv Preußischer Kulturbesitz, Ministerium der Justiz, Rep. 84a/14408-14413.
Gordon, H. J. (1957), *The Reichswehr and the German Republic, 1919-1926*, Princeton University Press, Princeton.
Grimm, F. (1930), 'Denkschrift über die Notwendigkeit einer Befriedigungsamnestie. Verfaßt im Auftrage des Ausschusses zur Förderung der Amnestiebestrebungen aus Anlaß der Rheinlandräumung von Rechtsanwalt Professor Dr. Grimm, Essen/Münster', printed manuscript, 20 January, Bundesarchiv, Abteilungen Militärarchiv (Freiburg), Nachlaß Hans von Seeckt, N247/128.
Gumbel, E. J. (1922), *Vier Jahre politischer Morde*, Verlag der neuen Gesellschaft, Berlin.
Gumbel, E. J. (1924), *Verschwörer. Zur Geschichte und Soziologie der deutschen nationalistischen Geheimbünde 1918-1924*, reprint, Fischer, Frankfurt, 1984.
Gumbel, E. J. (ed.) (1924), *Denkschrift des Reichsjustizministers zu 'Vier Jahre politischer Mord'*, Malik-Verlag, Berlin.
Gumbel, E. J. (1929), with collaboration from Berthold Jacob and Alfred Falk, '*Verräter verfallen der Feme'. Opfer/Mörder/Richter 1919-1929*, Malik-Verlag, Berlin.
Gumbel, E. J. (1930), 'Edmund Heines, der "Femerichter"', *Acht Uhr Abendblatt*, 3 November.
Hannover, H. and Hannover-Drück, E. (1987), *Politische Justiz 1918-1933*, Second edn., Lamuv, Bornheim-Merten.
Holborn, H. (1982), *A History of Modern Germany, 1840-1945*, Princeton, Princeton University Press.
Johnson, E. A. (1999), *Nazi Terror: The Gestapo, Jews, and Ordinary Germans*, Basic Books, New York.
Kaes, A., Jay, M. and Dimendberg, E. (eds) (1994), *The Weimar Republic Sourcebook*, University of California Press, Berkeley.

Kirchheimer, O. (1961), *Political Justice. The Use of Legal Procedure for Political Ends*, Princeton University Press, Princeton.

Koch, H. W. (1989), *In the Name of the Volk. Political Justice in Hitler's Germany*, St. Martin's Press, New York.

Kolb, E. (1988), *The Weimar Republic*, trans. Falla, P. S., Unwin Hyman, London.

Kuenzer (1926), Reichskommissar für die Überwachung der öffentlichen Ordnung (Commissioner for the Observation of Public Order), report to the Reichsminister des Innern, 20 February, in Bundesarchiv Deutschland, Abteilung Koblenz, Akten der Reichskanzlei, R431/2732, p. 101 (microfilm reel 557, frame 83).

Kuhn, R. (1983), *Die Vertrauenskrise der Justiz (1926-1928). Der Kampf um die "Republikanisierung" der Rechtspflege in der Weimarer Republik*, Bundesanzeiger, Cologne.

Kuttner, E. (1913), *Klassenjustiz*, P. Singer, Berlin.

Luetgebrüne, W. (1928), 'Femeprozess und Recht', *Völkischer Beobachter*, 9 October.

Müller, I. (1991), *Hitler's Justice. The Courts of the Third Reich*, trans. Lucas Schneider, D., Harvard University Press, Cambridge, MA.

Nagel, I. (1991), *Fememorde und Fememordprozesse in der Weimarer Republik*, Böhlau, Cologne.

Noakes, J. and Pridham, G. (eds) (1990), *Nazism 1919-1945*, Shocken Books, New York.

Oberstaatsanwalt bei dem Landgericht III, Berlin (1927), 'Strafsache gegen Stantien u. Gen. (Mord an Wilms)', 28 January, Bundesarchiv Deutschland, Abteilung Koblenz, Nachlass Walter Luetgebrüne, N1150/65.

Ottwalt, E. (1931), *Denn Sie wissen was Sie tun*, Berlin.

Petersen, K. (1988), *Literatur und Justiz in der Weimarer Republik*, Metzler, Stuttgart.

Preußischer Landtag (1924/28), *Sitzungsberichte*, Drucksache Nr. 8924-8.

Quack, S. (1986), *Geistig frei und niemandes Knecht. Paul Levi-Rosa Luxemburg. Politische Arbeit und persönliche Beziehung*, Revised edn., Ullstein, Frankfurt.

Reichsgesetzblatt (1934), Band 1, p. 529.

Reichstag (1924/28), III. Wahlperiode, 27. Ausschuß, (Untersuchungsausschuß) Feme-Organisationen und Feme-Morde, in Bundesarchiv Deutschland, Abteilungen Berlin-Lichterfelde (BAB), R101/1645-1648.

Schmitt, C. (1934), 'Der Führer schützt das Recht', *Deutsche Juristen-Zeitung* Band 39, Heft 15, 1 August, pp. 945-50.

Schulz, B. (1982), *Der Republikanische Richterbund (1921-1933)*, Peter Lang, Frankfurt.

Schulze, H. (1969), *Freikorps und Republik, 1918-1920*, H. Boldt, Boppard.

[Seeckt, Hans von] (1928), 'Einige Hinweise für ein militärisches Gutachten zu dem Rechtsgutachten des Herrn Professor Dr. Grimm', typescript, undated, Bundesarchiv Deutschland, Abteilungen Militärarchiv (Freiburg), Nachlaß Hans von Seeckt, N247/126.

Sinzheimer, H. (1929), 'Die Legalisierung des politischen Mordes', *Die Justiz*, V. Band, Heft 2, November, pp. 65-9.

Stern, H. (1963), 'The *Organisation Consul*', *Journal of Modern History*, Vol. 35(1), March, pp. 20-32.

Stern, H. N. (1966), 'Political Crime and Justice in the Weimar Republic', Ph.D. diss., Johns Hopkins University.

Stolleis, M. (1998), *The Law under the Swastika. Studies on Legal History in Nazi Germany*, trans. Dunlap, T., University of Chicago Press, Chicago.

Waite, R. G. L. (1970), *Vanguard of Nazism. The Free Corps Movement in Postwar Germany 1918-1923*, Reprint, Harvard University Press, Cambridge.

Wehler, H-U. (1991), *The German Empire 1871-1918*, trans. Traynor, K., Berg, New York.

10 Legitimizing 'Justice': Lynching and the Boundaries of Informal Justice in the American South

Susan Jean and W. Fitzhugh Brundage

Introduction

On June 25, 1900 in Polk County, Florida, a black man was lynched for the murder of a white man. The local *Bartow Courier-Informant* opened its article on the lynching with the headline, 'Bloody Scene at Kingsford'. The newspaper recounted an unexplained difficulty that had occurred at the Kingsford Phosphate Mine between a black man named Sam Smith and a white man named Joe Hendricks. The row ended when Smith struck Hendricks fatally in the chest with an axe. When word of the killing reached the local sheriff, he formed a posse to search for Smith. By the time they found him late that night the posse had metamorphosed into a mob. For more than an hour, the officers staved off the mob's attempts to seize the prisoner, but the lynchers finally triumphed. They snatched Smith, dragged him off, and shot him dead. The reporter commented, 'Thus, two men within the same twenty-four hours were sacrificed to what was, in its beginning, in all probability, a trifling'. He concluded that 'the killing *may* have been a violation of the law, the lynching *certainly* was, and it is hoped that at least the leaders of it may be brought to trial and made to answer for the violent deed' (emphasis added).[1]

In striking contrast, the *Tampa Tribune* reported an entirely different version of the event. Underneath the headline, 'BEHEADED BY NEGRO BRUTE', the *Tribune* reporter told a story that unfolded not with a possible violation of the law, but with a 'peculiarly atrocious murder'. In this version the perpetrator was Bob Davis, 'a notorious negro', who 'waylaid' Will Hendrix, respected white citizen of Brandon. First, Davis struck Hendrix to the ground and then used an axe to chop off his victim's head. Upon discovering Hendrix's decapitated trunk and severed head, which had rolled down the road, a crowd of Hendrix's friends began to hunt for Davis. The crowd was 100 strong by the time they found him that night. Davis

157

confessed to the murder, and the lynchers marched him back to the scene of the crime and riddled him with bullets.[2]

If the local paper reported something approaching the facts, we must conclude that somewhere in the transmission from Bartow to Tampa the events of June 25 twisted from a mob murder with ambiguous origins into a stereotypical lynching. No longer did the original killing stem from a quarrel. Instead, the white man was cravenly ambushed. One fatal blow to the chest turned into a brutal beheading. The black man became notorious, the white man respected. The posse had no longer thwarted a sheriff's honourable attempts to uphold the law, but was instead an uprising of friends bent on meting out justice. This time, Davis confessed to his crime and was not just shot, but riddled.

Had the events transpired as the *Courier-Informant* reported them, the lynching would have been far less 'laudable'. Rendered as a stereotypical lynching story, featuring a desperate black murderer and an innocent and respectable white man, the incident affirmed white southerners' ideal of lynching as an honourable practice that upheld the defense of white civilization from the 'black brute'. Employing a scale that rated implied or actual violence against a white woman as the most dire offense and accidental or reciprocal violence against a white man as a lesser offense, the *Tribune* reporter upgraded the lynching victim's crime from a lesser transgression to a more reprehensible violation – the unprovoked, psychopathic murder of a white man. This desperate crime provided a justifiable motivation for the now valiant lynch mob and sustained a more positive interpretation of the lynching.

Given the penchant of white southern journalists to describe the actions of lynch mobs in scripted, laudatory terms, the *Tribune* reporter's use of poetic lynching licence is unsurprising. More striking is the *Courier-Informant*'s comparatively candid report that expressed disapproval of what it deemed to be the mob's inappropriate behaviour. The discrepancies between the two reports signal no difference in the papers' attitudes toward lynching in general; on other occasions the *Courier-Informant* published viciously racist and sensational lynching reports. Rather, a comparison of the reports highlights the *Tribune*'s attempt to applaud one type of lynching – a 'warranted' lynching – and the *Courier-Informant*'s attempt to denounce another type – an 'unwarranted' lynching. In these conflicting reports are displayed some of the ongoing efforts of white southerners to define and to formalize boundaries on mob violence.

By the close of the nineteenth century, lynching had become the most notorious and conspicuous form of informal justice in the United States. Precisely because lynching had, according to prominent white Methodist bishop Atticus G. Haygood, 'become so common that it no longer surprises', white southerners sought to confine mob violence to what they believed to be its proper, legitimate jurisdiction (Haygood, 1893). As an extralegal and informal form of justice, lynching was seldom subject to any form of legal regulation. Only in the rarest circumstances between 1880 and 1930 were southern whites ever indicted, let alone prosecuted, for lynching. Consequently, only informal norms regarding mob violence stood between southern society and uncontrolled, chaotic violence. As the *Atlanta Constitution* urged in 1893, white southerners needed to refrain from uncontrolled mob violence. 'It may be hard to draw the line,' the newspaper pleaded, 'but it must be done somewhere. The stern justice administered by the people in their sovereign capacity must not be made too common.'[3]

The Historical Evolution of Lynching in the American South

With obscure origins (traced by some to seventeenth-century Ireland and by others to eighteenth-century America), the practice of organized mobs summarily punishing alleged wrongdoers was an established custom in North America by the late colonial period.[4] During the American Revolution, zealous patriots whipped, and less often hanged, Loyalists and British sympathizers. After the Revolution, lynching expanded across the frontier, as mobs used whipping, rituals of humiliation, and occasionally hangings to enforce 'justice' and impose social order (Brown, 1963; Percy, 1959; Ross, 1983, pp. 55-75; Waldrep, 1998). During the first half of the nineteenth century, mob violence became a truly national phenomenon. In the North, mobs murdered abolitionists, Mormons, Catholics, immigrants, and blacks. In California during the Gold Rush, vigilante justice invaded mining camps and boom towns, reaching a climax in the San Francisco vigilance committees of the 1850s (Brown, 1975, esp. pp. 91-180; Cutler, 1903; Gilje, 1987; Richards, 1970). In the South, lynch mobs defended slavery by keeping a watchful eye for suspect slave behaviour, inflammatory abolitionist literature, and unorthodox attitudes. When conditions warranted, mobs silenced both real and imaginary abolitionists and savagely suppressed slave uprisings. By the close of the antebellum era, the tradition of mob violence had evolved into an integral part of southern culture (Ayers, 1982; Eaton, 1942; Wyatt-Brown, 1982; Waldrep, 1998).

The informal justice of the lynch mob took root in the American South in part because of the legal institutions that distinguished the South from the rest of the nation. In the North the accelerating pace of economic development and the growth of cities required the permanent and dependable exercise of state authority on behalf of capital and property. Consequently, courts and law enforcement agencies, including recently-created urban police forces, were charged with preserving order, protecting property, and discouraging extralegal violence. In the South, planters were wary of any powerful legal institutions that might challenge their autonomy. White southerners developed 'an intense distrust of, and, indeed, downright aversion to, any actual exercise of authority beyond the barest minimum essential to the existence of the social organism' (Cash, 1941, p. 35). Although white southerners readily employed the formal courts to settle property disputes and punish many crimes, they also routinely relied on a code of honour and extralegal punishment to safeguard community morals and punish miscreants (Friedman, 1984; Hindus, 1980; Waldrep, 1998).

The Civil War and the subsequent abolition of slavery unleashed an unprecedented wave of extralegal violence in the South. The circumstances of the postbellum era served both to perpetuate and to enlarge the role of informal justice in southern culture. At the root of the postwar bloodshed was the refusal of most whites to accept the emancipated slaves' quest for equality and autonomy. Mob violence, to an even greater degree than before, became a tool for enforcing conformity to prescribed racial roles. The dismantling of slavery left a void in the enforcement of white supremacy, threatening to deprive whites of their traditional prerogative of disciplining blacks as they chose. Planters who were unable or unwilling to renounce the free-handed discipline of slavery, whipped, shot, and killed hundreds of blacks for failing to display sufficient deference or for arguing over working conditions. Simultaneously, the Ku Klux Klan and other paramilitary groups defended the interests of the Democratic Party, the avowed party of white supremacy, by waging systematic political terrorism (Crouch, 1984; Foner, 1988; Rable, 1984; Stagg, 1974; Trelease, 1979; Wright, 1990; Zuczek, 1996).

The epidemic of lynching that swept the South in the late nineteenth century persisted after the 'reconstruction' of the former Confederacy ended. Following an ebbing of violence in the late 1870s and early 1880s, the number of lynchings in the South increased again. The new wave of racial violence climaxed in 1892, when mobs executed an estimated 71 whites and 155 blacks, the largest number of lynchings in the history of both the South and the nation. With each succeeding decade, the proportion of lynchings that occurred in the South rose, increasing from 82 per cent of all lynchings in the nation during the 1880s to more than 95 per cent during the 1920s. Indeed, casualties of mob violence in some southern states equalled or exceeded the totals of entire regions outside the South. Quite likely, southern mobs executed more than 4000 victims between 1880 and 1930. At the same time, the connection between lynching, race, and ethnicity became starker. Outside the South, blacks comprised less than twenty per cent of mob victims. In the South and the border states, in contrast, 85 per cent of the victims were black (Tolnay and Beck, 1995; Brundage, 1993; Work, 1931; Wright, 1990).

In general terms, southern whites used lynching as a tool to intimidate black men and check the threat whites imagined they posed – to white women physically, to white men socially, and to white civilization fundamentally. To southern whites, black men who explicitly flaunted racial conventions of deference and servility posed the biggest threat of all.[5] It is thus predictable that in Florida, where much of the material for this essay was gathered, lynchings often erupted at or near the turpentine camps and phosphate mines that abounded in the northern and central parts of the state. These labour camps created pockets of relatively independent communities of young black men working and living together, which fact represented a serious threat to southern whites. Moreover, the exploitative system of labour in the camps engendered deep tensions between black workers and their white managers, and lynching victims were frequently charged with 'crimes' that stemmed from their altercations with white employers.

In Florida 94 per cent of lynching victims were black, and the incidence of lynching in the state ebbed and waned in the same general pattern as in all southern states. Yet population pressures unique to Florida in the twentieth century encouraged tension later in the state, and the steady toll of lynchings into the 1930s and 1940s in Florida placed the state among the very worst offenders in the nation during these final decades of lynching. For these reasons, Florida is a useful setting in which to study lynching; while patterns of lynching in Florida responded to conditions particular to the state, they still generally mimicked those in the rest of the South and are consistent with the findings of scholars who have studied lynching in states such as Georgia, Virginia, and Kentucky. In short, conditions in Florida created the same environment that encouraged whites across the South to draw the line separating the races in the most violent fashion.

Even in the act of lynching itself, whites drew a line separating the races. The profoundly racialized nature of southern lynching was evident in the different rituals and violence associated with the lynchings of whites and of blacks. The small mobs that typically lynched white men were as intent on expressing and affirming traditional values as the mobs that lynched alleged black rapists. Yet, the mobs, in the minds of their members, were responding to menaces of entirely different magnitudes. Whites viewed the crimes committed by white wrongdoers as the products of aberrant personalities rather than of criminality innate to their race. Content simply to purge the community of an offending individual, mobs that lynched whites performed modest group dramas that were sufficient to establish that certain rules could not be broken without reprisals (Beck and Tolnay, 1997; Brundage, 1993, pp. 91-2; Ross, 1983, pp. 204-5, 211-12). In contrast, the (perceived) constant menace of black criminality demanded that whites adopt far more conspicuous measures to maintain and reconfirm the boundaries of proper black conduct. Consequently, the lynchings of blacks, with which mobs intended to intimidate all blacks, all too often took the form of a public spectacle of mockery, humiliation, and torture.

As the practice of lynching became pervasive across time and place and conspicuous in its brutality, white southerners grappled with the fact that lynching itself, which they justified as a crucial tool for the defence of civilization, could, if unrestrained, pose a threat to organized society. Ignoring the horrors that mobs inflicted on their victims, white southerners instead fretted about the anarchic potential of mob violence. At the very least, mundane considerations of public safety explained their concern. The mob that lynched Jim Glover, a black man charged with the rape of a thirteen year-old white girl, in Cedartown, Georgia, in 1904, demonstrated the hazards of unco-ordinated mob violence. A mob of 500 formed a circle around Glover and opened fire on him. Stray bullets from the fusillade killed one lyncher and seriously wounded at least four others.[6] In other instances, after punishing the alleged wrongdoer, lynchers engaged in ongoing and indiscriminate attacks on blacks. After the lynching of two blacks for the rape of a white girl in Forsyth County, Georgia, for example, white tenant farmers in the area used violence and intimidation to drive virtually every black from Forsyth and neighbouring Dawson counties.[7]

Even more threatening were mobs that made manifest the threat lynching could pose to formal justice and public authority. For instance mobs on occasion attacked militia troops who protected alleged black criminals. In 1904, at the request of local authorities, Governor James M. Terrell of Georgia sent militia companies to protect Paul Reed and Will Cato, two black turpentine hands charged with the murder of a white family in Statesboro. The militia prevented any lawlessness during the trial of the men, but at the conclusion of the trial a mob stormed the courthouse, overpowered the troops, and seized the prisoners. The mob then chained them to a stump and burned them alive. Unsatisfied by the immolation of the two men, white marauders, without pretext, murdered and whipped an undetermined number of blacks in the surrounding area. Eventually the flight of black labourers from the county prodded white planters, who worried about a pending shortage of labour, to halt the violence. But no face-saving measures could erase the humiliation of the militia or the precedent it established.[8]

More destructive still was the mob that lynched Thomas Smith in Roanoke, Virginia in 1893. Smith, a young black man, allegedly choked, beat, and robbed a 'respectable' white woman. Once Smith was arrested and placed in jail, an immense mob gathered outside. Ignoring the pleas from the Mayor and other city officials, and disregarding the presence of armed militia and the city's police force, the mob attacked the jail. In the chaos that followed, shooting erupted and seven mob members were killed and another twenty-five were wounded. Initially repulsed, the enraged mob regrouped and then targeted the militia and public officials who had defended the jail. The mayor fled the city and the terrified militia men went into hiding. Thwarted in their pursuit of vengeance, the mob set about locating Smith, who had been spirited from the jail during the street battle. When the mob eventually captured him, they quickly executed him and burned his body. Even then, the lynchers harboured grievances stemming from the previous night's clash. For three days, they encamped in front of the jail, demanding the removal of the mayor, the chief of police, and several police officers. Only protracted negotiations between prominent businessmen and mob leaders led to the restoration of the city's constituted authorities.[9] The tumult in Roanoke, Statesboro, and elsewhere reminded white southerners that however much they agreed that lynching was a defensible complement to formal justice, the violence wrought by lynch mobs could be capricious and dangerously unpredictable.

In addition to these real and practical concerns about the threat that lynch mobs could pose to the social order, white southerners felt compelled to justify mob violence as a result of the national and international censure elicited by southern lynchings. As the toll of lynch mobs mounted during the 1890s, black activists, ranging from Ida B. Wells and Frederick Douglass to W. E. B. Du Bois, protested that whites who participated in or condoned mob violence violated the very notion of civilization by which they justified their own racial superiority. It was the blacks who campaigned against lynching and the protection of civil rights, anti-lynching activists insisted, who were upholding civilization in the face of the barbarism of the lynch mob and its defenders. Wells's efforts to mobilize British public sentiment during her controversial tours of Great Britain in 1892 and 1894 were a manifestation of this strategy conducted on an international scale. One measure of her success in redirecting public discussion of lynching by creatively exposing white hypocrisy was the intensity of southern white denunciations of her tour. Subsequently, increasing numbers of white northerners, and even some white southerners, joined with black anti-lynching activists in their campaign to mold public sentiment and to restrain white southern mobs (Bederman, 1995; Carby, 1985).

Neither the censure of outraged critics of lynching nor the threat that mobs posed to social order, however, provoked white southerners to prosecute lynchers.

Although anti-lynching laws were adopted in several southern states during the 1890s, white southerners in practice were wary of establishing any real precedent for the prosecution of mob members. White southerners engaged in vigorous discussion of lynching between 1880 and 1930, but prior to 1910 there was little visible evidence of any significant shift of popular sentiment against mob violence. What 'progress' in public attitudes towards lynching had been made was riddled with compromises with the very values that gave legitimacy to mob violence. Contemporaries would have needed the skills of a trained logician to distinguish most public criticisms of lynching from justifications. The tortured arguments of whites who did not unequivocally champion mob violence reflected the tug of competing values. Torn between a commitment to law and order and sympathy for the traditional justifications for lynching, concerned whites were immobilized by indecision and confusion. Some white southerners might periodically wring their hands over the excesses of mobs but they retained their faith that mob violence, when all was said and done, was in the natural order of things (Brundage, 1993; Hall, 1979).

Consequently, neither the law officers who were complicitous in lynchings nor mob members themselves had reason to fear legal penalty. White southerners who were concerned about the boundaries of mob violence instead looked to non-judicial and informal methods to influence public opinion and behaviour. They debated the merits of lynching from the lecture podium, the church sanctuary, the printed page and any other fora available to them. By any measure, newspapers were the most important venue for representations of and justifications for lynching in no small part because they compiled virtually the only public record of lynchings. Newspapers had the power to represent lynchings in whatever manner they found expedient and to define the practice as they saw fit. Newspapers also could and sometimes did choose to remain silent about lynchings, thereby wielding the power to erase events from the historical record. Furthermore, editorial pages provided an ideal setting in which white southerners could rebut critics of mob violence and defend southern 'civilization'.

The discussion white southerners engaged in over lynching was a struggle to bound the definition and representation of the phenomenon. Lynching opponents within and without the South were engaged in a similar contest, arguing strenuously amongst themselves for varying definitions of lynching. Some anti-lynching activists hoped to make the term as inclusive as possible in order to underscore the magnitude of the problem; others argued for a narrower definition, insisting that white southerners would stop lynching when it appeared that lynchings were becoming increasingly rare (Waldrep, 2000). Supporters of lynching tried to impose their own definition on the phenomenon, but with the opposite aim, hoping not to eliminate the practice, but to defend it. When white southerners engaged in this complex calibration of the discourse surrounding lynching, they revealed how important perceptions of legitimacy and justice were to lynching as an enduring practice.

Legitimizing Lynchings as a Form of Informal Justice

In the eyes of white southerners, all lynchings were not created equal. A particular kind of lynching dominated the front pages of southern newspapers; it seemed to affirm to southern whites the meaning and the value of the practice, and it remains with us even today as the prevailing image of lynching. This lynching featured key recognizable elements, such as a black man committing a crime against a white woman (or, less frequently, an esteemed white man), communal expression of outrage over the incident, and communal execution of 'justice'. This model of lynching was familiar and acceptable to contemporary observers; it was 'like a text that white southerners read to themselves about themselves', and whites found in it a confirmation of the 'honorable', 'redemptive' nature of lynching (Brundage, 1993, p. 17). Indeed, many of the lynching reports that appeared in newspapers bolstered this ideal and blended to form a powerful voice in the struggle to define the parameters of lynching.

When a young white woman was murdered in 1901 in Bartow, the local *Courier-Informant* responded with a frenzy typical of reports describing 'honorable' lynchings. On May 29, the following headline blazed on the front page: 'BLACK BRUTE'S HEINOUS CRIME! A Well Known White Woman Murdered Near Peace River Bridge – Men Scouring Country – Lynching Almost Certain'. According to the *Courier-Informant*'s report, a black man had witnessed the woman's murder the day before and had alerted whites about the identity of the murderer, 16-year-old Fred Rochelle. A search party recovered the body of young Mrs. Ed Taggert, who was 'well known to almost everybody in the community and connected with some of the oldest families in South Florida'. A posse of whites immediately began tracking the alleged murderer. At the time the newspaper went to print, the posse had surrounded Rochelle in a swamp, 'and it is only a question of time until [...] he will undoubtedly meet the only justice possible'. Although the *Courier-Informant* alluded to the inevitability of lynching, it predicted, 'While there is an air of quiet determination about the men of the community, there is no undue excitement apparent, and it is safe to say that cool judgment prevails, and nothing will occur to further mar the spotless character of this vicinity'.[10]

In its next printing, under the headline 'BURNED AT THE STAKE', the *Courier-Informant* concluded the tale. Later that Wednesday, Rochelle had been seized by whites who then brought him to Bartow, 'where a crowd of cool-headed citizens took charge of him, despite the sheriff and his deputies'. Here the *Courier-Informant* reminded its readers, 'To the credit of this community, it should be remembered that the whole affair was conducted so quietly that those living three blocks away heard nothing of it'. The lynchers took their prisoner to the scene of his alleged crime, where they hoisted him onto a hogshead filled with inflammable material, piled wood around it, and poured coal oil on top. Unrepentant, Rochelle claimed he was ready to die, and Mrs. Taggert's husband lit a match and tossed it onto the pile. 'In eight minutes there was only a charred mass to tell the tale. Awe-struck the throng turned homeward, and by midnight the town was as peaceful as ever, and ever since has been trying to forget.'[11]

The *Courier-Informant* filled its editorial page that day with justifications for the lynchers' actions. The arguments rested largely on the nature of the lynching itself, which was, in the newspaper's words, 'the spontaneous work of practically all the best citizenship of this place'. As evidence of the virtuous nature of the lynching, the editorial noted that 'there were no masks or attempts at disguise and it was done in the full light of day. The men who did it are the same who are on our streets today doing the business of the community. Not a man of them would deny for a moment whatever share he took in the tragedy.' In short, the *Courier-Informant* found the conviction of the lynchers to be ample proof of their righteousness, and the core of its defence was the simple assertion that 'all that was done, was done decently and in order by sober and serious men, possessing the full average of kindly instincts, and on this we rest the case'.[12]

The *Courier-Informant*'s reporting was typical of portrayals of 'honorable' lynchings. The most conspicuous and widespread feature of such reports was the salacious language used to describe the black victims, their alleged crimes, and the lynch mobs' actions. These sensational representations reflected the tradition of the turn-of-the-century 'penny press', which employed shocking images to attract and titillate readers. But such headlines did more than just lure readers. Newspapers that branded a lynching victim a 'black brute', an 'inhuman fiend', or an 'imp of inferno' were from the start helping to exonerate the lynch mob. In depicting the bestiality of the black man and by contrast the sweet, delicate, and innocent nature of his alleged victim, reporters were courting the fury of their readers and encouraging them to identify with the lynchers.

Yet even the most lurid news accounts of lynchings offered lessons about the appropriate behaviour of mobs. Reporters often described and applauded lynch mobs as being free of any rash emotion. While the 'circumstantial chain' was being collected against Charlie Pittman for alleged rape and murder in 1908, it was 'with commendable patience [that] the outraged community bided its time and would not be swayed by blind passion. When a white mob lynched Charles Scarborough for alleged attempted rape in 1909, 'There was no excitement in the matter at all'. The people were determined that the negro should pay the penalty for his attempted crime: that was all. After the lynching of Amos Smith in 1909 for alleged attempted rape, the *Arcadia Champion* described the victim's riddled body; then, a week later, the paper printed this correction of the apparently erroneous detail: 'Nothing could have been further from the truth. The people who punished the negro considered that they were doing their duty to their community, and they went about the business in the most orderly manner, and no unseemly passion or excitement was shown whatever.'[13]

In the white southern imagination, 'honorable' lynchings were executed sombrely by men who derived no undue pleasure from them. Local newspapers often reported on the absence of whisky drinking or excessive violence in an attempt to fashion these lynchings as sober, earnest affairs. When whites in Marion County lynched Robert Larkin for the alleged rape of 18-year-old Fannie Alexander in 1893, the *Florida Times-Union* dwelled on the purported grave resolution of the mob, which was comprised of 'quiet but determined men'. The men who captured Larkin were 'two of the most gentlemanly boys that Citra affords' and after Larkin was identified, 'the hearts of the Citra people were bowed down in grief to know that a duty was to be performed'. 'Three hundred of the best citizens' overpowered the court at the preliminary trial and 'with the greatest forbearance' set about the lynching. 'There was no excitement much as is looked for at such times', 'there was not a drop of whiskey in the crowd', and the placard left by the body read, 'Done by 300 of the best citizens of this county'.[14]

The 'forbearance' of lynchers, according to white newspapers, stemmed not only from a solemn understanding of their duty, but, more fundamentally, from their upstanding moral fibre. Thus 'honorable' lynchings were conducted by mob members who were not only local members of the community but also their area's 'best citizens'. In 1904 the lynchers of alleged murderer Washington Bradley 'were among the best people of Levy County', who wanted revenge for one of the most hideous crimes known in the history of that section, and they got it in a well-planned and orderly manner. The mob that lynched Richard Anderson for alleged rape in 1916 consisted of '300 prominent citizens of Marion, Levy and Alachua counties'. No strangers or suspicious characters appeared in these reports – only local gentlemen responding to the imperative of communal duty.[15]

Given the makeup of such mobs and their purported motivations, 'honorable' lynchings necessarily drew unanimous support from the community. After the lynching of Walter Austin in 1892 for the alleged murder of a prominent white man, the *Florida Times-Union* concluded that 'the citizens all approve of the lynching, and it will have a salutary effect on the negroes'. About the lynching of Lee Bailey for alleged attempted rape in 1891, 'All felt that it was time to teach such brutes that they must expect vengeance, swift and sure. The lynching is fully indorsed [sic] by all the best citizens here, both white and black.'[16]

When the lynching victim was a 'brute', the lynchers were good and level-headed men, and all the best citizens commended their actions, the finishing touch to the 'honorable' lynching was the redemption of the community. Reporters sometimes waxed poetic on this subject. In 1909 the *Tampa Tribune* reporter detailing the lynching of Jack Wade in Polk County for the attempted rape of a young white woman described the wake of the lynching in the following inspirational terms: 'Almost like the lifting of a fog when the morning sun bursts forth was the change in spirit of the city today after vengeance had been claimed and justice meted out to the negro.' A coda to the report, which serves also as a reminder of the familiarity of such episodes to southern readers, states, 'Once more the honor of southern womanhood had been protected and a life had paid the penalty of transgression'.[17]

'Illegitimate' Lynchings and Informal Justice in the American South

Given the way white southerners liked, indeed needed, to conceive of the role of lynchers, we can imagine their distaste upon reading about lynchings that subverted their notion of 'honorable' lynching. Lynchings for exceedingly petty crimes or lynch mobs which clearly acted out of personal interest seemed to cross the line of propriety. These lynchings were not merely unseemly; they attracted unwanted attention to the problem of lynching, and to approve of such lynchings would be to allow a state of lawlessness that would call into question the legitimacy of lynching itself. Instead, white southerners attempted to regulate the practice by participating in a discourse against certain kinds of lynching.

The murder of Charles Jones in Baker County in 1896 was a clear case of behaviour that was indefensible to 'upstanding' southern whites. On the night of May 3, three black men were returning from church when they stumbled across five white men sprawled out on the railroad tracks. Without provocation, the white men opened fire, killing Jones instantly. Jones's companions managed to escape into the swamp, and they made it into town the next morning and alerted the sheriff about the murder. Jones's body was found shot dead with a large gash on the head and 'most mysterious of all a piece of flesh about as large as a silver dollar was cut out of the top of his head as though the murderers had scalped him'. The *Florida Times-Union* reported that the murderers were surely strangers to the community and that 'the citizens are justly indignant over the affair as Jones, though a colored man, was regarded as an humble, peaceable negro'. And in an editorial the next day, the *Times-Union* reasoned that 'in the darkness it was difficult to see how the men who perpetrated the murder were known to be white men'. In this wanton murder of an unassuming black man, whites apparently found no positive expression of southern lynching values; thus they not only denounced the murder, but they also refused to call it a lynching and even implied that the murderers may not have been white.[18]

In this and other instances white southerners refused to apply the label of lynching, and all that it suggested, to everyday murder of blacks by a few whites. (Admittedly, the definition of the word 'lynching' is problematic and there is still no universally accepted definition of the term.) Although a present-day reader may infer that five white men casually gunning down an unarmed black man constituted a lynching, it is almost certain that whites in 1896 did not consider the execution to have been a lynching. But even if Baker County whites did not define the incident as a lynching, the reasons why are nonetheless enlightening. The murderers, surely foreigners in the opinion of the white journalist, were acting without the support of the community, and their victim was an 'inoffensive' black man. In short, there was nothing 'honorable' or 'redemptive' about the white men's actions.

But even seemingly unambiguous lynchings could draw the reproach of southern whites. During the night of December 4, 1891 in Marianna, the daughter of W. G. Holloway woke to the sound of someone moving in her bedroom. When she rose to investigate the noise, a man jumped out the window and escaped. Suspicion for the offence fell upon one of Holloway's employees, a black man named John Ely. Holloway and a friend launched a search for the suspect and after several days they found him in a neighbouring town. Holloway contacted the sheriff and informed him that he and his friend would bring Ely to the Justice of the Peace. When the justice received the prisoner, he placed him under the watch of a special constable. But that night a mob overpowered him and seized the prisoner.[19]

The next day a group of white men from the neighbourhood who suspected foul play began to search for Ely. They visited Holloway's property, but Holloway ordered them to leave and threatened to kill all of them. The next day the town judge ordered the sheriff to organize a posse to search for Ely. The posse headed straight for Holloway's water mill, where they found Ely's body buried in an earthen dam. Holloway then appeared and began firing at them. When he refused to stop firing, the lawmen shot and killed him.[20]

The *Florida Times-Union* opened its report on the affair with the headline, 'MOST COWARDLY MURDER. A MAN BRUTALLY KILLED AND HIS BODY HIDDEN. They Fire in Defense and Kill the Man Who Hid the Body – The Murdered Man Suspected of Entering a Girl's Room – No Opportunity to Prove His Innocence'. When contrasted to the headlines concocted for 'honorable' lynching reports, the remarkable nature of the *Times-Union*'s wording is manifest. This time the black man was only suspected of breaking into a girl's room. And this time he was not the guest of honour at a necktie party – he was brutally killed. Although the article acknowledges that his murder was the work of several men, it does not once refer to the crime as a lynching, and it ends with the assertion that 'the citizens of Greenwood and Marianna are justly indignant and aroused, and doubtless further investigation of the affair will be had'.[21]

Apparent white indignation over the lynching of Ely reveals the fluid nature of the phenomenon. Each lynching had its own actors, circumstances, and situation in time and space, and there is no way to predict with certainty the reception any lynching would receive in its community. We can only surmise the reasons Marianna residents may have found Ely's lynching unacceptable. The fact that a group of white men from the neighbourhood took it upon themselves to search for the missing black man suggests that Ely had supporters in the white community.[22] This possibility is strengthened by the article's assertion that Ely had no chance to prove his innocence, when of course no lynching victims ever had any opportunity to do so. It is possible, too, that Holloway was a 'suspicious character' in the eyes of the community, for the paper emphasized his strange behaviour and the claim that all his accomplices came from out of town. Although the crime of entering a white girl's room often inspired communal outrage against a black man, in this instance Marianna residents, or at least the *Times-Union* reporter, evidently found lynching to be a grossly unwarranted response.

When Will English was lynched twenty-one years later for another alleged 'crime' against a white girl, whites in Manatee County purportedly responded with similar indignation. English was placed in the Bradenton jail after a young white woman reported that he had made 'proposals that called for vengeance'. Yet while the lynchers who seized and shot English dead may have believed they were justly defending the virtue of white womanhood, local citizens apparently did not concur, and 'more than a score of the leading citizens had gone to Sheriff Wyatt to tell him they'd assist in every way to uncover the identity of the men'. For whatever reason, local whites, according to news accounts, did not believe English's behaviour justified such extreme measures, and they wished to divorce from the lynching any appearance of respectability or community support. The *Tampa Tribune* reported that 'the people of Bradenton do not believe the mob had in it a single reputable citizen of that town'. Instead the mob that lynched English purportedly came from a distance and 'was made up of men who are not recognized in their own section as being men of affairs or of prominence in any walk of life'. Here again the community and the press were setting limits around the proper scope of lynching and placing 'unwarranted' lynchings and their perpetrators outside of these limits.[23]

An especially telling example of white denunciation after a lynching occurred in 1895 in Columbia County, when a black man was lynched for allegedly raping the daughter of his white employer. Despite the grave charge levelled against the victim, Lake City residents were so angered by the lynching that they pushed for justice and even tried the alleged lynchers. Early on July 4, 1895, a dozen white men, including Constable John Walker, crept into the Hope Henry Church just outside of Lake City, Florida and arrested Robert Bennett, a black man, for the alleged rape of the daughter of Brantley Padgett, his employer.[24] The mob then drove off with Bennett. About a mile down the road, they stopped their wagon and dragged their victim out. There they fired at him with their guns, sliced his throat, cut off his ears, and either 'shot or beat out his brains'. The lynchers then loaded the dead man's body into a wagon and carried it to a site where a large crowd was waiting. Although disappointed to find Bennett already dead, the crowd strung up his 'terribly and horribly mutilated' body and pinned on a warning to rapists.[25]

When the lynching was discovered, local blacks were outraged to learn that, although the alleged assault had occurred over a month earlier, Bennett had continued to work for Padgett unmolested until the time of the lynching. According to the *Florida Times-Union*, 'The negroes believed the charge trumped up for the purpose of getting rid of Bennett for other reasons, and few persons believed the lynching was justified'. White and black citizens of Lake City met together in the courthouse to protest 'indiscriminate' lynchings, and 'this particular one' in unmeasured terms. Governor Henry Mitchell offered a $500 reward for the apprehension of and evidence to convict the guilty parties. On July 14, Bennett's stepfather swore out a warrant for the arrest of Walker, Padgett, and three other suspected lynchers. The next day deputy sheriffs set out to make the arrests but were chased away from the suspects' homes with warnings to leave 'before the other boys got there'.[26]

Later that day the wanted parties descended on the town with a heavily armed mob of supporters, hired a lawyer, and immediately posted bond. The group returned for the preliminary examination the next day 'fifty or sixty strong, in full battle array'. When their attorney warned them that a carload of armed black men was making its way from Jacksonville, the mob agreed to disarm. The circus-like atmosphere on the street prompted the mayor to order all bars closed and to call for extra police protection. By the time the trial started, at least 150 supporters of the defendants lined the street in front of the courthouse. The *Times-Union* reported, 'It was freely hinted that if any of [the defendants] were sent to jail that it would be raided and the men liberated'.[27]

An equal number of blacks and whites stuffed into the courthouse where a succession of witnesses testified that they had recognized Constable Walker and the Padgetts in the lynch mob. Despite corroboration by several witnesses for the prosecution, the evidence against the defendants was deemed insufficient. The men were discharged, and they and their friends left town 'triumphant'.

The *Times-Union* closed its report with the observation that 'this probably ends the matter and demonstrates the almost utter impossibility of obtaining evidence to convict in such cases'.[28]

Though the attempt to bring the lynchers to justice was predictably ineffective, its significance should not be overlooked. Given the setting in which Bennett's lynching took place, the very fact that the lynching aroused indignation is remarkable. Lake City hosted more lynchings than any other town in Florida; indeed this was its seventh lynching in just five years. And with nine lynchings claiming fifteen victims, 1895 was a peak year for lynchings in Florida. Moreover, Robert Bennett was charged with the most 'lynchable' offence in the eyes of whites. Yet Lake City residents were incited not only to denounce, but to prosecute, this particular lynching. Again, we can infer potential reasons from the newspaper article. It appears that Bennett had enjoyed a favourable reputation in the white community, for the *Times-Union* noted that 'Bennett has been rather well spoken of here'.[29] It is also possible that Lake City residents did not wish to be cast as dupes in the schemes of 'foreign' men trying to cover up their own misdeeds. But their reaction in no way implies any sort of anti-lynching sentiment. The wording of Lake City residents' protest is crucial: they were opposed to *indiscriminate* lynchings. In other words, white southerners had a duty to uphold when they lynched – a duty to lynch discriminately. It was when whites neglected this duty that 'unjustified' lynchings took place and the legitimacy of mob violence was threatened.

Conclusion

The urgency with which white southerners rehashed defences of lynching reminds us that the power to define informal justice was never as complete as they would have liked. Even in a society like the American South, which was marked by extraordinary extremes of power and repression, blacks could not be coerced into accepting lynching as legitimate. Admittedly, some blacks did participate in lynchings; at least 148 southern blacks died at the hands of mobs that were either composed entirely of blacks or were integrated (Beck and Tolnay, 1997; Brundage 1993, p. 45). These instances suggest that under certain conditions, blacks did not view all lynchings as an inherent expression of racial repression directed against them. When community standards were offended by especially notorious rapes or murders, blacks on occasion did inflict informal justice upon alleged black perpetrators. Confronted with an unresponsive white-controlled criminal justice system, blacks may have preferred to rely upon their own communal methods of punishment. Whites complained about the 'law's delay', but it was southern blacks who truly understood how capricious it was. Even so, the frequency of black-on-black lynchings should not be exaggerated; the number of blacks lynched by fellow blacks almost certainly was fewer than five per cent of the total of blacks lynched in the South. Equally important, these isolated examples were overshadowed by the vocal and unceasing opposition of black leaders, both local and national, to mob violence. They, along with a small but growing number of white allies, chipped away at the defences of lynching until, during the 1930s, the practice lost virtually all of its legitimacy. But until then, white southerners had laboured strenuously to convince themselves and others that mobs had executed thousands and thousands of victims in the name of civilization and law and order.

The language that white southerners used to define and describe lynchings, as well as the behaviour of lynchers themselves, reveals much about white southerners' conceptions of power and justice. White southerners refused to acknowledge the contradiction between their use of extralegal violence and their professed commitment to law and order. Indeed, they insisted that lynch law enhanced formal justice and affirmed their dedication to it. White southerners blamed the failings of the legal system for their need to resort to extralegal methods. In a growing chorus of disenchantment with the legal system, newspaper editors, ministers, and lawyers complained of the 'law's delay' during the late nineteenth and early twentieth centuries. Many of the complaints about the criminal justice system reached a crescendo during the 1890s and struck a responsive chord in the South and the rest of the nation. Beset by serious problems, the southern legal profession faced attacks from both within and without the legal community. At the same time that state law associations began the difficult processes of setting professional standards and of weeding out 'pre-professional', old-time lawyers, the profession was the target of harsh criticism from the Populist Party and cynicism from the general citizenry (Haber, 1991; Hylton, 1986; Keller, 1977, pp. 343-70; Paul, 1960).

The surge in both crime and in mob violence in the 1890s gave added urgency to calls for reform of the system of justice. Many southern observers, including leading southern legal minds, insisted that lynching was a response to problems that were not being met effectively by the courts. They argued that mobs resorted to summary justice because of a legitimate fear that due process of law actually was hampering the suppression of crime and the punishment of criminals. Discontent focused on the complexities of the law of evidence and of trial procedure, both of which led to a staggering number of technical errors in criminal cases. State supreme courts had little choice but to reverse large numbers of erroneous lower court decisions (Thompson, 1888; Strickland, 1899; DeLacy, 1899; Arnold, 1901). In addition to 'shyster lawyers' who took advantage of legal loopholes and incompetent judges who failed to conduct their courts with a firm hand, the governors' pardoning powers undercut the legitimacy of the courts. A governor's respite or pardon of a condemned criminal frequently aroused calls for communities to substitute their own, informal punishment for the less certain punishment of the state (Brundage 1993, pp. 99-101). Running through these critiques of the southern legal system was the presumption that the legal crisis had driven southerners to resort to lynching. Thus, rather than evidence of southerners' lawlessness, lynchings demonstrated their commitment to law and order by whatever means necessary.

The solicitude about the legitimacy of mob violence was not a ruse intended simply to deflect criticism of white southerners and their penchant for summary justice. To the contrary, the ongoing efforts to demarcate the boundaries of legitimate mob violence were crucial to the broad support that the practice enjoyed among white southerners. Lynching, like other forms of informal justice, required legitimacy in the eyes of its practitioners and a significant portion of citizenry if it was to endure as a complement to formal modes of justice.[30] Just as the constitutive power of formal law depends on the ability of legal institutions to legitimate its power, so too the social utility of lynching was dependent upon its capacity to garner legitimacy.

Essential to the legitimization of lynching was the claim, made by white southerners, that widely held and enduring criteria constrained mobs. Through the stories that white southerners told about lynching they denied that lynching represented power unfettered by the restraints of justice (Ewick, 1998). As Bryant G. Garth and Austin Sarat have observed, whether with regards to informal or formal modes of justice, 'The ability to hold power accountable, or to be seen to do so, is crucial to legitimation' (Garth and Sarat, 1998, p. 11). News accounts and editorials proclaimed that when white southerners surrendered their devotion to the letter of the law they nevertheless followed procedural regularities that paralleled those of formal justice. An essential component of the legitimacy of extralegal violence was not only the aim of the lynchers – to punish heinous criminals – but also the purported procedures that lynchers scrupulously obeyed. News accounts left the impression that lynchers were scrupulous to bring the alleged criminals before their accusers, to secure confessions, to allow their prisoners to pray, and to conduct themselves with the decorum befitting the occasion. Indeed, in some instances, mock trials were conducted and the gathered mob rendered a verdict on the basis of the evidence presented. Given the unlimited violence and power that lynchers had over their victims, it is almost paradoxical that lynchers would adhere to any trial procedures or conventions of legal execution even while they violated the rule of law with impunity. But however token these ritualized acts and processes may have been, in the eyes of white southerners, they were testimonials to the fundamental propriety of informal justice. It was the combination of the aims and behaviour of mobs that enabled white southerners to deny that there was a meaningful distinction between formal and informal, legal and extralegal justice.

As journalists and editorialists scrutinized the alleged details of lynchings, winnowing the illegitimate from the 'honorable' acts of summary justice, they demonstrated that legitimacy was acquired through a dynamic process. It rested on a concatenation of conditions and circumstances regarding the precipitating crime, the victim, the alleged wrongdoer, and the response of the community. Unwilling to rely solely on the courts to prosecute alleged lawbreakers and unwilling in particular to use the courts to restrict extralegal violence, white southerners instead relied on public debate to define the standards against which the conduct of mobs would be measured. Representations of lynchings (especially in newspapers), rather than legal rulings or administrative procedures, were the mechanism that granted legitimacy to lynchings and held mobs accountable.

White southerners were not alone in their need to legitimize lynching. Although the overwhelming majority of lynchings after 1880 took place in the former states of the Confederacy, lynchings did occur with shocking regularity in the American West, especially the Southwest. There the transgressors often were Mexican desperadoes rather than alleged black rapists and the specific circumstances of western lynchings necessarily differed from those of southern lynchings. But the use of narrative conventions in news accounts to legitimize informal justice in the West and Southwest was strikingly similar. Western lynchers and their defenders, no less than southerners, had to justify the use of extralegal and informal modes of justice despite the existence of a robust system of formal justice. Not surprisingly, the tropes and cliches that infused the published accounts of and editorials on western lynchings often were indistinguishable from their southern counterparts. It is testimony to the success of the contemporary narrators of western lynching that the mention of western lynch mobs conjure up images of cowboys, cattle rustlers, and a generally wholesome tradition of frontier justice. Lynching, in these accounts, represented a lamentable but necessary stage in the conquest and settlement of the West; westerners no less than white southerners pointed to lynchings as a means to defend 'civilization' from the threat posed by labour anarchists and Mexican banditry. Thus, while this essay has focused upon the legitimization of lynching in the American South, the patterns of discourse that it traces is relevant to the phenomenon of mob violence beyond the Mason-Dixon line.[31]

Lynchers, whether in the South or elsewhere, were at pains to demonstrate that, in light of the precipitating crimes, summary justice was reasonable rather than cruel and excessive. They insisted that the penalty of mob-inflicted death was imposed evenly and fairly and that like crimes elicited like punishments. In the same vein they dwelled on the stable and transcendent ideals that virtually compelled the application of mob justice. With seemingly unlimited stamina, defenders of mob violence recited the mantra that lynching was a defence of 'white womanhood' and 'civilization' from black 'savagery' or Mexican predators. The invocation of these nineteenth century (white) ideals as justification for the vengeance of mobs mitigated, at least in the eyes of whites, the extralegal nature of lynching and its associated brutality.

Notes

1   *Bartow Courier-Informant*, 27 June 1900.
2   *Tampa Tribune*, 28 June 1900.
3   *Atlanta Constitution*, 19 May 1893.
4   The essential starting point for research on lynching is Moses, N. H. (1997), *Lynching and Vigilantism in the United States: An Annotated Bibliography*, Greenwood, Westport, CT.
5   Women, both black and white, were victims of southern mob violence. Perhaps as many as 130 women, most of whom were black, died at the hands of lynch mobs. Although the lynching of women underscores the complex role of gender in mob violence, it is still important to recognize that black male victims outnumbered women victims of mob violence by approximately 30 to one. See Feimster, C. N. (2000), 'Ladies and Lynching': The Gendered Discourse of Mob Violence in the New South, 1880–1930, Ph.D. thesis, Princeton University.
6   *Atlanta Constitution*, 23 August 1904.
7   *Atlanta Constitution*, 13 October 1912.
8   *Savannah Morning News*, 16-20 August 1904; Moseley and Brogdon, 1981.

9   *Roanoke Times*, 21-27 September 1893; Waits, 1972; McKinney, 1977; Alexander, 1992.
10   *Bartow Courier-Informant*, 29 May 1901.
11   *Bartow Courier-Informant*, 5 June 1901.
12   *Bartow Courier-Informant*, 5 June 1901.
13   *Madison New Enterprise*, 6 February 1908; *Arcadia Champion* quoted in *Tampa Morning Tribune*, 22 June 1907; *Bartow Courier-Informant*, 29 April 1909.
14   *Florida Times-Union*, 18 July 1893.
15   *Gainesville Sun*, 7 September 1904; *Florida Times-Union*, 11 June 1895, 8 September 1891, 29 January 1916.
16   *Florida Times-Union*, 19 July 1890, 28 September 1891, 19 December 1891, 16 February 1892; *Tampa Morning Tribune*, 6 December 1903.
17   *Tampa Morning Tribune*, 14 February 1909.
18   *Florida Times-Union*, 5, 6 May 1896.
19   *Florida Times-Union*, 16 December 1891.
20   *Florida Times-Union*, 16 December 1891.
21   *Florida Times-Union*, 16 December 1891.
22   On the suspicion of 'outsiders', see Ayers, 1992, pp. 157-8; on white 'protectors' of blacks, see Brundage, 1994.
23   *Tampa Tribune*, 3 July 1912.
24   *Florida Times-Union*, 5 July 1895.
25   *Florida Times-Union*, 5 July 1895.
26   *Florida Times-Union*, 21 August 1895.
27   *Florida Times-Union*, 21 August 1895.
28   *Florida Times-Union*, 21 August 1895.
29   *Florida Times-Union*, 5 July 1895.
30   The tradition of defending purported community values through acts of extralegal 'justice' endured in the South well into the twentieth century. Aroused southerners at times engaged in behaviour which followed the conventions of charavari and 'rough-music' in early modern Europe and punished individuals who had offended communal values and social propriety. An informal code of violence also regulated labour disputes, which were only sometimes settled through formal legal channels. In an era when unemployment was virtually criminalized as vagrancy, white planters, like their slave master predecessors, vouched for the healthy effects of intimidation and an occasional flogging on dilatory labourers. County officials condoned such irregular forms of 'justice' because they too held the widely shared belief that 'any crime which occurs among the propertyless Negroes is considered a labor matter to be handled by the white landlord or his overseer'. Whippings and beatings were just increments on a continuum of violence that concluded with lynchings; mob violence, as sociologist Oliver C. Cox observed, was 'the culminating act of continuing white aggression against the Negro'. See Brundage, 1993, pp. 109-10; McMillen, 1989, pp. 125-7; Palmer, 1978; Raper, 1932, p. 56.
31   See Carrigan, W. and Webb, C., 'Muerto Por Unos Desconocidos (Killed By Persons Unknown): Mob Violence Against African Americans and Mexican Americans' (forthcoming), and Pfeifer, M. (1998), 'Lynching and Criminal Justice in Regional Context: Iowa, Wyoming, and Louisiana, 1878-1946', Ph.D., University of Iowa.

References

Alexander, A. F. (1992), '"Like an Evil Wind": The Roanoke Riot of 1893 and the Lynching of Thomas Smith', *Virginia Magazine of History and Biography*, Vol. 100, pp. 173-206.

Arnold, R. R. (1901), 'Delays and Technicalities in the Administration of Justice', *Report of the Eighteenth Annual Session of the Georgia Bar Association*, Vol. 18, pp. 114-27.

Ayers, E. L. (1982), *Vengeance and Justice: Crime and Punishment in the 19th century American South*, Oxford University Press, New York.

Ayers, E. L. (1992), *The Promise of the New South*, Oxford University Press, Oxford.

Beck, E. M. and Tolnay, S. E. (1997), 'When Race Didn't Matter: Black and White Mob Violence Against Their Own Color', in Brundage, W. F. (ed.), *Under Sentence of Death: Essays on Lynching in the American South*, University of North Carolina Press, Chapel Hill, pp. 132-54.

Bederman, G. (1995), *Manliness & Civilization: A Cultural History of Gender and Race in the United States, 1880-1917*, University of Chicago Press, Chicago.

Brown, R. M. (1963), *The South Carolina Regulators*, Harvard University Press, Cambridge.

Brown, R. M. (1975), *Strain of Violence: Historical Studies of American Violence and Vigilantism*, Oxford University Press, New York.

Brundage, W. F. (1993), *Lynching in the New South: Georgia and Virginia, 1880-1930*, University of Illinois Press, Urbana.

Brundage, W. F. (1994), 'The Varn Mill Riot of 1891: Lynchings, Attempted Lynchings, and Justice in Ware County, Georgia', *Georgia Historical Quarterly*, Vol. 78, pp. 257-80.

Brundage, W. F. (1997), *Under Sentence of Death: Essays on Lynching in the American South*, University of North Carolina Press, Chapel Hill.

Carby, H. (1985), '"On the Threshold of Woman's Era": Lynching, Empire and Sexuality in Black Feminist Theory', *Critical Inquiry*, Vol. 12, pp. 262-77.

Cash, W. J. (1941), *The Mind of the South*, Knopf, New York.

Crouch, B. A. (1984), 'A Spirit of Lawlessness: White Violence, Texas Blacks, 1865-1868', *Journal of Social History*, Vol. 18, pp. 217-26.

Cutler, J. E. (1903), *Lynch Law: An Investigation Into the History of Lynching in the United States*, Longmans, Green, & Co., New York.

DeLacy, J. F. (1899), 'The Necessity of Reforms in the Criminal Law', *Report of the Sixteenth Annual Session of the Georgia Bar Association*, Vol. 16, pp. 191-8.

Eaton, C. (1942), 'Mob Violence in the Old South', *Mississippi Valley Historical Review*, Vol. 29, pp. 351-70.

Ewick, P. (1998), 'Punishment, Power, and Justice', in Garth, B. G. and Sarat, A. (eds), *Justice and Power in Sociolegal Studies*, Northwestern University Press, Evanston, pp. 36-54.

Feimster, C. N. (2000), '"Ladies and Lynching": The Gendered Discourse of Mob Violence in the New South, 1880 – 1930', Ph.D. thesis, Princeton University.

Foner, Eric (1988), *Reconstruction: America's Unfinished Revolution, 1863-1877*, Harper & Row, New York.

Friedman, L. M. (1984), 'The Law Between the States: Some Thoughts on Southern Legal History', in Bodenhamer, D. J. and Ely, Jr., J. W. (eds), *Ambivalent Legacy: A Legal History of the South*, University Press of Mississippi, Jackson.

Garth, B. G., and Sarat, A. (1998), 'Justice and Power in Law and Society Research: On the Contested Careers of Core Concepts', in Garth, B. G. and Sarat, A. (eds), *Justice and Power in Sociolegal Studies*, Northwestern University Press, Evanston, pp. 1-18.

Gilje, P. A. (1987), *The Road to Mobocracy: Popular Disorder in New York City, 1763-1834*, University of North Carolina Press, Chapel Hill.

Haber, S. (1991), *The Quest for Authority and Honor in the American Professions, 1750-1900*, University of Chicago Press, Chicago.

Hall, J. D. (1979), *Revolt Against Chivalry: Jesse Daniel Ames and the Women's Campaign Against Lynching*, Columbia University Press, New York.

Haygood, A. G. (1893), 'The Black Shadow in the South', *Forum*, Vol. 16, pp. 167-75.

Hindus, M. S. (1980), *Prison and Plantation: Crime, Justice, and Authority in Massachusetts and South Carolina, 1767-1878*, University of North Carolina Press, Chapel Hill.

Hylton, Jr., J. G. (1986), 'The Virginia Lawyer From Reconstruction to the Great Depression', Ph.D. thesis, Harvard University.

Keller, M. (1977), *Affairs of State: Public Life in Late Nineteenth Century America*, Harvard University Press, Cambridge, MA.

McKinney, G. B. (1977), 'Industrialization and Violence in Appalachia in the 1890s', in Williamson, J. W. (ed.), *An Appalachian Symposium: Essays Written in Honor of Cratis D. Williams*, Appalachian State University Press, Boone, N. C., pp. 131-44.

McMillen, N. R. (1989), *Dark Journey: Black Mississippians in the Age of Jim Crow*, University of Illinois Press, Urbana.

Moses, N. H. (1997), *Lynching and Vigilantism in the United States: An Annotated Bibliography*, Greenwood, Westport, CT.

Moseley, C. and Brogdon, F. (1981), 'A Lynching at Statesboro: The Story of Paul Reed and Will Cato', *Georgia Historical Quarterly*, Vol. 65, pp. 104-18.

Palmer, B. (1978), 'Discordant Music: Charavaris and Whitecapping in Nineteenth-Century North America', *Labour/Le Travailleur*, Vol. 3, pp. 49-60.

Paul, A. M. (1960), *Conservative Crisis and the Rule of Law: Attitudes of Bar and Bench, 1887-1895*, Cornell University Press, Ithaca.

Percy, A. (1959), *Origin of Lynch Law, 1780*, Percy Press, Madison Heights, VA.

Pfeifer, M. (1998), 'Lynching and Criminal Justice in Regional Context: Iowa, Wyoming, and Louisiana, 1878-1946', Ph.D. thesis, University of Iowa.

Rable, G. C. (1984), *But There Was No Peace: The Role of Violence in the Politics of Reconstruction*, University of Georgia Press, Athens.

Richards, L. L. (1970) *'Gentlemen of Property and Standing': Anti-Abolition Mobs in Jacksonian America*, Oxford University Press, New York.

Ross, J. R. (1983), 'At the Bar of Judge Lynch: Lynching and Lynch Mobs in America', Ph.D. thesis, Texas Tech University.

Stagg, J. C. A. (1974), 'The Problem of Klan Violence: The South Carolina Upcountry, 1868-1871', *Journal of American Studies*, Vol. 8, pp. 303-18.

Strickland, J. J. (1899), 'Are the Courts Responsible for Lynchings, and if so, Why?', *Report of the Sixteenth Annual Session of the Georgia Bar Association*, Vol. 16, pp. 184-90.

Tolnay, S. E. and Beck, E. M. (1995), *A Festival of Violence: An Analysis of Southern Lynchings, 1882-1930*, University of Illinois Press, Urbana.

Thompson, S. D. (1888), 'More Justice and Less Technicality', *Report of the Fifth Annual Meeting of the Georgia Bar Association*, Vol. 5, pp. 107-43.

Trelease, A. W. (1979), *White Terror: The Ku Klux Klan Conspiracy and Southern Reconstruction*, Harper & Row, New York.

Waits, J. A. (1972), 'Roanoke's Tragedy: The Lynch Riot of 1893', M.A. thesis, University of Virginia.

Waldrep, C. (1998), *Roots of Disorder: Race and Criminal Justice in the American South, 1817-80*, University of Illinois Press, Urbana.

Waldrep, C. (2000), 'War of Words: The Controversy Over the Definition of Lynching, 1899-1940', *Journal of Southern History*, Vol. 66, pp. 75-100.

Work, M. (ed.) (1931), *The Negro Yearbook: An Annual Encyclopedia of the Negro, 1931-1932*, Negro Year Book Publishing Co., Tuskegee.

Wright, G. C. (1990), *Racial Violence in Kentucky, 1865-1940: Lynchings, Mob Rule, and 'Legal Lynchings'*, Louisiana State University Press, Baton Rouge.

Wyatt-Brown, B. (1982), *Southern Honor: Ethics and Behavior in the Old South*, Oxford University Press, New York.

Zuczek, R. (1996), *State of Rebellion: Reconstruction in South Carolina*, University of South Carolina Press, Columbia, SC.

Index

Zehr, H. 64, 65, 74n
Zeitfreiwilligenverbände 138
Zero Tolerance 92

Zizek, S. 19
Zuczek, R. 160